ARCHISPEAK An illustrated guide to architectural terms
TOM PORTER

With contributions by:

Steve Bowkett
Alan Brookes
Walter Grondzik
Richard Hayward
Craig Huffman
Mike Jenks
Conway Lloyd Morgan
Thorbjeorn Mann
Henk Mihl
Byron Mikellides
Enn Ots
Martin Pawley

Larry Peterson
Clare Pollard
Richard Rose-Casemore
Ron Shaeffer
Geoffrey Spyer
Peter D. Stone
Jane Tankard
Mark A. Tarmey
Maelee Thomson Foster
Karel Vollers
Edward T. White

Spon Press
Taylor & Francis Group

LONDON AND NEW YORK

First published 2004 by Spon Press
11 New Fetter Lane, London EC4P 4EE

Simultaneously published in the USA and Canada by Spon Press
29 West 35th Street, New York, NY 10001

Spon Press is an imprint of the Taylor & Francis Group

© 2004 Tom Porter

Typeset in Din by Sutchinda Rangsi Thompson
Printed and bound in Great Britain by T J International, Padstow, Cornwall

British Library Cataloguing in Publication Data
A catalogue record for this book is available from the British Library

Library of Congress Cataloguing in Publication Data
Porter, Tom
  Archispeak : an illustrated guide to architectural terms / Tom Porter
    p. cm.
    ISBN 0-415-30011-8 (alk. paper) — ISBN 0-415-30012-6 (pbk : alk. paper)
    1. Architecture—Terminology. 2. Architectural design—Terminology.
I. Title
NA31 .P67 2004
720'.3—dc22
                            2003021736

ISBN 0-415-30011-8 (hb)
      0-415-30012-6 (pb)

The author pays tribute to the memory of a good friend and colleague, the late Layla Shamash.

List of contributors

Steve Bowkett is a Senior Lecturer at the schools of architecture at Southbank University, London, and Oxford Brookes University. He is also a partner in the Tankard Bowkett architectural practice.

Alan Brookes is Professor of Building Technology at the Faculty of Architecture, TU University, Delft. Previously a partner in Brookes Stacey Randall, his buildings and structures are internationally known. He is the author of several books, including *Cladding of Buildings* (1998) and *Innovation in Architecture* (2003).

Walter Grondzik is an architectural engineer and a Professor at the School of Architecture, Florida A&M University, Tallahassee. His research interests include building environmental control systems and building perform-ance, and he is the past-President of both the Architectural Research Centers Consortium and the Society of Building Science Educators.

Richard Hayward is Professor and Head of the School of Architecture and Construction at the University of Greenwich, London. He is executive co-editor of the quarterly refereed journal *URBAN DESIGN International*, and author of *Architecture: An Invitation* (with Paul Oliver) (1990) and *Making Better Places: Urban Design Now* (with Sue McGlynn) (1992).

Craig Huffman is co-founder and Design Principal of the Tallahassee based firm of Huffman/Tarmey Architecture PA, which specializes in urban design, architecture and preservation. He is also an Associate Professor at the School of Architecture, Florida A&M University, Tallahassee.

Mike Jenks is Head of the Department of Architecture, Oxford Brookes University. His research into sustainable urban forms and the compact city is well known and widely published.

Conway Lloyd Morgan is an editor, publisher and author of many books, including the award-winning *Virtual Architecture* (with Guiliano Zampi) (1995) and *Jean Nouvel: The Elements of Architecture* (1998).

Thorbjeorn Mann is a Professor Emeritus at Florida A&M University, Tallahassee, where he taught architectural design and programming, design analysis and methodology, building economics and drawing. He authored *Building Economics for Architects* (1992) and *Time Management for Designers* (2003).

Henk Mihl is a practising architect and Assistant Professor in the Faculty of Architecture, Delft University of Technology, Holland. He is the editor of several books, including *Architectural Design and Composition* (2002).

Byron Mikellides is an environmental psychologist and Professor at the School of Architecture, Oxford Brookes University. He is the co-editor of *Colour for Architecture* (1976) and author of *Architecture for People* (1980).

Enn Ots is a practising architect and the Associate Dean at the School of Architecture, Florida A&M University, Tallahassee. He teaches theory and design courses to graduate and undergraduate students.

Martin Pawley is an architectural critic and, currently, columnist for the *Architects' Journal*, and he has written widely on architecture and design. Apart from radio and television work, his many books include *A Private Future* (1974), *Buckminster Fuller* (1990), *Theory and Design in the Second Machine Age* (1990) and *Terminal Architecture* (1997).

Larry Peterson is a Professor at the School of Architecture, Florida A&M University, Tallahassee. He specializes in exploring new ways of thinking about architecture. He has authored many articles (and editorials) on architecture and sustainable planning, and has contributed chapters to several books.

Clare Pollard is a poet. She won an Eric Gregory Award in 2000 and took part in the First Lines young poets tour in 2001. She has published two collections of her work, the most recent of which is *Bedtime* (2002), and she has presented two TV documentaries for Channel 4.

Richard Rose-Casemore is Director of the architectural practice Design Engine, with offices in London and Winchester, and he also runs a Diploma Course unit at the Oxford School of Architecture. He has received numerous RIBA citations and was awarded the Stephen Lawrence Prize in 2001.

Ron Shaeffer is a Professor Emeritus of the School of Architecture at Florida A&M University, Tallahassee. Ron is a registered engineer specializing in lightweight structures and is the author of several books and numerous technical papers.

Geoffrey Spyer is an Emeritus Professor at Middlesex University. He has practised architecture for 50 years in Denmark, West Africa and Greece, as well as in the UK.

Peter D. Stone is an Associate Professor at the School of Architecture, Florida A&M University, Tallahassee. Peter is a practising architect specializing in residential design, with an emphasis on energy efficiency and sustainability. He is currently preparing a text for architects, entitled *The Form of Enclosure*.

Jane Tankard is Senior Lecturer at the School of Architecture, University of Westminster, London, and is also a partner in the Tankard Bowkett architecture practice.

Mark A. Tarmey is co-founder and Managing Principal of the Tallahassee-based firm of Huffman/Tarmey Architecture PA, which specializes in urban design, architecture and preservation. He is a visiting critic to the School of Architecture, Florida A&M University, Tallahassee.

Maelee Thomson Foster, Professor Emerita at the School of Architecture, University of Florida, Gainesville, is also an ACSA Distinguished Professor and held the Beinecke-Reeves Distinguished Chair in Architectural Preservation between 1999–2002.

Karel Vollers is an award-winning architect focusing on materializing an architecture of free geometry. Published in 2001, his doctorial thesis is enshrined in the book *Twist & Build* (2001). He is currently Assistant Professor at the Faculty of Architecture, TU University, Delft, where he leads the Blob and Technology Group.

Edward T. White is a Professor at the School of Architecture, Florida A&M University, Tallahassee. He is the founder of Architectural Media Inc., and he is co-author of *Post-occupancy Evaluation* (1988) and the author of several books, including *Images of Italy* (1997) and *Path, Portal, Place: Appreciating Public Space in Urban Environments* (1999).

Preface

During my year as Visiting Professor at the School of Architecture, Florida A&M University in Tallahassee, I attended a Fifth Year design review. Within minutes of the opening student presentation and the ensuing debate, there had been an outpouring of architectural terms including 'co-mingling space', 'layering', 'articulate' and 'transition'. It was then that my eyes met the quizzical look on the face of my colleague for the day — visiting critic and practising architect, Mark A. Tarmey. With raised eyebrows he said: 'Fine, but what does it all mean?'. It was amid the ensuing howls of laughter from both students and tutors that the idea for *Archispeak* was born.

During the design review, I began a compilation of a growing list of architectural jargon terms — a list that has continued to expand ever since. What began with a sense of fun has continued with the help of colleagues at the School in Tallahassee and at the Oxford School of Architecture. While confirming that the currency of *Archispeak*, apart from some slight differences in meaning, is international in its usage, and with a little help from friends in the Faculty of Architecture at TU University, Delft, what follows forms a personal bridge between the institutions and the countries in which I have spent much of my teaching life.

Tom Porter
September 2003

Acknowledgements

I would like to thank the following contributors of definitions for their generosity, scholarship and friendship:

Tallahassee: Walter Grondzik, Craig Huffman, Thorbjeorn Mann, Enn Ots, Larry Peterson, Peter D. Stone, Ron Shaeffer, Mark A. Tarmey and Edward T. White.

Oxford: Steve Bowkett, Mike Jenks, Byron Mikellides and Richard Rose-Casemore.

Delft: Alan Brookes, Henk Mihl and Karel Vollers.

Special thanks are also due to Richard Hayward, Conway Lloyd Morgan, Martin Pawley, Clare Pollard, Geoffrey Spyer, Jane Tankard and Maelee Thomson Foster.

Finally, I would like to offer my warm thanks and sincere gratitude to Enn Ots and Peter D. Stone in Tallahassee who have played an extraordinary role in this project from the very beginning. Together with Richard Rose-Casemore in England, they have made contributions, suggested additional terms, as well as acted as transatlantic editors in the development of definitions.

All line drawings are by Sue Goodman, unless otherwise credited.

Illustration credits

Alsop Architects: Blob architecture (Blobmeister) (b), p.16; Branding
    (naming), p.17 (photo: Roderick Coyne)
Ateliers Jean Nouvel: Black box, p.15 (photo: Philippe Ruault); Layering (a),
    p.111 (photo: Philippe Ruault)
Roderick Coyne/Alsop Architects: Robust, p.158
Farrell & Partners: Crystalline, p.42 (photo: Andrew Putler); Decorated
    shed, p.49 (photo: Richard Bryant/ARCAID); Layering (b), p.111 (photo:
    Andrew Putler)
Maelee Thomson Foster: Sacred space, p159
Foster and Partners: Blob architecture (Blobmeister) (a), p.16; Servant/
    served, p.166; Serviced shed, p.167
Gehry Partners, LLP: Gesture, p.90
Hodder Associates: Working wall, p.208 (photo: Andrew Wray)
Huff+Gooden Architects LLC: Scrim, p.162 (photo: Jerry Ballinger)
Craig Huffman: Conceptual drawing, p.34
Metropolitan Board of Parks and Recreation, The Parthenon, Nashville,
    Tennessee: Simulacrum, p.171 (photo: Gary Layda)
Henk Mihl (photo): Sacrificial, p.160
National Aeronautics and Space Administration: Virtual reality, p.205
Holly Porter: *Assemblage* (conceptual model), p.10
RIBA Library Photographs Collection: Constructivism, p.36
Phillip Rittner: Dynamic, p.63
Richard Rose-Casemore: Analytical drawing, p.5; Breathe, p.19; Diagram,
    p.57; Erosion, p72; Metaphor, p.119; Site appraisal, p.171
Socrates Yiannoudes: Interaction, p.100
Edward T. White: Consequence triangle, p.35; Diagramming, p.58

Introduction
The 330 most used terms in architectural debate

Widely used in architectural circles in the heat of discussion, the recurrent use of particular terms has evolved into a language of building design. Commonly found in architectural literature and journalism, in critical design debate, and especially in student project reviews, *Archispeak* can seem insular and perplexing to others and, particularly to the first-year architectural student, often incomprehensible.

Architects enjoy engaging and articulating these terms. Indeed, when in full flow, they are prone to modify and adapt the meanings of existing words or, when stuck for a term, will often spontaneously invent a new one. However, drawing from a diversity of sources, the emergence of this subculture also reflects the need to translate architectural design concepts into spoken commentary — each term embodying a precise and generally accepted architectural meaning. Inadvertently, this unique form of expression can also disclose a critical 'wish list' that emanates from a consensus of issues and strategies considered crucial to an idealized design approach. Therefore, if we explore the vocabulary of this language we gain insight to a collective understanding of what constitutes 'good architecture'. Hopefully, if the first-year student can understand the nuances of the language, he or she will be better able to address and communicate these issues and strategies, and, thereby, improve the quality of their design commentaries. This is the core purpose of this book.

To make *Archispeak* easily understandable and accessible to the reader, each term is defined in the context of its architectural usage; while many definitions are illustrated, all are cross-referenced. Also, some of the definitions are written by architects and educators whose work and criticism draws from a use of particular terms. Finally, *Archispeak* is intended as a primer, each definition being offered as an appetizer, which, hopefully, will provide a springboard to further reading and a deeper understanding.

Allegory

An *allegory* is a story where figures, in the form of humans, animals or superhumans (gods and fantasy figures) are used to illustrate abstract concepts, qualities or situations. Showing one thing and meaning another, *allegory* is a mode of representation, usually naturalistic, that uses the veneer of one narrative to disguise the deeper meaning of another. Usually referring to some outstanding quality or exceptional situation, allegorical meaning remains hidden. Therefore, like an illusion, *allegory* is elusive; it is a palimpsest that awaits its inner message to be disclosed and decoded. In *Signs and Symbols* (1989), Adrian Frutiger writes that the majority of allegorical figures in Western culture are derived from the mythology of ancient Greece and imperial Rome. However, their investment with attributes were later assigned, possibly in the Middle Ages and especially during the Renaissance, when 'Truth' was a principal tenet of humanism. An allegorical layer of meaning was inscribed by Andrea Pisano's sculpture on the lower sections of Giotto's campanile, built in fourteenth-century Florence. Carrying 'comic-strip' bands of sculpture, each façade represents a 'page' of cryptic 'text' that codifies the virtues, the sacraments, the arts, the planets and so forth.

An *allegory* can convey a message with moral overtones; *allegory* personifies the values of a culture that create it. The combination of the historical figure with symbolic object produces an abstract statement with a message that is allegorical. For example, the winged female form shown here is the generally understood representation of victory and peace, the blindfolded female figure holding a sword in one hand and a pair of scales in the other represents justice, and the Statue of Liberty, carrying a torch for freedom to light the way, extends the hand of friendship to the displaced. These robed women are not merely symbols that connect the visible and an invisible world, but are an allegorical picture of a real phenomenon.

Frutiger suggests that in the wake of the fading allegorical images of the past, new forms are emerging. For instance, all the robed variants of Superman and Superwoman, together with the science fiction heroes of outer space, will probably provide the replacement models of a future allegorical expression.

See also:
Anchoring • Didactic • Narrative •
Palimpsest • Semiology • Sign

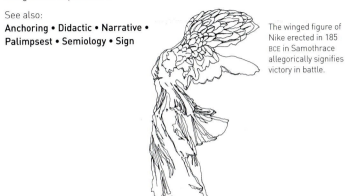

The winged figure of Nike erected in 185 BCE in Samothrace allegorically signifies victory in battle.

Ambiguity

Ambiguity is a double entendre, an enigmatic or equivocal characteristic that appears in art, literature and architecture. Like its bedfellows, paradox and contradiction, it is a consequence of a balance of opposing forces at work. *Ambiguity* plays upon our educated vision and induces in the viewer the confusion of a bifocal vision — a mixed register that results from either deliberately cryptic intention or the dubiousness of inexact expression.

Ambiguity is the condition of not being able to believe your eyes in which what you get is not necessarily what you bargain for. It is experienced in the optical conundrums posed by Maurice C. Escher's graphical illusions and in the light sculptures of James Turrell, where the interface between matter and space becomes diffused. Architectural *ambiguity* is famously exploited in Jacques Tati's movie *Playtime*, in which he uses the anonymity of International style sets to blur differences between interior and exterior and between one building use and another. In order to further confuse both the screen character and the audience as to what is real and what is illusion, Tati exploits to the full the ambiguous duality of transparency and reflectiveness in glass — the symbolic material of Modernism.

The ancient Greeks were anxious to avoid *ambiguity* in the formal appearance of their temples. In order to do so, they employed '*entasis*', i.e. a subtle inflection of the contour of mass as a means of correcting the apparent distortion caused by excessive straight edges. By contrast, *ambiguity* was heavily promoted by many post-modern architects and critics who argued for a layered complexity of allusion, metaphor and contradiction as a means of enriching the experience of architectural form and of placing the onus of its interpretation upon the spectator. Obviously, one antidote to *ambiguity* is to use an unequivocal primacy and a clear hierarchy in the ordering of events.

See also: **Analogue • Complexity • Disjunction • Metaphor • Paradox • Sign**

Analogue

Analogies are forms of inference: from the assertion of similarities between two things is then reasoned their likely similarity in other respects. — Albert C. Smith

There are basically two forms of architectural *analogue*. The first is the architectural drawing or model, which is an *analogue* of the building it represents. The architectural drawing was invented over 5,000 years ago so that ideas could be tried out before the building is built. Drawing grids and tools, such as the T-square, predetermined that Euclidean geometry would be the language of architectural form. In a similar way, computer software is now influencing potential building forms. One could not imagine designing Frank Gehry's Museum in Bilbao with a T-square. *Analogue* takes over — that is, predetermining the range of possible building forms; but the means by which the drawing or model is executed may be more powerful than we realize.

The second type of *analogue* is the building that looks like something else that is not a building at all. The most famous of these is the Dinosaur building featured in the cult movie *PeeWee's Big Adventure*. Charles Jenck's in *The Language of Post Modern Architecture* (1977) featured buildings as hot dogs, running shoes, as well as human genitalia. Other well-known *analogue* buildings are Cinderella's Castle at Disneyland and most of the newer casinos in Las Vegas, especially New York, New York, which is a building that is analogous to an entire city.

Analogies are forms of inference: from the assertion of similarities between two things is then reasoned their likely similarity in other respects. (EO)

See also: **Allegory • Metaphor • Sign • Semiology • Symbolism**

Analytical drawing   ▌

The purpose of the *analytical drawing* is to visualize the spatial character-istics of a building. In order to do so, analysis is a process of reduction — essentially omitting all relevant data from a design drawing so that only information essential to the study remains. The art of making such a drawing is deciding what use is to be drawn and what left out. Such drawings should make sense at a glance and should be self-explanatory rather than requiring explanation. Often, a series of drawings with a limited quantity of data is much easier to read than a single drawing containing a great deal of information.

See also: **Diagram • Diagramming • Morphology**

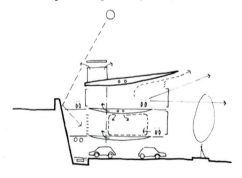

All reductive drawings and diagrams that selectively process, filter or distil information are analytical in intent.

Anchoring   ▌

The excessive weight attached to the question of where one is, goes back to nomadic tribes, when people had to be observant about feeding-grounds. — Robert Musil

Anchoring is a term using to describe the physical and metaphysical rooting of a building to the context of its setting. Literal *anchoring* devices include the sculptural or architectural plinth, which, like the base of a column or the emphasized ground line in an elevation or section drawing, establish the form as 'growing' from the earth while simultaneously mediating between ground and edifice. The link between the building and the earth upon which it stands is sometimes expressed with a lower band of coarse stonework, such as in the rusticated first-floor levels of

Renaissance palaces. Also, while external staircases 'stitch' together ground and building, columns will appear to spring from the earth to hold up (and hold down) a sheltering plane that appears to belong to the sky. Historically, stone-based and clay-based settlements were built from the substrate on which they stood, masonry or brickwork precisely reflecting the geological nature of their setting. Even a lick of local colour can function as a rooting device. For example, rather than be gilded to symbolically commemorate the 1849 gold rush, as originally planned, San Francisco's Golden Gate bridge was painted in its existing oxide red to visually anchor its structure to the colour of bedrock on each side of the bay.

However, Steven Holl proposes that a metaphysical or poetic *anchoring* is more appropriate for modern life. For instance, when a new architecture is fixed into a place in space and time, a more profound connection can be evoked through memory and through the architectural inscription of historical traces on a site. This is a strategy in which materials can speak of disconnected points in time — like the frosted glass planes on Holl's competition project for Minnesota's State Capitol archive, which echo the primordial glaciers that formed the local terrain in the Pleistocene period. There is also his incorporation into the same design of an abstract footprint of the original buildings, which forms a fossilized impression of Minnesota's first State Capitol. These are not literal reconstructions but, as Holl points out, are 'compressed allegorical accounts of the history of Minnesota'.

The concept of *anchoring* finds an echo in Peter Eisenman's notion of 'trace' — a type of critical regionalism taken to a poetic level. It also has roots in Martin Heidegger's and Christian Norberg-Schultz's phenomenological ideas about site, together with Gottfried Semper's 'stereotonics' — an aspect of buildings that sees hearth and masonry as locked into a site and grounded in the earth.

See also: **Allegory • Focal point • Memory • Place • Trace**

Animate

Animate means to give life or make lively. When heard in architectural debate, the term usually refers to the need to breathe life into a drawing or a design. In other words, it is usually employed as a critical kick-start to schemes or their representation that appear dull or lifeless.

Animated drawings are those apparently created with the spontaneity of the quick sketch, i.e. drawings whose lines that, resulting from the immediacy of directness of thought and purpose, appear to trace the essential dynamic of an idea. Many tutors will preach the exploitation of line weight as an antidote to bland and inanimate-looking drawings; others will recommend that life is breathed into more rigid and wooden-looking hard-line drawings by tracing over them in freehand.

Architectural design schemes appear animated when their form and space appears to imply movement — not actual movement but an implied dynamic. Animation is the technique of filming successive drawings or positions of models to create an illusion of movement when the film is shown in sequence. Similarly, computer flythroughs and walkthroughs *animate* a design proposal in this cinematic form.

See also: **Articulation • Breathe • Dynamic • Modulate • Morphing** (metamorphosis) **• Rhythm • Transformation • Transition**

Anthropomorphic

Nature influences many channels of architectural creativity. It is ever-present and unclassifiable, powerful inspirationally and as a tool.
— Anthony C. Antoniades

The term *anthropomorphic* applies human characteristics, motivation, or behaviour to those of animals, natural phenomena or inanimate objects. For instance, anthropomorphism takes place when we project proportional and symmetrical systems based on the human body into the design of buildings. Also, in verbal descriptions of architecture we make constant reference to gender (male and female components) and to human body parts: to the 'skin' of a building; to its 'heart' (hearth), 'womb', 'underbelly', 'hat', 'feet', 'eyes', 'mouth', 'finger' and so forth.

In an *anthropomorphic* reading of buildings, façade becomes 'face' and elevation becomes 'portrait'. When the architectural expression is vacant, the face appears 'blank' — a common indictment of modern architecture. While more literal *anthropomorphic* references historically abound in architecture, such as the entrance to the Palazzo Zuccari in Rome shown here, it was Le Corbusier's famous portrayal of the house as a 'machine for living in' that reinforced the attempt to break with this humanizing language of the past. However, having said that, when Le Corbusier referred to a window he used the term 'organ' rather than 'element' because the window is first thought of as an eye.

Anthropomorphism can cut both ways. While we can project human characteristics into buildings, we can also reciprocate by 'becoming buildings'. For example, there is the famous photograph of the Beaux Art's ball, where the architects of noted buildings in New York, such as Van Allan, dressed up as their building. Also, in the annual Tallahassee Homecoming street parade in Florida, architecture students and their teachers design and wear their favourite building to create a 'walking skyline'.

See also: **Breathe • Corporeality • Frontality • Golden section • Ken • Kiss • Metaphor • Modulor • Place**

Humanoid window in the Palazzo Zuccari, Rome.

Archetypal image

If we trace the artistic forms of things made by man, to their origin, we find imitation of nature. — W. R. Lethaby

The term 'archetype' emanates from the psychological work of Carl Jung and his theories concerning the 'collective unconscious'. It describes an original notion or image from which other forms might be contrived. Therefore, an *archetypal image* is a deeply rooted, primitive symbol, motif or schema which becomes distilled as prototypes to constantly influence our world of imagination. Although not scientifically confirmed, certain archetypal forms are thought to be inherited from humankind's earliest ancestors and are presumed to be present in the collective subconscious. One such image is the mandala (a square contained by, or enclosing, a circle). Described by Jung as holding a deeply emotional significance, the mandala provides a footprint upon which many buildings have been formed.

Other basic archetypal images include the 'arch cross' (cruciform), the 'arch clew' (spiral), and their superimposed combination, the 'cross-clew'. The arch cross motivates those bent on right angles, i.e. the pragmatic and mathematically orientated. Those driven by the spiral arch clew favour circular forms; they are more romantic and emotional than their pragmatic arch cross counterparts. The cross-clew archetype compels those who work with a combination of the two archetypes. If Mies van der Rohe's work is representative of the arch cross, and that of Erich Mendelssohn's the arch clew, then the architecture of Alvar Aalto presents a prime example of the cross-clew.

Julani Pallasmaa describes Aalto's architecture as often exhibiting sensuous associations that appear to derive from the image of Primordial Female or Earth Mother. Also, a particularly recurrent aspect of Aalto's work is the repeated appearance of certain patterns, such as the wave-like flowing line — drawn from the fox's tale in Finnish folklore, the distorted grid and the tree-like radiating fan which denotes the dynamism of growth. Pallasmaa further suggests that the frequency with which these archetypal images occur in Aalto's work invites psychoanalytic interpretation.

See also: **Precedent • Sign • Symbolism • Typology**

Archigram

Conceptual architecture: the architecture that would-be real world designers do when they admit to themselves that their drawings will never get them into business. — Martin Pawley

Archigram was a 'paper architecture' phenomenon that began at the onset of the 1960s. Its fantastic ideas were influenced by images of zeppelins, submarines, spacecraft, molecular structures, computers and fashion girls, with designs drawn in a subversive space comic and techno magazine style. All students at the Architectural Association in London, the *Archigram* principals included Warren Chalk, Dennis Crompton, Peter Cook, Ron Herron, David Greene and Mike Webb. They celebrated popular taste and the potential of the new technology, bringing it to architecture in the form of capsule dwellings and plug-in units.

Archigram has been a phenomenon twice. First, there were the 'mechanisms'. These represented the triumph of the early phase — Greene's 'Cushicle' (a combination house and vehicle) and 'Suitaloon' (a combination suit and dwelling), together with many others, such as Rokplugs and Logplugs, occupied the middle ground between product design and architectural design.

Archigram's second phase was architectural art. Incredibly influential at the time, and still so, their drawings were widely published, exhibited and bought and sold. Their conceptual architecture, including motorized tents, pods and capsules, the celebrated Walking City and Plug-in City, etc., drew from aerospace, automobile and consumer technology. Such projects eventually gave way to a more professional conceptual architecture that was made for display in galleries and the group's eventual assimilation into the architectural mainstream — their acceptance by the establishment culminating in the award of a RIBA Gold Medal in 2002.

See also: **High-tech (low-tech) • Utopia**

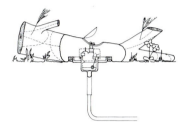

Logplug living — Archigram's plug-in habitable log capsule.

Arcology ∎

A compound of 'architecture' and 'ecology', *arcology* is an idealized vision of the city as organism, first visualized in the early 1960s by the Turin-born architect Paolo Soleri. Arcology refers to a city that is fully integrated with its natural environment and includes a plethora of unrealized projects, such as 'Novanoah 1' — a floating city for 40,00 people — and 'Arcodiga' — a city structure of hanging gardens and houses using the face of the Hoover Dam as its armature. By appropriating the site of a dam, the latter project capitalizes on the 1:7 ratio of redundance in the safety coefficiency in dams built in the US to transform a monolithic, non-cellular system into one that is articulated and cellular. Funded over the years by sales of Soleri's bells and wind-chimes, and the volunteer efforts of countless architectural student pilgrims, the city of 'Arcosanti', being built piece by piece since the late 1960s, is Soleri's physical, utopian expression of *arcology* in Arizona's (re-christened 'Aridzona' by Soleri) Nevada desert.

See also: **Sustainability • Utopia**

Articulation ∎

As in speech, where the term *articulate* refers to the coherent expression of ideas and the distinct pronunciation of words, its use in archispeak embodies the same meaning except that 'expression' refers to 'design language' and 'words' refer to 'building elements'. Therefore, to *articulate* architectural elements is to clearly distinguish the parts that constitute the whole — especially at the points of their connection. Consequently, the roles of each of the constituent elements in a design become accentuated.

As opposed to slurred speech in which words roll into one and become confused, clear speech relies upon interval. Similarly, like the couplings on an *articulated* truck, architectural articulation relies upon strategic breaks in the continuity of its expression. Articulation exists when the integrity of two elements, such as walls and floors, or two materials, is maintained at their point of connection — either through direct contact, the insertion of a void — as in the architectural 'kiss', or by a specifically designed 'node'. Such emphasis on the clear architectural expression of connections and junctions between one building component and another demands extreme sensitivity to detailed design that operates within a voracious design approach.

See also: **Composition • Interface • Intersection • Kiss • Kit of parts • Node • Transition**

Assemblage (conceptual model)

An *assemblage* is a physical version of the conceptual drawing. It is a subjective scale-model built as a thinking mechanism; a template for defining and testing the invisible. It uses found material (*objets trouvés*) to create three-dimensional objects. Although a technique associated with art, *assemblage* occurs in architectural design when models and physical diagrams are quickly fabricated from junk materials to symbolize the components and relationships of an idea. Albeit temporary, a highly opportunistic form of *assemblage* also operates at the dining table when, in earnest conversation, people spontaneously use condiments and cutlery to illustrate a topographical point under discussion.

See also: **Bricolage • Collage • Montage**

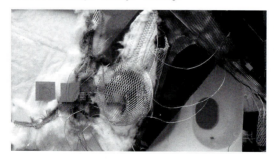

Initial design realization as an assemblage of found materials.

Avant-garde

The modern arts have a special obligation, an advanced or avant-garde duty, to go ahead of their own age and transform it. — Ezra Pound

Avant-garde describes a group, as of writers and artists, considered ahead of their times, i.e. regarded as pre-eminent in the invention and application of new techniques in a given field.

The term was originally used by the French military to refer to a small reconnoitre group that scouted ahead of the main force. It also became

associated with left-wing French radicals in the nineteenth century who ▌
were agitating for political reform. At some point in the middle of that century the term was linked to art through the idea that art is an instrument
for social change. Only toward the end of the nineteenth century did l'art
d'*avant-garde* begin to break away from its identification with left-wing
social causes to become more aligned with cultural and artistic issues.
This trend toward increased emphasis on aesthetic issues has continued
to the present. *Avant-garde* today generally refers to groups of intellectuals,
writers and artists, including architects, who voice ideas and experiment
with artistic approaches that challenge current cultural values. *Avant-
garde* ideas, especially if they embrace social issues, often are gradually
assimilated by the societies they confront. The radicals of yesterday
become mainstream, creating the environment for a new generation of
radicals to emerge.

   Although the *avant-garde* has a strong tradition in the US in the areas
of art and literature, in architecture the so-called *avant-garde* has recently
tended to look to the past or to other cultures for validation and imagery.
In an editorial in *Progressive Architecture* (1993), Thomas Fisher also
berates the lack of vitality of the current *avant-garde* in the US, reminding
the architectural profession that, in spite of the influence of *avant-garde*
Modernist architects escaping the fascism of Europe in the 1930s, the
architects of the early Modern *avant-garde* had a very specific social, as
well as artistic, agenda. In order that it be a positive, creative force for
change, Fisher argues for broadening the focus of the *avant-garde* beyond
the concerns of aesthetics and style to the original, and toward a more
inclusive concept of the *avant-garde*. (PDS)

See also: **Constructivism • Cubism • Cutting edge • Futurism • Modernism •
Parameters • Suprematism**

Axis

**Sequences of space . . . spaces aligned along a common axis — all are
specific architectural organizations, from Egyptian temples through
the churches of the quattrocento to the present. All have emphasized
a planned path with fixed halting points, a family of spatial points
linked by continuous movement.** — Bernard Tschumi

Like the spine that supports the body, or a pole that holds up a tent, the ▌
axis is an ancient representation of an enduring principle which supports
reality. One of the earliest architectural design instruments, the *axis* is
the invisible principle that connects and unifies mind and matter. When
functioning as a pathway, the *axis* is associated with the ceremonial, the
processional, formality and power.

   Used as a basic planning device, the *axis* enlists a regulating line that,
functioning like an invisible tightrope, connects two defined points to provide
a directional force about which the planes of figures can be organized or
rotated in a variety of ways. Axial arrangements can be symmetrical or
asymmetrical, dramatically relentless or subtle in nature, but always
denoting physical and visual movement along its pathway. When defining
planes are punctured, lateral views are provided across its trajectory.

However, axial pathways can also be precarious, making it easy to 'fall off' to either side.

The daddy of all axes is the *Axe Historique de Paris*. This is an urban straight line unique in the world. It began in 1572, when André Le Nôtre (designer of the gardens at Versailles) planted an alignment of trees from the Louvre through the Tuileries Gardens. Since then, each successive century has preserved the sight line of this shaft of space and seen the *axis* extended and respected by architecture, avenues of trees and marked by monuments. Connecting the Arc de Triomphe of the Carousel, the Place de la Concorde and the Place de l'Étoile, the *Axe Historique* was projected out in 1883 to the Rond-Point, located at what is now the business district of La Défense, where it is now enshrined by its twentieth-century marker, the Grande Arche de La Défense.

See also: **Axis mundi** • **Edge condition** • **Erosion** • **Ley lines** • **Linearity** • **Regulating lines** • **Sight lines**

Axis mundi

This important ridgepole rose symbolically from the navel of the world — the central mound of omphalos — the pole star. — Tom Chetwynd

Give me a point of support (fulcrum) and I shall move the world. — Archimedes

An architectural axis is typically understood as an imaginary line about which groups of buildings or building elements are arranged. The *axis mundi* (world axis) is a very special form of axis that is formed by the imaginary line between a significant or sacred place and the centre of the earth or the stars. In early societies, the *axis mundi* is often marked with a sacred tree. It is symbolically the notional centre of the known world. The *axis mundi* was important in, among others, the cosmology of early Roman, Egyptian and Nordic cultures. Typically, the mythical *axis mundi* rises from the navel of the earth to the pole star. It represents the centre pole or column of the house that is the cosmic world.

New Age communities have a renewed interest in the *axis mundi* in sacred place-making. Coincidentally, the architectural community has also rediscovered the architectural *axis mundi* — a designed place that is exceptionally powerful, analogous to the existential centre of a particular world. Few modern designed places qualify for this special distinction — perhaps the plaza at Louis Kahn's Salk Institute offers a rare example.

A related concept is the phenomenological notion of the *genius loci*, or 'spirit of place', championed by the Norwegian architect and educator Christian Norberg-Schultz. An *axis mundi* is perhaps a special, transcendental manifestation of *genius loci*. (EO)

See also: **Axis** • **Context** • *Genius loci* • **Sacred space**

Balance   ▌

The horizontal–vertical construct is the basic relationship of humankind to its environment. As equilibrium, i.e. the need to stay upright in a horizontal world, is the strongest form of visual reference, *balance* is a most important psychological as well as physical influence on human survival. Balance is a design stratagem in which equal or appropriate proportions of elements are arranged around a centre of gravity to achieve and retain a sense of equilibrium.

Equivalence of *balance* can be achieved in two ways: symmetrically (axial balance) and asymmetrically (counterbalance). In the former, units on one side of a centre line are mirrored on the other side to produce a predictable and simple resolution. However, such compositional distributions can appear static and even visually tedious. Of much more interest to the eye is the asymmetry of counterbalance involving variation in weight distribution and placement. The result of this kind of equilibrium comes from complex forces that move us away from simplicity to a condition involving weight and counter weight, action and counteraction.

See also: **Composition** • **Dualism** • **Modulation** • **Rhyme** • **Symmetry** • **Proportion** • **Yin-Yang**

Bespoke   ▌

Like the customized Levis you can order on the internet, customized architecture is naked until the client moves in to give it meaning. Examples of architectural 'open' systems that can be tailored to 'fit' include Polykatoika in Greece, the Corbusian Do-min-o system and the Plattenbau in Berlin. — Richard Woditsch

Bespoke describes the tailor-made article; the unique, one-off artefact that is made to order. In a sense, all architect-designed buildings are *bespoke* products, i.e. specifically made to the requirements of the client and the specification of the designer. Although there have been changes over the last 50 years in the use of 'open systems' of the interchangeable components, pioneered by Ezara Ehrenkra in California, and the prefabrication of industrial components, principally led by the architect Renzo Piano, major buildings continue to be made to order. For instance, each element of the construction for Norman Foster's Hong Kong and Shanghai Bank was designed, developed and custom-made in collaboration with product manufacturers: cladding from the US; fire protection from the UK; staircases from Japan; external sunscoops from Germany; inner sunscoops from Austria; floor finishes from Finland; and refuse disposal from Sweden. Mock-ups and prototypes were built and tested until their performance met with the architects' approval. In some respects, one could regard this building as the ultimate in *bespoke* architecture.

In his thesis on technology transfer, Martin Pawley refers to how much architects can learn about industrialization from the automobile industry. While it is true that the building industry also uses factory-made products, the essential difference is that, whereas the design of a car is a prototype for many similar models, the design of a building is usually a made-to-measure one-off. (AJB)

See also: **Kit of parts** • **Site specific**

Best practice

For those who wish to know how I obtain certain effects, it is sufficient to say that I regard these as very personal forms, obtained by the violation of accepted principles in the process of working . . .
— Man Ray

Much like 'benchmarking', *best practice* has become a buzzword in the corporate world. *Best practice* describes those methods or procedures that through experience have traditionally proved themselves to be tried and true. *Best practice* principles affect architecture in all its formative phases from conception to detailed design and construction. However, *best practice* techniques can case-harden into convention. The term is also open to interpretation and can provide an easy way out of situations that demand specificity. Moreover, an unquestioning acceptance of the basic rules of the game can blind the opportunity for innovation. The main dilemma is how to introduce a basic methodology while simultaneously encouraging freedom of thought when teaching building technologies to architects. In practice, leading-edge architectural firms will prototype and test new ideas but, owing to the time and risk involved, will tend to introduce not more than one innovation into a building at a time.

Rigid adherence to architectural *best practice* may account for the fact that, compared with other industries, the building industry is slow to accept change. For example, compared to the 40,000–80,000 materials available to the automobile industry, the number of materials in a palette of building construction that is used by most design offices can be counted on two hands. While the world of the intelligent building and smart materials is upon us, but still awaits exploration, we continue to build walls by the messy practice of heaping one brick on another. Indeed, back in 1902, H. G. Wells wrote: 'I find it incredible that there will not be sweeping revolution in the methods of building during the next century. The erection of a house wall, come to think of it, is an astonishingly tedious and complex business: the final result is exceedingly unsatisfactory.'

Therefore, while unbridled experimentation and true innovation can break all the rules, *best practice* procedures, although worthy, feed and inform mainstream thinking. (AJB)

See also: **Convention**

Black box

The *black box* is one of the early classics of cybernetics. It derives from the black chamber of the camera, and its most famous incarnation is as the unfortunate location of Schrodinger's cat. The function of a *black box* is to transform an input and to output the result. Its importance as a concept lies in our not needing to know how the transformation is made in order to use the box. Therefore, the *black box* is also the notional location where the act of designing takes place. This is the abstract 'engine room' or the 'hot house' in which decisions are made and issues are resolved, and where ideas about material forms and spaces are brought together to represent the definitive design. However, it might be more precise to say that ideas are formed within the vicinity of the 'box'. While predictable and conventional thinking is said to emanate from 'within the box', more innovative, questioning and unconventional thinking is generally applauded and rated as being derived from 'outside the box'.

Black box also refers to the product of a design process that avoids custom-designed or intrusive statements. For example, some museums and theatres are described as *black box* buildings because they provide curators and directors with a blank canvas with which to work and the freedom to tailor its function to a particular show or exhibit. Jean Nouvel's Onyx Cultural Centre in France is both a reality and a metaphor of the *black box*. Clearly defined in shape, this 600 seat auditorium (shown below) betrays no function. It is anonymous — a non-object.

See also: **Chora** • **Concept** • **Design genesis** • **Lateral thinking** • **Problem solving** • *Tabula rasa*

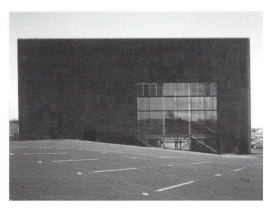

Culture in a caddy. Jean Nouvel's literal *black box* building — the Onyx Cultural Centre, St Herblain, France.

Blob architecture (Blobmeister)

Aficionados of Steve McQueen will remember his starring role as a teenager in the horror movie *The Blob* in which the first homogeneous, gelatinous-shaped non-monster gobbles up people.

'Blobs' in architecture are more politely known as 'free-formed shapes' and have now become more respectable than ever. Even the critic Charles Jencks, writing in *Architectural Review* (February 2003) identifies this as a new paradigm in architecture when he refers to the 'Blobmeisters', such as Greg Lynn, Eric van Egeret and Kees Osterhuis, as 'those determined to capture the field with blob grammars and obtuse theories based on computer analogies'. Norman Foster can be said to have joined the gang with his 30 St Mary Axe (the Swiss Re building) in the City of London, the offices for the London Mayor and Gateshead's new music centre. Meanwhile, Will

Alsop's Fourth Grace for Liverpool's Pier Head is a blob par excellence.
   Blobmeister's themselves claim the early influence of Frank Gehry and the 'Bilbao effect'. Certainly, Gehry's means of translating free-formed models into real buildings using computer-aided prediction and measuring techniques gave others confidence that it was not just a form-finding exercise. The challenge now is to find constructional techniques, such as the explosion forming of metal and twisted glass, which can be used to build these forms within economic restraints. (AB)

See also: Typology

Blob in the landscape: Foster and Partner's 30 St Mary Axe, London, and Will Alsop's proposed Fourth Grace in Liverpool.

Boundary

In his *Elements of Architecture* (1990), Pierre von Meiss describes *boundary* as the interface between two places — a demarcation involving co-dependence of both separation and connection. He suggests that before architects build they have to first define and limit an area of site as distinct from the rest of the cosmos and assign a particular role to it. When demar-cated, a *boundary* can define both micro and macro worlds: the limits of a room, a building, a site, a city, a county and a country are all marked in some way. Boundaries ring-fence containment and denote 'inside' from what lies beyond; they imply control by encumbents on what happens within them. Once limits are established, boundaries are to be defended. Where the edges of boundaries are crossed, these represent points of control and special places of transition that are marked with thresholds, portals, gateways and bridges.

As opposed to site boundaries, which demarcate the extent of physical territory, visual boundaries are limited only by the acuity of our eyes. This *boundary* moves with us as we move through space; its dynamic dramatically expanding and contracting in direct response to the edges of spatial containment or release in the surrounding mass.

See also: Edge condition • Gateway • Interface • Interpenetrating space • Intersection • Parameters • Threshold • Zoning

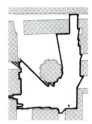

Mapping the visual limits of public space. Drawing made while its author rotates 360 degrees in a city square.

Branding (naming)

If we equate 'communicating' with 'selling' in design presentation, it is important to remember that language can function as an influential publicity tool. Marketeers and admen know that words used to describe an object or an idea can strongly influence the way the object or idea being described will be viewed and dealt with. For instance, to invest a building design with a nickname can bring a sense of identity to the form; in other words, it can idealize or 'brandmark' the design in a manner to suit the intention of the project.

For promotional reasons, most major international cities attract nicknames, such as 'The Big Apple' and the 'City of Dreaming Spires'. Similarly, buildings of note and projects on paper are often invested with names. These names are sometimes given by the designer, sometimes

Hôtel du Départment in Marseilles, France, nicknamed the 'Big Blue'.

affectionately appropriated by the users who often invent such labels as a means of domesticating unusual forms, for example 'Blue Whale' (Cesar Pelli's Pacific Design Centre, Los Angeles), 'Big Blue' (Will Alsop's Hôtel du Départment, Marseilles) 'Paddy's Wigwam' (Basil Spence's Liverpool Cathedral) and 'Fred and Ginger' (Frank Gehry's office building in Prague).

In communication terms, naming can often encapsulate, poeticize and quintessentially represent the design concept. For example, two award-winning student projects nicknamed respectively 'Fogcatcher' and 'Theatre of the Void' immediately capture their functions in words: one a mist-collecting, water-conversion screen structure in the Namibian desert; the other a subway station in London's theatreland given over to busking and street performance. Even a characterizing nickname formed from acronyms can provide cache: MOG (Mobile Operational Gateway) describes another student project for a moveable ticket office.

Through characterization, naming can be persuasive; labels metaphorically capturing a specific quality that is often quite prominent in the design.

See also: **Brandmark (brandscape)** • **Metaphor** • **Narrative** • **Symbolism**

Brandmark (brandscape)

Brandmark is an abbreviation of the term 'branded landmark'. It is an aspect of architectural education that questions the relationship among globally advertized products, architecture, and the urban landscape.

In order to discriminate their existence and to communicate persuasive concepts about lifestyle, the ethos of brands — known as 'brand value' — can transcend the nature of a product. Corporate structures that market brand values using a global vocabulary invade the city to create the 'brandscape' — an invasion that appears to erode local identity and contextual formalism. The result is what tutors at the Royal College of Art and the Architectural Association in London describe as the creation of 'a new typology', that is, an urbanscape more concerned with global marketing than with socio-political issues or questions of context. Their student projects study brands and branding techniques as a means of articulating aspects of our culture and to revitalize the city. To do so, brand values, image and the style of product that are studied, while challenging the privatization of public space, attempt to create a three-dimensional architectural response.

See also: **Branding (naming)** • **Typology**

Breathe

We talk of ' breathing' and 'breathing space' in metaphorical and literal ways. One way refers to the fundamental right of a good building to be experienced from all sides and from all angles. It should be given room to *breathe*. Clearly, some sites and conditions allow for greater space around buildings than others. However, even in the tightest of sites, we can find 'moments' when the architecture is allowed to *breathe*, to be fully appreciated by the viewer. So, we talk of buildings being allowed to *breathe*, but building elements, too, benefit from space around them. As Wassily Kandinsky points out, a curve needs to *breathe* to be appreciated — otherwise, it will work less effectively next to another. A curve in space, or a curve as a counterpoint to a line or plane, will allow its inherent qualities to be read and understood.

Breathing space, just as in prose, is a chance to catch breath, slow the pace and prepare for the next move. Even the simplest buildings can cause a degree of disorientation to the user, and a spatial device which invites room to pause, find bearings and give direction is often valuable.

The last example of *breathe* is a more literal use of the term. Expressions such as 'breathing wall' and 'breathing skin' are used to describe the passive or moving parts of a building which help its performance in operation. Often, movement in a façade is in response to the external influences of the sun, wind or rain, or from drawing anatomical references. Although Renzo Piano is considered the master of the 'soft machine', Jean Nouvel's L'Institut du Monde Arabe (1987), which uses metal diaphragms and glass lenses to control sunlight through a south-facing wall, is perhaps the best-known example of such a breathing wall or reactive skin.

An example of a passive breathing wall can be found in Design Engine's headquarters building for Gifford Consulting Engineers. Here, the cedar-clad external skin is 'cracked' along strategic lines to encourage the natural movement of air into the wall construction. From here, it is assisted by fans through air plena and finally out into the internal working environment through floor grilles. The breathing wall is part of a carefully designed system of natural ventilation systems and contributes to the very high BREEAM (Building Research Environmental Assessment Method Consultancy) rating for the building as a whole. (RR-C)

See also: **Interaction** • **Lung** • **Modulate** • **Proximity** • **Rhythm**

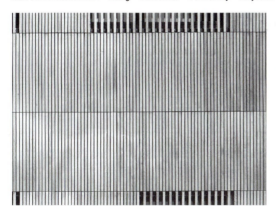

Heavy breathing. Ventilated cedar-clad skin on Design Engine Architect's headquarters building for Gifford Consulting Engineers, Southampton.

Bricolage

The French word *bricolage* refers to a basic form of recycling that involves the opportunistic adoption and reuse of existing materials and the secondary use of existing structures for other purposes. The term usually describes a kind of ad hoc architecture — one that incorporates the recycled fragments of previous constructions or demolitions. But the term also covers the reuse of waste products or architectural salvage as building components. In art, *bricolage* is represented by the litter, yesterday's papers and found objects amalgamated in the collages and assemblages of the Dadaists and Cubists.

The '*bricoleur*' is one who practices *bricolage*. He or she is viewed as a 'primitive' handyman, an odd jobber who, like Simon Rodia's do-it-yourself Watts Towers in Los Angeles, works with a non-scientific mindset and who is operating outside the exclusivity of any rigorous design discipline, and invents and builds with society's flotsam and jetsam. While some cities that are patchworked from the layers, pockets and parts of previous periods can be considered *bricolage*, architectural examples abound. There is the use of ancient clay bottles over 1,500 years ago by the early Italian dome-builders at San Vitale in Ravenna, Italy, and the Drop City domes in the US built from recycled industrial waste in the 1960s by hippie *bricoleurs*. There are also examples of a 'garbage architecture' made from recycled aluminium cans, car tyres and beer bottles, the common incorporation of parts from older buildings in vernacular structures (a technique also found in postmodernism), and the assimilation of industrial and agricultural components into the 1970s 'high-tech' chic.

See also: ***Assemblage*** (conceptual model) • **Collage** • **Montage** • **Serendipity** • **Vernacular**

Brief (program)

Usually issued by the client or a tutor (the surrogate client) the brief — known as the '*program*' in the US — represents instructions and specifications given for a design task. Depending upon their needs, such as the difference between a professional brief and one for an ideas competition, briefs can vary in detailed information but usually comprise site documentation and a list of physical requirements. However, educational briefs that do not include aims and objectives are not worth the paper they are written on. This is because the success or failure of the design response to an open-ended *program* is difficult to measure at the later debriefing stage, that is, the design review or critique.

The initial phase of analysing a brief, i.e. when a brief may be challenged, is known as 'interrogating the brief'.

See also: **Design intent** • **Mission statement**

CAD monkey

Also known as a 'CAD-jockey' or 'computer jockey' and as a 'CAD drone', a *CAD monkey* is the contemporary version of the poor 'drawing-board hack', and is a term usually heard on the lips of graduating students. This is because it describes the kind of role in practice — usually the work-fodder role in big practices — that most creative students desperately want to avoid. A *CAD-monkey*, therefore, is a person cheaply hired to spend their working lives sitting in front of a monitor screen churning out production drawings and the like. Consequently, *CAD-monkeys* are easily spotted away from their station: they wear thick-lensed spectacles, wear elbow patches on their jackets and walk with a pronounced slouch!

Cantilever

A *cantilever* is a load-carrying structure or part of a structure, usually horizontal, that is supported only at one end. The other end is free. The supporting end must be capable of providing reactions to rotational (moment) effects as well as resisting vertical and horizontal forces. Such a support is often called a fixed or rigid connection.

Some of the earliest known applications of the principle were in Japan where it has long been customary to bridge streams by embedding a bulk of timber in the bank at each side and adding a third timber resting on the ends of the other two. In the mid-twentieth century, the cantilever was used to achieve visually dramatic structural effects by designers such as Pier Luigi Nervi and Frank Lloyd Wright.   (RS)

See also: **Tension**

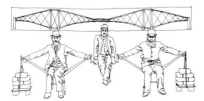

Human chain. Demonstration of the cantilever-suspended structural system for the Firth of Forth Bridge, Scotland.

Cartesian grid

The curious, unsettling sense of revelation such a radial spatial model contains underscores the extent of our acceptance of and dependence on the rectangular Cartesian grid.
— Kent C. Bloomer and Charles C. Moore

The ancient Egyptians seem to be the originators of the grid. Later, the Pythagoreans developed a system of geometry that was the basis for Euclidean or descriptive geometry. It was the French philosopher and mathematician René Descartes who, in the seventeenth century, built upon these developments to provide an analytical, or Cartesian, geometry that showed how every point in a plane could be defined by two numbers, known as 'coordinates'. In his *La Geometrie* (1637) he set out the idea that a pair of numbers can determine a position on a surface: one number as a distance measured horizontally; the other number as a distance measured vertically. Descartes showed that, with a pair of intersecting lines, a whole network of reference lines could be constructed on which numbers could be designated as points. Furthermore, if algebraic equations were represented as points, they would appear as geometric shapes and, in turn, geometric shapes could be translated into sequences of numbers represented as equations. The consequence was the birth of the graph and the grid.

Not only did Descartes' coordinates give ensuing mathematicians a new and stimulating way of analysing mathematical information, but it also gave architects a neutral means of visualizing and organizing space. However, although beloved by the modern architect, the notion of architectural space as governed by the *Cartesian grid* is not every designer's cup of tea. Some see it as a characterless spatio-formal construct and accuse the Cartesian tradition of abstracting objects from pure geometry as the cause of the idealization of the cube and, with it, the proliferation of a rectilinear built environment and the gridiron city. Others question Descartes' idea of substance as having an 'independent existence' and blame it as the reason for our perceptually conditioned, contained and essentially visual approach to architectural design. In other words, Descartes' definition of substance as the 'essential attribute' of form (while sensory output is relegated to the private sensations of the beholder) causes a diminution of the multi-sensory experience.

See also: **Euclidean space • Grid • Matrix • Order • Ordering systems • Platonic solids • xyz space**

Catenary curves

Catenary is the mathematical curve usually associated with the shape taken by a cable loaded by its own self-weight when suspended from two supports to create a span. When the sag-to-span ratio is small, the shape is very close to that of a parabola.

Catenary curves were employed famously by Antonio Gaudí (1852–1926) in his structural investigations to determine the proportions and shape of the brick-arched construction of his Chapel at Santa Coloma and Sagrada Familia in Barcelona. Working with engineer Eduardo Goetz and the sculptor Bertran, he used compositions of string and balance weights hung upside down to form loops shaped by gravity. The idea was simple yet ingenious, i.e. if gravity pulled the construction into its correct shape, this same composition, if built pointing upward and duplicating the same *catenary curves*, would transfer the load from pure tension to pure compression.

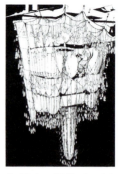

Upside down thinking. Inverted wire and canvas model through which Antonio Gaudí studied building structure.

Catenary curves were also employed earlier

by Isambard Kingdom Brunel as hanging wrought-iron chains carrying the 190 metre span of his Clifton suspension bridge, completed in 1864 in Bristol. The later invention of steel cables by John Roebling and his son, Washington, allowed suspension bridges to be built with a span eight times as long as that at Clifton. The first major use of spun cable was on Brooklyn Bridge — designed by Roebling and built by his son.   (RS)

See also: **Tensegrity**

Celebrate

To *celebrate* in the architectural sense is to mark a special event. Celebratory devices can include framing (framing a view or an important feature), orientation (positioning an object or building in recognition of some nearby event), gesture (the use of architectural posturing to make a point) and marking (distinguishing or decorating a feature so as to call attention to itself).

Therefore, when we *celebrate* we adopt a perceptual targeting strategy in order to deliver a punchline message. For example, entrances are perennial targets for the celebration of the sense of arrival, but they can also act as a mark of privilege, prosperity and social status. The act of celebration can involve a change in scale and usually coincides with the greatest amount of visual contrast. For instance, Alberto Giacometti describes the celebratory power of a spot of luminous red in a grey visual field when he writes: 'It is the Sunday in a row of grey weekends; it is the festival'.

See also: **Context** • **Contrast** • **Focal point** • **Framing (enframimg)** • **Gesture** • **Hierarchy** • **Place** • **Scale**

Chaos theory

Chaos occurs when a deterministic (that is, non-random) system behaves in an apparently random manner. — Ian Stewart

When exploring the mathematics of unpredictability, coincidence and accident, J. A. Paulof in his book *Once Upon a Number* (1999) turns to a technique devised by topologist Steve Smale to illustrate the evolution of chaos. Smale asks us to imagine a cube formed in white clay; through its middle is a thin seam of red dye. The cube is then squeezed and pulled into a shape that is twice its length before being folded back on itself in an attempt to reform the cube. This procedure of squeezing, stretching and folding is repeated many times over until the red dye is dispersed throughout the white clay in a continuous and highly intricate pattern. The result is a form in which all the points in the dye and the clay that were in close proximity in the original cube are now distant, while all the points that were distant are now in close proximity. Many similar stretching and folding operations occur in the natural world; it is argued that all chaos results from such stretching, squeezing and folding in a 'suitable logical space'.

Chaos gives rise to unpredictability, disproportionate response and the familiar butterfly wing effect commonly enlisted to illustrate the catastrophic consequences in one part of the planet as a consequence of microscopic atmospheric disruptions in another. The serious study of chaos began in the late 1960s; the term *Chaos theory* appearing later at the end of the 1980s. *Chaos theory* has applications in diverse specialist fields such as physics, ecology and economics. It embodies two main standpoints: that random or irregular processes, like a leaf floating down a mountain stream, may actually conform to discoverable laws; that some processes, hitherto thought to be unpredictable, have now been shown to be chaotic.

Chaos theory appeared in archispeak around the beginning of the 1990s and was used a term to describe all manner of formal splintering, shattering and deconstruction that did not appear to conform to any obvious mathematical underpinning. When the term is architecturally applied, one is drawn to the concept of randomness and to the visual manifestations of strange attractors, the Mandelbrot set, Julia sets and fractals. However, it was Vitruvius who first expressed the notion that the part should relate to the whole when designing architecture. In *Chaos theory* this is referred to as 'self similarity'.

See also: **Complexity • Fractal • Order • Topology**

Charette

Charette is an *École des Beaux-Arts* term from France. The *charette* was the cart that was wheeled around to collect student drawings for submission to L'École (and was also the cart that collected heads from Madame La Guillotine).

The term has lingered on — particularly in North American Schools — having attained the meaning of any short intensive student sketch design project. In recent years, *charette* has come to more general worldwide usage as an alternative to the clumsy R/UDATs and UDATs (Regional/ Urban Design Assistance Teams), where expert teams from elsewhere jet in to fix bits of the city in a week or two. The Congress for New Urbanism (CNU) affiliation of architects and urban designers — most prominent in the US under the effective leadership of the Miami-based academics and practitioners Andres Duany and Elizabeth Plater-Zyberk — has developed the *charette* further. According to their approach, when they work well, *charettes* avoid the pitfalls of 'expert workshops' of the past by ensuring that a multi-disciplinary local team is involved in the preparation of the materials, as well as participating in the workshop and also by planning for continued work when the star team has left. Most CNU *charettes* also involve the widest lay communities that they can reach to participate in agenda setting, but more particularly are able to respond critically to the three-dimensional visualizations of proposals that are an essential part of the design development process. Thus, there are a number of cycles of critique and debate, then the re-formation of proposals and visualizations, which means that by the end of the workshop all the participants can feel much more confident than in many other design processes that they know: what they are going to get; why it is the way that it is; and how it is going to be realized.

In this light, the *charette* is a worthy bandwagon for positive urban change. (RH)

See also: **Design intent** • **Design genesis** • *Esquisse*

Chora

Chora is a concept of an invisible, indeterminate receptacle or place. It is a term that emanates from the discourses surrounding the attempt to find common ground between the philosophy and architecture of Deconstructivism. In their book *Introducing Derrida* (2000), Jeff Collins and Bill Mayblin recount its initial use by Plato in his *Timaeus* (the first Greek chronicle of the Creation by a divine Maker) in which Plato maintained that every object has both an ideal form and a changing sensible copy. *Chora* is the abstract non-space, a matrix, the virtuality where this copy is created. This obscure environment, in which a thing is developed, together with its feminine, womb-like metaphors, was later explored by the French philosopher, Jacques Derrida. According to Derrida, rather than a place, *chora* is a spacing that is the necessary receptacle for everything to take place — a 'space' that defies presence, depiction and, it seems, definition.

Chora became part of Peter Eisenman's deconstructive work beginning in the late 1970s. His definition of the indefinable *chora* suggests that, like sand on a beach, it is something between container and contained; it is '. . . not an object or a place, but merely the record of the movement of water'. Decompositional variants of the term give 'chord', 'chorale' and 'choral', and Eisenman's unbuilt project 'Choral Work' excavates a non-existent, fictitious site history and archaeology. Using extracts from Derrida's writings, references from one of his earlier projects, and even drawings imported from another architect's work, he included and superimposed them all to inform his design.

See also: **Black box** • **Matrix** • **Trace**

Closure

A long straight road has little impact because the initial view is soon digested and becomes monotonous. — Gordon Cullen

While a dictionary will define *closure* as the act or process of closing — the drawing of lines of finality under events — its use in archispeak refers to an aspect of our bodily movement through spatial sequences. It refers to the creation of a perceived break in a chain of connected spatial events that, while momentarily containing the eye, does not restrict nor eradicate the sense of progression beyond. *Closure* occurs both in interior and urban space. For example, progression through Oxford's serpentine High Street is to walk through a series of identifiable spatial pockets — each seemingly enclosed as we pass through them. However, their closure is illusory as each are connected by a continuum of space — the result of this apparent 'containment' increasing anticipation and arousing curiosity of what lies beyond.

Closure is also an important aspect of visual perception. In this context it refers to our capacity to optically close, or visually 'paint-in', incomplete information in a stimulus. The term derives from the Gestalt psychologists who, in 1912, studied visual perception as an interactive and creative process involving both the viewer and the viewed. Their theories stress that, in seeking harmony and unity in visual data, our perception first sees a 'gestalt' (image) as a unified whole before an identification of its constituent parts. Also, as part of this visual reconstruction process, our tendency to perceptually group elements into simple units is governed by proximity (the relative nearness of elements to one another) and similarity (the relative sameness of elements). In terms of visual resolution, the power of *closure* over proximity and similarity is exemplified in this optical illusion shown below — the eye preferring to reconstruct the ghost of the white triangle rather than accept recognition of the individual parts.

There is also the term 'premature *closure*' which, drawn from the world of creative writing, refers to a form of mental constipation in problem solving. Those architects and students of architecture who avoid any extensive search for options before commitment, and thereby fail to push new ideas to the limit, appear to suffer from this condition. Conversely, the exhaustive design processes of architects like Louis Kahn, Charles Moore and Carlo Scarpa seem to have the opposite problem, i.e. frustrating their clients by continuing to explore different avenues of possibility well beyond their deadlines.

See also: **Intersection • Parameters • Processional space •** *Promenade architecturale* **• Resolve • Serial vision**

Spatial closure in Oxford's serpentine High Street and the perceptual closure of an optical illusion which induces the ghost of a white triangle.

Coda

The term *coda* carries musical overtones. It refers to the closing stages of a passage or final movement of a piece of music, or the concluding section of a dance. Its adoption in archispeak, especially in the writings of Steve Holl, describes an architectural caveat, i.e. a concluding event or series of events that form an addition to a basic architectural structure. For example, a *coda* can be an endpiece, a terminating element in a chain of buildings. It can also describe the concluding experience of a journey through a building where, what was the entry threshold, later becomes the *coda*, or point of exit — an entrance experienced in the opposite direction.

See also: **Engage (***dégagements***) • Threshold**

Collage   ∎

Collage is the juxtaposition of disparate things and the twentieth-
century mode of manifesting paradox 'par excellence'.
— Lebbeus Woods

In art, *collage* is the process of gluing down fragments of paper onto a
surface, often unified with lines and colour. Invented by Pablo Picasso
and Georges Braque during their Analytical Cubist phase, it involved introducing cut-out pieces of newspaper and pre-printed material into their
painted compositions. The technique was later adopted by Dadaist artists
such as Kurt Schwitters and Max Ernst. However, this latter use was
associated more with notions of chance and randomness. For example,
Hans Richter recounts the apocryphal moment when a frustrated Hans
Arp tore one of his paintings to shreds and, before leaving his studio, threw
its pieces into the air. On his return, Arp realized that the chance abstract
pattern created by the fallen fragments had achieved a power of expression that his earlier efforts had failed to achieve and glued all the pieces
to the floor. The Dadaists also used 'found' images to create irrational
conjunctions, deliberate spatial disharmonies and incongruities of scale.

Sigfried Giedion questions the idea that *collage* was invented by the
Cubists. He describes Antonio Gaudí's mosaic of broken pieces of glazed
tiles on Barcelona's Guell Park seating as exemplifying a form of collage
that predates that of Picasso and Braque by more than a decade. However,
the use of collage in architectural design is widespread. Here, exploiting
both chance and deliberation, it is used to heighten visual engagement in
the presentation of an idea and, more importantly, to release hidden associations in the issues of a design project. Also, the manoeuvring of painted
paper elements, their trial arrangement, and ultimate sticking down in the
manner of Henri Matisse, has been associated with those architects who
exercise a type of free-form planning. The ability of *collage* to transform
old meanings into new ones has, in the words of Lebbeus Woods, become
a convention, '. . . permeating consumer culture, advertising, fashion, movies,
and post-modern architecture'.

See also: Cubism • Dada • Fragment • Montage • Serendipity • Superimpose

Co-mingling space   ∎

A term mainly heard within the American design fraternity, *co-mingling
space* refers to that part of a building or the built environment where people
can spontaneously assemble, move about and mix together. *Co-mingling
spaces* occur when two or more spaces, each with its own function, overlap
to cause a common meeting ground.

Co-mingling spaces are found in lobbies, foyers, corridors, landings and,
indeed, in any space that, either by accident or design, allows people to
congregate and associate. Informal and adapted *co-mingling spaces* exist
wherever people hang out: street corners, the steps of public buildings
and underneath awnings and bridges, etc. Impromptu spaces are often
co-opted by people who pause when in transit, or who are caught in the
rain. Sometimes they are 'non-spaces' or what Lebbeus Woods calls

C | 28   Commodification

'freespace', that is, leftover urban spaces that have been momentarily commandeered.

Co-mingling spaces also exist more formally in the boulevards, arcades, markets, parks and plazas of the world. Successful public spaces are often enlisted as wishful-thinking precedents for gathering spaces in or around proposed designs. Among the most cited are the courtyard spaces in and around London's Covent Garden, the frontage of Richard Meier's Museum of Contemporary Art in Barcelona and the stage-like square outside the Centre Pompidou in Paris where the city spills into its fore-court. Often described as 'theatrical' in atmosphere, the square teems with people who, while being entertained by street performers, mill, idle and relax against the mechanical backdrop of its main façade.

See also: **Dualism • Interpenetrating space • Intersection**

Commodification

Commodification is a term that emanates from Walter Benjamin's influential, critical texts on modernity and city life. *Commodities* represent the dream world products of capitalist industrial production. *Commodification* entails the magical creation of mass-produced, consumable objects that become enshrined in the showrooms and shopping malls where the devoted consumer comes to pay tribute. Prototyped in the glassy halls of Paxton's Crystal Palace (1851), these temples of consumerism commodify a recycling of fashion. The accelerated tempo of work associated with the production and distribution of products leads to the *commodification* of time — an essentially modern sensibility in which time is equated with money. One of the consequences of *commodification* is the idolizing of products, i.e. the investment of inordinate value to commodities. Deification of products leads to fetishism — the projection of sexual passion and desire onto the inanimate object.

Along the shopping galleries and arcades of the late nineteenth-century and early twentieth-century lingers one of Benjamin's tragic, recurrent characters — the dehumanized prostitute. As the figure of greatest suffering, she represents the *commodification* of the woman's body — a symbolic, street-walking fusion of both the consumer and the 'mass-produced' object.

Meanwhile, today, fake dormers, plastic porches, and shutters and curtains in the garage, together with the schlock and styles associated with house types, all come to commodify the ideal home.

See also: **Branding (naming) • Brandscape • Temporality**

Commodity, Firmness and Delight

Well building hath three conditions: commodity, firmness and delight.
— Sir Henry Wotton

First recorded in *Elements of Architecture* (1624), Henry Wotton's quote *Commodity, Firmness and Delight'* (later made famous in 1914 by Geoffrey

Scott's *The Architecture of Humanism* (1974)) is a restatement of the recipe found in *The Ten Books on Architecture* by Vitruvius: '*Haec autem ita fieri debent, ut habeatur ration firmitatis, utilitatis, venustatis.*' It appears that Vitruvius wrote his famous treatise as a marketing effort to secure the favour of the Emperor Augustus. He failed, as only one insignificant building can be attributed to him.

He goes on to elaborate the attributes of '*venustatis*' as 'Order (*ordinato or taxis*), Arrangement (*dispostio*), Eurythmy, (*eurythmia*), Symmetry (*symmetria*), Propriety (*decor*) and Economy (*distributio or oeceonomia*)'. 'Order' is the relationship of the part to the whole; 'Arrangement' is putting things in their proper places; 'Eurythmy' refers to proportion; 'Symmetry', the proper balance between the parts of the building and the whole; and 'Propriety' refers to following the established rules for designing in the correct style for a particular building type. 'Economy' is a broad term, including the appropriate use of the Classical Orders and the relationship between the house and the occupant.

As can be seen from the above, the popular understanding of Wotton's '*Commodity, Firmness and Delight*' has become synonymous with late modern architecture, whereas both Vitruvius and Wotten were referring to classical revival architecture. It should also be noted that the statement by Wotton is an English translation of a Latin translation of a Greek text and may be more off the mark than we know.

'*Commodity, Firmness and Delight*' is a convenient cliché that takes its place alongside 'Form Follows Function' (Sullivan) and 'Architecture is Frozen Music' (Schelling) as a little understood architectural sound bite.
(EO)

See also: **Corporeality** • **Materiality** • **Order** • **Proportion** • **Symmetry**

Community indicators   ▌

Community indicators are measures and trends that describe the factors contributing to healthy neighbourhoods and communities. *Community indicators* usually have most of the following characteristics: they are relevant, understandable and usable to the community; they show the links among the economy, environment and social aspects of the community; they focus on the long term; they promote local sustainability, and they are based on available, reliable and timely data.

Some examples of good *community indicators* are: the per cent of housing units within walking distance of schools, shop, transit, employment; average incomes of the bottom and top 20 per cent of local residents; acres of natural and restored areas available to local residents; water use per capita relative to supply; number of housing units at different income levels compared to people at those levels; electricity consumption per person from non-renewable supplies; and acres of accessible park lands per person ratios of local jobs to housing.

The best *community indicators* are slightly complex and they contrast or compare multiple factors that are necessary for healthy neighbourhoods and communities in such a manner as to illuminate and aid in making long-term community planning decisions.

Community indicators can also be useful in guiding local government's investment in infrastructure to leverage desired private investment in a neighbourhood or community. A good walkability study of existing neighbourhoods in a town or city can reveal how a relatively small investment in enhancing the pedestrian infrastructure — making it safe, secure and pleasant — can increase the property values in local neighbourhoods and attract private investment into an existing area instead of supporting sprawl on the fringe.   (LP)

See also: **Ecological footprint • Sustainability • Walkability**

▎Compact city

The *compact city* is based on the belief that the physical form of towns and cities can positively affect sustainability. The European Commission (CEC, 1990) was an early and influential advocate, defining it as a high density, mixed use compact urban form. The argument is that the *compact city* will reduce urban sprawl, protect agricultural and amenity land, lead to the more efficient use of existing urban land, and ensure that the functions of work, leisure and living are in much closer proximity.

The *compact city* form claims to provide benefits in environment, social and economic sustainability. Because facilities are closer together, there is less need to travel, and hence it will be easier to walk or cycle. Higher densities mean that there are more people to support good public transport systems. Thus, there will be environmental benefits as there will be less dependency on cars and a consequent reduction in greenhouse gas emissions. Mixed uses and more people living and working in the same place gives rise to social and cultural vitality, with facilities in easy reach of everybody. Also economically, higher densities mean that local businesses become more viable, as there is a larger population to serve.

While the *compact city* is relatively easy to define as a physical urban form, its success in achieving sustainability is not. Caution is needed as few of the claimed benefits have been tested. Recent research suggests that not one single form, but a number of urban forms may be sustainable. The compact city may be one of them (for a definitive review see *The Compact City: A Sustainable Urban Form?* (Jenks *et al.*, 1996); Achieving *Sustainable Urban Form* (Williams et al., 2000); *Compact Cities: Sustainable Urban Forms for Developing Countries* (Jenks and Burgess, 2000)).   (MJ)

See also: **Dense • Sustainability**

▎Complexity

Complexity is wonderful unless it is invented by project managers who invent it to justify themselves. — Will Alsop

In the dictionary sense, *complexity* deals with intricacy, elaboration, convolution and multiplicity — characteristics that are diametrically opposed to straightforwardness, uncomplication and the obvious. *Complexity* is associated with the writings and design approach of Robert Venturi who, in his influential book *Complexity and Contradiction in Architecture* (1966), advanced a design approach that associates its antonyms with the trite and the superficial. In promoting his vision of aesthetic ambiguity and visual tension, Venturi's visionary book marked the advent of architectural post-modernism.

According to Venturi, *complexity* in architecture is loaded with ambiguity (such as double-functioning building elements) and contradiction (such as the disjunction between interior and exterior), as well as contrast, tension and paradox. Such a multiplicity of meaning and content in a building can involve both the real and the abstract. Venturi argues that *complexity* is a symptom of a period in flux. Simple buildings, he suggests, are created by those who are over-selective about the problems they choose to solve; complex buildings result from embracing much wider, hybrid and often conflicting issues. While not denying simplicity as a valid goal, Venturi describes *complexity* in architecture as a condition that, in responding to intricate programmes rather than a need for the 'easy unity' and of an exclusive expression, allows opposites and a doctrine of 'both and' (rather than 'either or') to coexist.

Countering the Modernist maxim 'less is more' with his own 'less is a bore', Venturi also suggests that the medium of architecture itself is too complex to be dealt with by the limitations of narrow doctrine. Indeed, he proposes that if the demands of the complexities of its aims are to be truly expressed, the business of creating architecture should be rigorously reappraised.

See also: **Ambiguity • Disjunction • Paradox**

Composition

. . . the notion of architectonic composition is connected with both the physical elements and the way the visual features of the whole are arranged. — Clemens Steenburgen, Henk Mihl and Wouter Reh

Composition is a vehicle for bringing order to chaos; it involves the unifying of elements into a whole so that each ends up in its proper place. In the words of Deborah Hauptmann, *composition* is a process 'which makes visible conditions that would otherwise remain inapprehensible to structures of thought and systems of action'. For instance, while compositions can integrate their constituent elements through both their similarities and their differences, those that display too many similarities will lead to ambiguity; those that display too many distinctions will lead to chaos.

Writing in *Design and Analysis* (1997), Bernard Leupen *et al.* suggest that the concept of the compositional assembly of architectural form was adopted from fine art techniques, such as the structuring of paintings that has been practiced since the Renaissance. The gradual ascendance of *composition* came to cause a shift from the earlier Vitruvian idea of 'distribution' and away from the emulation of prescribed models to a new means of designing. It was one that, rather than division and subdivision and using hierarchy as its regulator, now directly dealt with the assembly of masses and spaces and the elements that define them. This approach offered a greater flexibility and more creative control; it was a design technique in which the individuality of the architect could feature more prominently in the outcome. Its full assimilation into architectural design as an ordering process became consolidated in the latter half of the nineteenth century in the teachings of the École de Beaux-Arts. It is one in which all the parts relate to the whole while the whole remains resonant of its parts.

Consequently, *composition* has become a central tool in the act of architectural problem-solving. From inception to resolution, architectural *composition* involves the complex orchestration of considerations, including the physical, visual and functional. All these considerations make their contribution to the *composition* as a whole.

See also: ***Assemblage*** (conceptual model) • **Collage** • **Montage** • **Order** • **Ordering systems** • **Reconfigure** • **Regulating lines** • **Resolved** • **Zone**

Composite drawing

A *composite drawing* occurs when two or more modes of drawing are brought together and are fused into a hybrid form of graphic representation. For example, the combination of a section and a perspective to create a section-perspective is a basic *composite drawing*. More recently, the *composite drawing* has resulted from more adventurous fusions involving variations in scale, type of drawing, reprographic technique, plus the use of repetition and overlapping elements. Eric Owen Moss, Henri Ciriani and Helmut Jahn are just a few of its exponents.

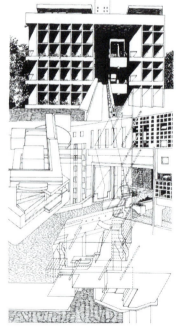

Although a large number of diverse drawings combined into one runs the risk of ambiguity, *composite drawings* offer opportunities to explore and experiment with a presentation, to emphasize, de-emphasize, compose and decompose specific parts of a design. A major influence on the evolution of the *composite drawing* has been the international design competition and the subsequent publication of prize winners in design journals. As a result of the restriction on size and the number of sheets, and the designer's need to catch the judge's eye in the preliminary rounds of selection, this more dynamic and adventurous approach to a condensed form of drawing has evolved. The competition layout is characterized by considerable variation in the scale of drawings and the squeezing together, overlapping and layering of graphic information. *Composite drawings* are carefully orchestrated, being reminiscent of

Detail from a compacted drawing by Henri Ciriani comprising an elevation, two overlapping perspectives and an axonometric drawing.

how an artist might plan an abstract composition. Indeed, the assembly of a series of multi-view fragments into the frozen dynamic of a complex drawing has obvious roots in Cubism and Constructivism.

See also: *Assemblage* (conceptual model) • Collage • Composition • Constructivism • Cubism • Montage • Superimpose

Concept

A concept, whether a rationally explicit statement or a subjective demonstration, establishes an order, a field of inquiry, a limited principle. — Steven Holl

The strength of a concept has to do with the clarity of its mandate to manage design of the scheme in a particular direction, how long the concept can continue to sustain this potency throughout the design process and how many kinds of design choices the concept can influence. — Edward T. White

Traditionally, during or following the act of digesting and interpreting the programme of requirements, or brief, the designer's next undertaking leads to the formation of a *concept*. However, as exemplified in the work of Frank Gehry and Bernard Tschumi, a *concept* can either precede or follow the outset of a design process; theoretical concepts either being applied to a project or derived from it.

A *concept* is a general notion, an abstract idea, a mental picture that forms in the 'soup' of all the related aspects. An initial concept need say nothing about the form the design is to adopt; essentially, it expresses the idea underlying a design and functions as a signpost to guide the direction of the ensuing design journey. While possibly feeding from the issues thrown up by the brief, or from the location or site of the proposed building, or deriving from a disassociated but parallel line of thinking, a *concept* can, depending upon its efficacy, inform, shape and advance a process of decision making, it can marshal thoughts and precedents and bring the field of opportunity into focus.

By feeding from a fertile imagination and a thorough understanding of the constraints, requirements and opportunities of a programme, *concepts* do not arrive to order. However, when a *concept* does arrive it can take on many forms. It can appear as a embryonic sketch, an object, an image, a word, or a text. A *concept* can emerge in the mind's eye at any time and in any place, such as in bed or in the bath. When not forthcoming, *concepts* have to be artificially teased out and then 'massaged' via brainstorming.

When realized, a good *concept* or network of concepts give direction and guidance to the designer at every level, from the global to the detail; it provides a framework for innovation.

See also: Black box • Conceptual drawing • Design genesis • Parameters • Problem solving

Conceptual drawing

How can I know what I think till I see what I say? — E. M. Forster

Every architectural design has started on a blank piece of paper, with a scribble whether in words or lines. For instance, Joseph Paxton's concept for his Crystal Palace began as a prophetic, rapid sketch on a telegraph form made during a train journey in 1850. Oscar Neimeyer's designs for the capital city of Brasilia, if his perpetuation of the legend is to be believed, were originated on the back of a cigarette packet, and Charles Moore would, in the manner of Pablo Picasso, doodle initial design ideas over a meal on table napkins. We tend to think of such gestures as casual and incidental, but these first impressions of an emerging design concept can be prognostic and represent an architecture at its purest and most basic.

Such marks begin what Robert Stern has described as the highly personal and idiosyncratic 'objective/conceptual drawing stage' that, using diagrams, advances the process of an idea. To externalise an idea, the conceptual drawing involves a language of abstraction in which hiero-glyphics and annotation combine to draft the potential relationships between mental concept and reality. Many educators see these inaugural marks as representing a precious moment in the design process — their fresh and uninhibited presence in a design review being as insightful as a polished presentation drawing. Furthermore, Frank Gehry has based his entire designing effort on maintaining the spirit of the conceptual doodle in the executed work.

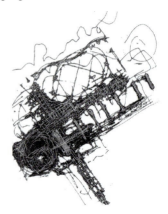

See also: ***Assemblage* (conceptual model) • Concept • Diagram • Diagramming • Design genesis • *Esquisse* • *Tabula rasa***

Concept drawing for the design of an elementary school.

Consequence triangle

Consequence triangle is a term that describes the interactive behaviours of key components in built environment situations. The *consequence triangle* facilitates thought and discussion about the consequences of design decisions, such as the impacts environments, people and sites have on one another. The *consequence triangle* can also question how each affects and is affected by the other factors involved in long-term occupancy and environmental performance.

When an environment is built and occupied, networks of cause-effect events are set in motion that last for the environment's lifetime. This event network affects the project's wear and deterioration, rate of repair, employee productivity, health and safety, site erosion and landscaping appearance.

The *consequence triangle* is composed of three elements: the environment, its occupants, and its surrounding situation or context. Each change is changed by the other two, and each changes itself by its own behaviours. Environment affects itself, occupants and context; occupants affect themselves, environment and context; and context affects itself, environment and occupants. Each emits and receives energies, forces, pressures, impacts and behaviour to provide a continual exchange of actions and consequences.

The *consequence triangle* reminds designers that environments are not just inert products to be delivered. Rather, they are settings for processes in continual evolution, motion and change. They are networks of behavioural interactions that hold important long-term consequences for people, natural systems and built environments.   [ETW]

See also: **Diagram • Diagramming • Synthesis**

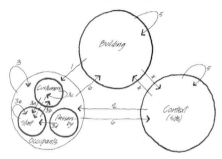

The *consequence triangle* showing the interaction of its three protagonists: the building, the users and the context.

Constancy scaling

As we have always occupied the horizontal plane, the human field of vision is horizontally biased, i.e. it is much more attuned to the lateral dimension than to the vertical. This bias has caused a phenomenon known as *constancy scaling*, which affects the apparent size of objects when seen over distance. For instance, as the size of an object appears to decrease with distance, it follows the law that its size will halve with each doubling of the distance from the viewer. However, this law refers to the retinal image and does not account for the 'zoom-lens' capacity of the brain, which uses *constancy scaling* to compensate for the shrinkage of objects over distance.

This can be tested by holding out both your hands, one hand nearer your eyes and the other hand at arm's length. Although a camera would record them as being quite different in size, their perceptual size as modified by the brain makes them appear quite similar and apparently little affected by distance. This discrepancy accounts for the fact that photographs taken of distant views make background features seem much farther way than when compared with their direct viewing.

The estimation of size and distance in the horizontal bears no relation to that of the vertical. Indeed, *constancy scaling* inverts when we look vertically up or down. The distance of the street, say, from atop tall buildings appears much farther away than it actually is, and can induce vertigo. Steeplejacks and 'sky monkeys' can, with experience, perceptually compensate and override this aspect of *constancy scaling*.

See also: **Depth cues** • **Parallax** • **Visual field**

Comparison of the shift in depth representation between the 'mechanical eye' of a perspective drawing and a quick student sketch.

Constructivism

The artist is turning from an imitator into a constructor of the new world of objects. — El Lissitzky

Constructivism was an anti-realist, abstract movement that manifested itself in Russia shortly before the Revolution. Considering easel painting and studies of nature bourgeois, they moved towards an art, architecture and theatre design that imitated the forms and processes of technology. They aimed to make art a detached, quasi-scientific investigation of the properties of materials, surfaces and their combination. From the 1920s their 'laboratory experiments' led them to make 'spatial constructions' using industrial materials and techniques. These were suspended in space in almost architectural fashion — a notable installation in 1920 was Alexander Rodchenko's 'spatial constructions'.

Architects have a real soft spot for *Constructivism*; particularly for Vladimir Tatlin's leaning tower 'Monument to the Third International' (1920). Although built only in model form, it comprised a double-helix steel framework inside which three glass volumes, a cube, pyramid and cylinder, respectively rotated once a month, a week and a day. Earlier in 1915, Tatlin had met Picasso in Paris and, inspired by his three-dimensional constructions, had returned to Russia to build polychrome reliefs. Fuelling dreams of an animated architecture and accompanied a decade later by the fantasy architecture of Iakov Chernikov, these free explorations of form uncannily anticipate some of the characteris-

Vladimir Tatlin's project for a three-speed 'Monument to the Third International' (1920).

tics of hi-tech structures. Indeed, their free explorations of architectural form provide perennial inspiration for successive generations of students and practitioners alike — from Mies van der Rohe to Zaha Hadid.

See also: **Animate • Diagonal • Suprematism**

Context   ∎

Context is an important idea in post-modernist design, and the machine metaphor denies this significance. An engine is an engine is an engine, and it always works the same way no matter where it is.
— Stephen Friedman

Architecture is an extension; a modification establishing absolute meanings relative to a place. — Steven Holl

In its widest sense, the term *context* refers to all the issues and circumstances that surround a design of which the nature of the setting is the most tangible. As the derivation of the word means 'weave together', the spirit of its meaning denotes an interdependence — 'weaving' or 'knitting' designs into existing site conditions and the striving for a sense of fit. *Context* refers to the fact that most buildings are designed and made for a specific place; the characteristics of which represent many of the constraints and opportunities in which a design is determined. Because architecture cannot detach itself from its *context*, and because *context* is never the same, it is essential that knowledge and insight be gained. The technique for gaining insight into a setting is the 'site appraisal' or 'site analysis', i.e. the systematic investigation of palpable (hard data) and intangible factors (soft data). Owing to the more subjective aspects of this analysis, the question of how the features of a site may impinge upon a design holds no clear-cut solution. This is under the control of the designer; it is subject to ideas on which he or she has to make a stand.

'Contextualism' is an approach that respects the setting in terms of its history, topography, memory, route and so on. However, respect for *context* does not necessarily mean that a design has to conform. Steven Holl describes the site for a building as the setting in which all its intentions are gathered together. The design for a specific place may mean an inversion of inherent conditions. These may be based upon other related frameworks for invention, such as esoteric or poetic linkages. Holl argues that today the link between situation and architecture must be formed in new ways, '. . . which are a part of a constructive transformation in modern life'.

See also: **Anchoring • Memory • Palimpsest • Site appraisal • Site specific**

Continuum   ∎

Within design education philosophies, concepts of space and form are usually separated and regarded respectively as the negative and positive of the physical world, a world where objects reside and void — the mere absence of substance — is a surrounding or contained atmospheric emptiness. However, since the beginning of the nineteenth century, there has been an alternative concept of space as *continuum*, as the continuously modified surface skin between the pressures of form and space in which the shape of the space in our lungs is directly connected to the shape of the space within which we reside — which is, in turn, just a layer of the space surrounding our planet. In this sense, space is perceived as an extension of the body, a dimension of its imagined extension — a continuous force field activated by the body's movement.

The fourth dimension, time, is a non-spatial *continuum* in which past, present and future occur in apparently irreversible succession. While space is the interval between point, surface and object, lapses of time are measured and marked by the intervals of recurring events.

Another related aspect of *continuum* is when no part of an object, such as a building, is distinguishable from adjacent parts. An architectural example is the Hancock Building in Chicago where hotel, office space and residential uses are indistinguishable on the exterior façades of the building.

See also: **Dimension • Temporality**

Contrast

Variety is not just the spice of life, it is the very stuff of life.
— J. J. Gibson

Thinking in terms of contrasts is not a confused way of thinking, for even contrasts can be united in a harmonious whole. — Emile Ruder

In *A Primer of Visual Literacy* (1973), Donis A. Dondis writes: 'All meaning exists in the context of polarities. Would there be understanding of hot without cold, high without low, sweet without sour?' *Contrast* is an important keyword: our ability to sense subtle and particularly sudden differences in our immediate environment — changes in temperature, movement, smell, sound, taste, etc. — functions as the crucial aspect of our biological survival kit.

Contrast is central to our visual perception, the basic operation of our eye detecting change in the field of vision and translating the spatial setting into an intricate network of 'perceptual patches'. Each shape in the network finds its existence through its degree of *contrast* with its neighbours; the resulting pattern, albeit illusory, being deciphered by the brain into a register of three-dimensional space. The incidence of this visual pattern responds to the direction of light — each shape in the network being differentiated by size, value, colour and textural attributes that communicate precise qualities, such as rough, smooth, glossy, matt, specular, etc. Without *contrast* a scene would appear as a uniformly dull event with little or nothing to be seen.

Contrast is a powerful design tool. Scales of *contrast* are the essential force in the articulation of design and communication; it is a powerful means of expression in the structuring of compositional unity and in the intensification of meaning. For example, when we look at a scene or a pictorial display, our eyes are immediately attracted to the areas of greater *contrast*, such as the flash of colour in a monochromatic field of value, and vice-versa. Therefore, when we design, we enlist the same vital force to structure and create two- and three-dimensional events as that used by our perception to make sense of our surroundings.

See also: **Composition • Depth cues • Figure–ground • Focal point • Juxtaposition • Message area • Pictorial space • Positive–negative space • Value • Visual field**

Convention

Let me say that there are two ways in which reality makes sense to us: there are those things we accept as being the way they are because we have no choice but to do so, and there are those things we accept as being the way they are because we want them to be that way.
— William Hubbard

A *convention* is a given, a rule, an established practice or ritual that is consolidated by majority consent. For example, social interaction is governed by conventions such the handshake (a declaration of being unarmed) and removing one's hat when entering a building (an act of deference). The practice of architecture is similarly riddled with *convention*: cultural 'street manners' and best practices that determine, for instance, how a building is drawn and constructed. Architectural drawing particularly is governed by a code of convention that determines everything from the appropriate thickness of a line to the direction of sunlight entering a plan or elevation.

However, *convention* can be shattered. For instance, the *convention* for the pictorial depiction of movement in space and time was suddenly demolished with the advent of new ideas in 1907. Hitherto, movement in time was expressed through successive images, and space was defined from the fixed viewpoints of linear perspective. Analytical Cubism came to reject this; their work enlisted a decomposition involving transparency, superimposition and interpenetration to introduce the notion of the simultaneous occupation of a picture by two different objects or by several aspects of a single object. Thus, new conventions can replace earlier codes of practice. Indeed, the cycle of architectural 'isms' each tend to question the conventions of those it purports to replace. For example, from a Deconstructivist standpoint, Modernism represents an artificial, cultural design prop — an uncritically accepted *convention* that suppresses the invention of individual subjectivity.

However, the true test of design conventions lies not in some absolute truth, but rather in their ability to achieve some desirable end. Designers are constantly faced with accepted rules of conduct and unwritten codes of practice informed by a particular culture or *convention*. However, while *convention* establishes axioms, some rules, even when golden, can be challenged. To do so holds the potential of putting one's foot in the door of innovation.

See also: **Best practice • Cubism • Didactic • Ghosting • Parameters**

Corporeality

The world articulated by the body is a vivid, lived-in space.
— Tadeo Ando

The philosophical alienation of the body from the mind has resulted in the absence of embodied experience from almost all contemporary theories of meaning in architecture. — S. Gartner

As distinct from spiritual awareness, *corporeality* refers to the physical, the sensate awareness of self and body. Consequently, to crack one's 'egg-head' on a beam is to experience *corporeality*. *Corporeality* becomes suppressed when we isolate ourselves from a primarily tactile appreciation in favour of surrogate representations of reality. 'Disembodiment' begins when our sight and mind insert abstract concepts to act as distancing agents between us and our physical setting. This is when we enter parallel worlds induced by thought, writing, reading and drawing, and, indeed, when we separate mind from body in the concept of 'telepresence'. In his *Understanding Media* (1964), Marshall McLuhan spells out the challenge of new forms of technology on our senses. He talks of the sensory desensitizing effect of our acquisition of the illusion of the third dimension and 'the private point of view'; both part of a narcissistic fixation in which we become what we behold. In other words, we substitute pictorial sensation for the sensate.

Writing in *Body and Building* (2002), Kenneth Frampton describes the multivalent presence of the corporeal in Tadeo Ando's architecture. Ando's body-centred approach is characterized by an adaptation of the Corbusian '*promenade architecturale*' in the ritualistic approaches to his church designs. Here, the tactile primacy of contact with the earth and our capacity to negotiate its plane is subtly articulated and intensified by discontinuities. These are intervals or pauses in the continuity of architectural space; moments when sky, water and surrounding vegetation are allowed to intrude. The idea of the pause in which the body is temporarily suspended in order to intensify *corporeality* is one associated with the concept of 'ma', a Japanese notion in which a momentary separation from an architectural event can paradoxically induce stronger experiential links in the chain of sensation.

See also: **Commodity, Firmness and Delight • Experiential • Materiality • Multi-sensory space • Tactility**

Crit

As far as desires go, there is really not such a great gulf between the one who creates and the one who appreciates. — Man Ray

Known as 'design review' in the US, the *crit* (short for 'critique') is feared by some and relished by others. *Crits* represent that moment when a project is made public and is open to debate. When they happen, three main forces are at work: the reviewer or critic, the ideas of the designer-presenter, and the setting in which this critical exchange of information takes place.

While two of these factors are directly under the control of the presenter, it is the critic or the review panellist that can provide the unknown. Therefore, *crit* presentations can often represent an anxious moment in the life of a design proposal. The only way of approaching them is to be well prepared.

While some schools of architecture operate reasonably democratic systems of criticism, the *crit* is seen by some reviewers as open season on students, i.e. when students become vulnerable to the whim and prejudice of panellists. One way of obviating this is to establish early in a presentation the central aims or objectives of the project. If generally accepted, then the ensuing *crit* should function to measure the level of success or failure in achieving those goals — the resulting measurement, hopefully, guiding the ultimate assessment.

See also: **Design intent • Design rationale • Mission statement • Moment**

Critical mass

Borrowed from the world of physics, *critical mass* describes the moment when the amount of fissile material is achieved to maintain a nuclear chain reaction. Its adaptation in archispeak generally refers to the moment in the process of design when a developing idea suddenly seems to assume the palpability of a life and identity of its own. This is the post-analytical moment of synthesis when the 'seed germ' of an idea takes root, when things come together and fall into place, and when the vacuum of uncertainty is filled.

Therefore, *critical mass* describes the realization that a concept is up and running, i.e. when its momentum and direction is being driven as much by the design idea as by the designer.

See also: **Moment • Synthesis**

Critical path analysis

Critical path analysis is a branch of operations research introduced in the 1950s to streamline industrial production. It is a method of organizing several closely related activities, some of which cannot begin until other sequences have been completed. Adopted in architectural design for the planning of buildings housing complex operations, it is now mainly a computer-based technique used to discover the best sequence of events in a complex process. Each operation is diagrammatically set out as a point in a network to show the order in which events occur and which tasks depend on the completion of the others. In order to ascertain the most economical sequence, each task is assigned a value, such as the time taken and the cost involved. *Critical path analysis* also 'brackets' tasks into 'early' versus 'late start' phases — any time lag between them being known as 'float' or 'wiggle room'.

When the network is completed, it becomes clear that while delays in some of the operations involved can be tolerated, delays in others will jeopardize the schedule of the entire process. Operations in this second group are said to lie on the critical path, i.e. when delays appear on or near the critical path. The advantage of identifying hiccups in the system means that resources can be concentrated upon them.

See also: **Diagramming** • **Lateral thinking** • **Problem solving**

Crystalline

Crystalline is a recurring metaphor defining an architecture of high transparency, or one that reflects the form or structure of a crystal. Glass crystal is the stuff of dreams and visions; it forms a ring of transparency around the parkland core of Ebenezer Howard's utopian dream of a radial ideal city in a garden, in the dome of Bruno Taut's vision of an architecture of the future and, albeit represented in a membrane of plastic, in the geodesic bubbles of Nicholas Grimshaw's Eden Project in St Austell, Cornwall.

The subconscious dimension of this influential design generator is touched on in John McKean's book *Crystal Palace* (1994) in which he describes the *crystalline* metaphor in context with our continued fascination with the memory of the transparency embodied in Joseph Paxton's monumental Victorian glass and cast-iron structure. Constructed to showcase the British Empire, the *crystalline* nature of Paxton's glass Palace came to provide a model for the site of consumerism — echoed in the transparency and sparkle of the shopping arcades and galerias that followed. These qualities, McKean suggests, evokes in us a latent, crystal dream: 'That magical, unworldly place deep in our subconscious stretches, as a crystal chain, from the castile in the Renaissance tale *Ariosto Furioso* via Paul Sheebart and Bruno Taut, to the filmed lair of Superman'.

See also: **Commodification** • **Fragment** • **Geodesic** • **Metaphor** • **Shard** • **Translucency** • **Transparency**

'Kryptonite' outcrop in Terry Farrell & Partners' design for 'The Deep', the Ocean Science Complex located in Kingston-upon-Hull.

Cubism

■

The cubist canvas was the locus where the painter simultaneously presented several aspects gathered successively with the purpose of suggesting a higher reality. — Marta Braun

Occurring during 1909–11 and claiming to be a realist movement, *Cubism* came as the mother of all the radical art movements which coincided with the transformation taking place on the world stage at the turn of the twentieth century, especially in the fields of science and technology. The paintings of its main protagonists — Pablo Picasso and Georges Braque — came to counterpoint the arrival of new and revolutionary theories of matter and the challenging concepts of space, time and energy embedded in Einstein's *Special Theory of Relativity* (1905). By allowing their paintings and collages to respond to a binocular (two-eyed) vision rather than a monocular (one-eyed) perception, *Cubism* came to shatter the single vanishing point of a Renaissance linear perspective into a multiplicity of viewpoints. By compressing and flattening several views of an object into a single composite, and by expressing the idea of the object rather than any one exclusive view of it, their experiments dramatically expanded the shifted viewpoints found in Paul Cézanne's later paintings. This also caused the two-dimensional image to fracture into tiny facets, and thereby release form from its hitherto naturalistic representation and move it towards its abstract conclusion.

   In parallel with the upsurge of a Modernist thinking, this shift toward fragmentation, which depended upon the relative position of the viewer, involved a temporal dimension. In its recording of the lapse of time, the dynamic of the artist's eye reflected that of shifting camera angles in movie-making — the ultimate image involving the 'simultaneity' of compressed time. This aspect of *Cubism* was profoundly influenced by the philosophy of Henri Bergson who saw time as an essentially intuitive experience and reality as resulting from a simultaneous flow of past and present into the future.

   Le Corbusier was well aware of the Cubistic mode of juxtaposing a multitude of meaning into the simultaneity of a single statement. Indeed, some of his buildings reflect this 'collage' approach in their elevations and in the layering of contrasting cultural and historical references.

See also: **Collage** • **Fragment** • **Layering** • **Modernism** • **Montage** • **Temporality**

Cutting edge

■

The term *cutting edge* usually refers to ground-breaking activities, or propositions resulting from such activities, that are considered to be innovative and original. This is the zone that exists at the forefront of new developments within a discipline and is characterized by a willingness to make creative leaps. Functioning as the sharp end of the leading edge, and often occurring where the boundary of one discipline overlaps another, the *cutting edge* can move into new ground or move a theory or concept into the territory of another discipline.

   The *cutting edge* is not for the cut and dried but the cut above who, in the cut and thrust of design, are intellectually prepared to cut a dash, cut both ways, cut across and cut corners.

See also: *Avant-garde* • Disjunction • Edge condition • Lateral thinking • Parameters

Cybernetics

In his book, *Cybernetics: or Control and Communications in the Animal and the Machine* (1948), the MIT mathematician Norbert Wiener identified the evolutionary model found in the organic world of living things as a blueprint for the development of adaptive systems in machines. In much the same way that periodic random mutations evolve into the dominant species in the animal kingdom, the science of *cybernetics* recognizes that the process of information feedback is the predominant agent for correcting or controlling the future behaviour of a mechanical (computational) system.

Within conventional reasoning the onus tends toward error correction, but an important distinction of the cybernetic model is that it can embrace chance encounter and error as part of its system, using this and other information (feedback) as a source for generating an evolved position. In effect, the system is learning and adapting to the changes and nuances in its surrounding environment as it progresses.

A feature of an adaptive system is that the total range of its outputs, that is, its variety of behaviour, determines its potential for survival and success in a world of unpredictability, and it is this that distinguishes its identity among its derivatives. This method of self-education by a form of trial and error in an organic structure is known as 'heuristic'.

Within the design process, the heuristic instruction incorporates the unexpected and unfamiliar as an opportunity for expression. Chance happenings or encounters are viewed as potentials for use and the adoption of the original direction of an idea manipulated to suit these new ingredients. As the late cybernetician Stafford Beer states in his book *Brain of the Firm: The Managerial Cybernetics of Organisation* (1972), one has to 'ride the dynamics of the system'.

While these ideas may now seem somewhat rudimentary in our present day electronically-driven world, the study of *cybernetics* has influenced innovation in a diverse range of subjects: from Stafford Beer's organizational business structures to Brian Eno's development of ambient and generative music. (SB)

See also: Cyberspace • Feedback • Simulacrum • Virtual reality

Cyberspace

The concept of *cyberspace* was first coined and defined in 1982 by William Gibson in his trilogy of novels which included *Neuromancer*. In his narrative, members of a science-fictional, technologically advanced but decaying society plug themselves into global computer networks. Quickly adopted in computer jargon, *cyberspace* describes the conceptual dimension through which electronic information — anything from a phone message to a fax to a television signal — is transmitted. In *cyberspace*, data are decomposed or 'liquefied' as the data are digitally transposed from one medium to another. In the abstract world, the building blocks are 'bits' rather than atoms. Using software to order and reorder them, it becomes possible to recreate digitally artificial versions of our physical reality and to construct dreamscapes: imaginary worlds at human scale that embody all the traditional notions of reality and conditions of human perception. Moreover, with the aid of the computer, it also becomes possible for us to recreate ourselves and to enter *cyberspace* and to interact with this digitized environment as freely and directly as we would in the real world.

According to Antonio Caronia, writing in *Ottagano* (1993), the concept of *cyberspace* has been with us for some time. It simply takes to extreme consequences a process that was already latent in television and computer games where our imagination becomes temporarily suspended between an imaginary, dreamlike state and the concrete reality of the everyday experience. It is a convergence where our imagination crashes in upon our physical reality in a profound way. Thus, it is a condition that involves the fragmentation of our body as it trespasses the boundaries of its mental and physical capabilities. At a basic level, this fragmentation of our body or, at least, its organs, is similar to the way that we use VCRs to watch television without being there, and answering machines to converse with others without lifting the receiver. If television has become an extension of our eyes, and the telephone an extension of our ears, we can also add the computer as an artificial intelligence existing outside our brain.

See also: **Cybernetic • Fragment • Simulacrum • Virtual reality**

Dada

Deliberately meaningless, the name *Dada* was adopted by an international anti-art movement that flourished from 1911. Its main centre of activity was the Cabaret Voltaire in Zurich where like-minded poets, artists, writers and musicians would gather to participate in experimental activities such as nonsense poetry, 'noise music' and automatic drawing. It was *Dada* that first introduced us to the concept of chance in design and to the idea of the 'ready made' or 'found object'.

Although not involving architects nor architectural projects, the move-ment is attractive to many designers. This is due to their interest in randomness and serendipity. One of its members was Arthur Cravan who became the subject of a Hollywood movie. Seen by some as the precursor of *Dada*, Cravan assumed a lifestyle that would tear 'bourgeois existence apart at the seams'. He lived out *Dada* on the principle that art was dead and that personal action should replace it. At the height of World War One he travelled the world on forged passports assuming different identities. In Switzerland he claimed to have committed the perfect burglary; in Spain he challenged the then world heavyweight champion, Jack Johnson, to a title fight (Cravan was floored in the first round); and in England he impersonated the Queen's Chancellor. His life ended in typical Dadaesque fashion, he disappeared while single-handedly sailing a tiny boat from the Mexican coast to Argentina.

See also: **Collage • Serendipity**

Datum

Datum is a known or assumed premise, benchmark, point or plane of origin from which inference can be drawn. For instance, in his book *The Concise Townscape* (1961), Gordon Cullen suggests that although the jargon of politics defines a person's persuasion in terms of being left or right of centre, the more usual classification of datum is in relation to the horizontal. In the context of our visual relationship with buildings and the landscape, Cullen refers to the significance of *datum* as, possibly, ema-nating from a primitive concept of heaven and hell. However, once sensed, we equate above *datum* or height with 'privilege', and below *datum* or depth with 'intimacy'.

In *Architecture: Form, Space and Order* (1979), Francis Ching describes *datum* as a bracing device that can take the form of a referential line, plane or volume. For example, functioning as a compositional ordering tool, an axial line serves as a *datum* that can either bisect formal arrangements or define their edge condition, while the plane of a grid can provide a neutral field against which the elements captured in its net are anchored and unified. However, Ching reminds us that a *datum* is not necessarily a straight line nor a flat plane. Indeed, *datum* can also function as a volume — the boundaries of a three-dimensional figure being used to either contain or to deploy elements around the pattern of their edge.

Every place has its *datum* line; one may be on it, above it or below it. However, an added complication to our understanding of *datum* is the fact that we each carry about with us our own inbuilt sense of *datum*.

See also: **Axis • Balance • Grid • Hierarchy • Order • Ordering systems**

Decision-making space   ▮

Decision-making spaces occur at collecting points and pathway intersections along journeys through the built environment. Moments of indecision
can be found at crossroads, car parks, building approaches, entrances,
foyers and in labyrinthine corridors where judgements have to be made by
the uninitiated about the next stage of passage. To be helpful, decision-
making requires ample physical space and a platform of clear information
on which to base a decision. Rather than resort to the banality of signage,
directions can be indicated by an architectural 'sign-posting' resulting
from a hierarchy of size and shape and the clarity of an en route incidence
of spatial elements.

'Wayfinding' and 'search behaviour' are aspects of decision making.
They are especially associated with the anonymity of large complexes,
such as hospitals and government buildings, that often present users with
significant problems of orientation and the associated feelings of stress
and incompetence. Studies by Kevin Lynch and others show that decision-
making relies upon the use of a cognitive version of physical maps called
'mental maps', the success or failure of which being determined by the
frequency of pathway intersection, circulation points of high encounter
with others and visual landmarks.

Decision-making space can also refer to the 'wiggle room' available to
the designer during the act of design. These are periods of reflection;
times when pause points are created in which to make decisions.

See also: **Breathe** • **Lung** • **Mapping** • **Moment** • **Node**

Deconstructivism   ▮

Railing against the architectural style and communication whipped up by
the advocates of stylistic post-modernism, a radical reaction to this reduction of architecture came in 1988 in an exhibition entitled 'Deconstructivist
Architecture' at New York's Museum of Modern Art. The work of seven
designers was featured, including that of Frank Gehry, Peter Eisenman
and Bernard Tschumi.

Philosophical deconstruction, as practised by Jacques Derrida, Paul de
Man and others, was advanced as a key to the Deconstructivists' pedigree,
but the new *rappel a desorder* was based more on the superficial similarities arising from fragmented and colliding geometries than on any

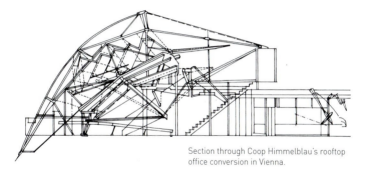

Section through Coop Himmelblau's rooftop
office conversion in Vienna.

shared body of ideas. In 'Decon' design, every element contorts as the 'suppressed alien' of the 'unconscious of pure form' is released. However, what the Deconstructivists clearly shared was a commitment to Modernist principles of composition, including techniques associated more with painting than design.

Built in 1989, Coop Himmelblaus Falkestrasse 6 in Vienna is an explosive confrontation on the roof of a traditional apartment building. It was proclaimed as one of the first built manifestations of deconstruction — or Deconstructivism — in architecture, but its revolutionary charge is purely aesthetic.

See also: **Deconstructed space • Disjunction**

Deconstructed space

Space has a history. — Gaston Bachelard

In the history of space we have now arrived at *deconstructed* space as the leading edge spatial paradigm of the moment. To arrive there we have travelled from the spherical, static, geocentric and limited space of the ancient and medieval world, through the constructed perspective space of the Renaissance, and more recently the relativistic space/time of the modern era. *Deconstructed space* is not space at all in the usual sense; it is the dimensionless, boundless space of the cyberworld. The very construct of space has been deconstructed and then reconstructed as cyberspace. Space has become a quickly traversed event space. The apparent limitations of this new conception of space are the human imagination and the speed of light. There is no longer a separation between space and the actors within that space — it is transitory. *Deconstructed space* does not exist unless someone engages it. The tree does not fall in the forest until someone is there to programme it to fall. Whether or not it makes a sound is dependent upon the volume button.

Architects are beginning to flirt with the possibilities of representing *deconstructed space* within the limitations of traditional tangible space. Daniel Libeskind's Jewish Museum provides a glimpse into *deconstructed space*. The play of the straight and fragmented zig-zag lines, representing sudden illumination or destruction, begin to approximate the experience of *deconstructed space*. Ultimately, there may be no place for tangible and predetermined architecture in the world of deconstructed space. In the architecture of *deconstructed space* even gravity, the weather and daylight are no longer relevant.

The video game is an ironic twist on the notion of *deconstructed space*. It constructs fantasy worlds of traditional Euclidean space that only exist in *deconstructed space* (one wonders if there will be future difficulty in making a distinction). (EO)

See also: **Cyberspace • Deconstructivism • Disjunction**

Decorated shed ▮

The d*ecorated shed* is one of two interpretations of architectural form involving symbolism discussed by Robert Venturi, Denise Scott Brown and Steve Izenour in their *Learning from Las Vegas* (1972). The other building type is referred to as the 'duck' — a term derived from a Long Island poultry shop housed within a building shaped like a duck. While the duck is a building that 'sculpturally' takes on the form and the image of its function, the preferred *decorated shed* is an otherwise conventional shelter fronted with applied symbolic ornament.

While Venturi and his associates designated many Gothic cathedrals as 'buildings behind billboards', and described Italian Renaissance palaces as 'decorated sheds par excellence', the term in critical use often carries undertones of superficiality. For example, a design approach that,

at the expense of a homogeneously considered architecture, exclusively focuses on the public face of a building or a group of buildings is dismissively described as 'façadism'. While the legacy of the original *decorated shed* is found in every retail park built since the 1980s, one of the best examples is the TVAM building in London designed by Terry Farrell.

See also: **Frontality • Ornament • Strip**

Terry Farrell's now defunct TVAM Building at Camden Lock, London, remains as an icon of the *decorated shed*.

Defensible space ▮

A 'defensible space' is a living residential environment which can be employed by inhabitants for the enhancement of their lives, while providing security for their families, neighbors, and friends.
— Oscar Newman

Coined by the architect and urban planner Oscar Newman in 1972 in his influential book *Defensible Space: Crime Prevention Through Urban Design* (1972), the concept of *defensible space* stems from his mainly New York-based research on crime in high-rise public housing. This highlighted the relationships between the occurrence of crime and housing project size, scale and layout. In order to reduce crime in dense residential settings, his basic strategy was to help residents establish more appropriate feelings towards their physical setting than the alienation and those sentiments of fear and anger that many people often hold in public housing.

According to Newman, through mutual surveillance comes the ability to monitor and 'defend' territorial spaces. A place would be safer because residents and other people could observe what was going on within their perceived 'sphere of influence'. Newman's notion was that through subdivision, the insertion of eye-catching features such as billboards and trees, and the clear articulation of the physical environment, public and private space could be designed to be naturally overlooked and monitored by its occupants. Despite ensuing criticism of what, for some, smacked of environmental determinism, Newman's ideas not only changed housing policy in terms of design in the US, but they also underscored the power of post-occupancy evaluation methods and their resulting benefits.

See also: **Determinism • Post-occupancy evaluation (POE) • Proximity • Sight lines**

Dense

The admonishing sense of *dense* and its colloquial equivalent, 'thick', is not too far from its wider meaning: crowded or closely compacted. Therefore, in environmental terms *dense* describes the compactness of population and a spatial compression caused by a close-knit structuring of form.

The author of *City of Bits* (1995), William J. Mitchell, compares the denseness of the city with a microchip. The electrical components of the silicon chip are packed tightly together because the closer their proximity, the faster the chip operates. So, too, cities are *dense* because many human transactions have traditionally necessitated face-to-face contact. Density is also key to Paolo Soleri's idea of the three-dimensional city infrastructure to improve efficiency of interaction and to conserve natural planetary systems.

See also: **Compact city • Contrast • Hierarchy • Proximity • Scale • Value**

Depth cues

Our visual experience of space relies upon a hierarchy of optical functions triggered by direct visual contact with the real world around us. The primary visual signals or cues that aid our perception of depth are binocular vision and motion parallax. Binocular vision can be subdivided into three related parts: *accommodation* (the ability of the eyes to focus on only one point at a time); *convergence* (the angle subtended by the eyes on the object in focus — a nearer object subtending a larger angle, a more distant object subtending a smaller angle); and *disparity* (each eye receiving a slightly different image). Our eyes give overlapping fields of view and stereoscopic depth vision; motions of the head and eyes give motion parallax; so movement at right-angles to a line of vision alters the relative positions of two unequally distant objects. When sight is removed, other depth-sensing receptors come into play to fine-tune our responses to acoustics, tactility and kinaesthetics.

When three dimensions are represented in the two-dimensional world of pictorial displays, they have to rely totally upon the secondary depth cues. These include *overlap* (a portion of one object in the field of view being partially hidden by another), *relative size* or *convergence* (the association of the decreasing size of objects with distance), *atmospheric haze*, also known as *aerial perspective* (the perceived greater clarity of nearer objects in contrast with those farther away), and *position in field* (objects seen progressively higher in the field of view appearing as more distant). When we draw a perspective many or all of these pictorial depth cues are utilized in the re-creation of a convincing illusion of space on the two-dimensional plane.

See also: **Cartesian space • Constancy scaling • Euclidean space • Matrix • Multi-sensory space • Parallax • Visual field**

Dérive   ▌

Guy Debord's text 'La Theorie de la Dérive' was first published in 1956 in the Belgian surrealist journal *Les Levres Nues*. Defined as the 'technique of locomotion without a goal', the *dérive* is an explorative journey through the city which offers the potential for the chance encounter, observation, interaction or exchange within a constantly changing, shifting and disorientating urban terrain.

Debord was the self-styled leader of the Situationist International, the formation of which, in 1957, heralded the beginnings of a radical revolutionary movement of academics, artists and thinkers whose rebelliousness and libertarianism culminated in writings, interventions and actions that attacked all aspects of life in the West in the latter half of the twentieth century. Despite its dissolution in 1972, the ideas and work of its members continue to inspire and challenge those who choose to critically examine and question the role of art and creativity within the late capitalist context.

The *dérive*, or psychogeographical shift, centres on a critique of the capitalist city. In his seminal work, *Society of the Spectacle* (1967), Debord describes a late capitalist society of passive consumption and production. The *dérive* is the notion central to the Situationists' proposed revolutionary reconstruction of the capitalist urban condition. The city, rather than a dumb machine, where the objectification of all aspects of modern everyday life result in *privatized, functionalist zoning and categorization*, becomes a physical landscape where the terrain itself offers the individual or group the possibility of direct creative action and interaction. The city is reconstructed as a site where freedom of choice in direction, experimentation and play could result in the liberation of the individual and society, creating the potential for the boundaries between politics, art and action to dissolve.

Unlike the traditional notion of the journey or stroll, where the observer or bourgeois Baudellairian '*flâneur*' wanders aimlessly looking at the 'other', the citizen engaging in a *derive* consciously interrogates, engages with and transforms the constructed landscape.

Representations of the *dérive* are rare, but include Debord and Jorn's 'mapped' collage 'The Naked City', Ralph Rumney's photographic collage 'Psychogeographic Map of Venice' and Constant's explorations of the Situationist city 'New Babylon'.   (JT)

See also: *Flâneur* • **Serendipity**

Design criteria

Design criteria are explicit benchmarks by which the success of a design effort may be measured. Such criteria are often, but not exclusively, quantitative, and may be confirmed by instrumented measurements, user surveys, interviews or data comparisons (such as a cost estimate versus a budget limit). Without *design criteria*, any solution to a design problem may be unilaterally declared 'successful' by any one of the numerous parties to the design (architect, interior designer, engineer, contractor). Such an 'anything goes' approach is generally undesirable and may result in less-than-satisfied clients and occupants.

Design criteria are the yardstick against which compliance with stated design intent is validated. For example, an intent to provide highly energy-efficient lighting may be proved by the measurement of lighting power density. An intent to provide a relaxing work environment may be proved by occupant responses to an appropriate questionnaire. An intent to provide a green building may be proved by a successful score on a consensus rating scale.

It is not difficult to establish appropriate and meaningful criteria (benchmarks) for many aspects of building intent. Many criteria (temperature, illuminance, floor area) can be easily validated with low-cost portable instruments. Other design objectives, however, may test the skill of the design team relative to evaluation. How, for example, would one prove that a roof is actually going to be 'maintenance free', a space really 'dazzling', a system truly 'innovative' or a building 'spiritually uplifting'? Although qualitative intents are more difficult to validate than quantitative, it is no less important that they be evaluated against valid criteria. Appropriate criteria for the qualitative are more likely to involve perceptual responses than instrumented measurements; they are more likely to involve complex patterns of variables than single-number measures.   (WG)

See also: **Design intent • Mission statement • Parameters • Vital signs**

Design genesis

What give our dreams their dreaming is that they can be achieved.
— Le Corbusier

Design genesis refers to the birth of an idea. This takes place in the mind's eye when our creative imagination triggers a concept that is imagined ('seen') as flashing, dimensionless images; images formed from a creative leap into the potential solution. These mental images can result from, or be subject to, prejudices, intuitions or a systematic analysis or reduction of criteria. Such mental pictures are impressions — incomplete, in a state of flux and somewhat vague. They originate from forces at work within the mind, including the nature of the immediate problem, and the past experience and personality traits of the creator — the latter influences lying beyond any conscious control. These factors continue to have some bearing on decision-making throughout the ensuing and evolving sequence of design.

It might be possible to generate and develop images from concepts in the mind alone. But spatial ideas can become so extensive and complex that they can no longer be contained. Externalization in some tangible form is needed so that they can be clarified, assessed and articulated. At this point the idea has to pass through space and be translated into two or three dimensions, as a descriptive model which allows the designer to experience and advance the nature of the idea. Newly represented, the model of the idea can inspire the creative imagination on to other mental images, which are, in turn, realized and evaluated, This two-way language of design is a continuous dialogue between concept and expression — alternating until the creative process is exhausted.

Louis Sullivan characterized the initial impulse of a design as the 'seed germ', a design catalyst that should be maintained throughout its many stages of development. Realization of newly-formed ideas can take the form of orthographic drawings. Of these, the plan view was famously described by Le Corbusier as the 'design generator'. However, less famously, the sectional view was promoted by Paul Rudolph as the most searching graphic vehicle when generating a design.

See also: **Black box • Conceptual drawing • Dialogue •** *Tabula rasa*

Design integrity   ▌

Design integrity refers to a state of completeness of design, a kind of cohesiveness in which the slightest modification or alteration would impair or destroy its unity. For instance, design integrity is threatened if we remove a leg from a chair. *Design integrity* also refers to consistency of resolve and, like a house of cards, quickly crumbles into compromise when we try to please everyone.

The movie *Fountainhead* is all about *design integrity* — Gary Cooper, playing its architect hero, Howard Roark, was prepared to dynamite his building as a consequence of its adulteration by others. Therefore, design integrity means devising a robust design concept and staying true to its principles when the freedom of its expression is threatened — even in the face of extreme criticism. However, *design integrity* can also provide a shield behind which a designer can camouflage a sham rectitude.

Structural integrity is a closely related concept. This refers to structural stability and the continuity of a structural system.

See also: **Robust**

Design intent   ▌

Design intent is a clear and concise statement that expresses the objectives of the design team relative to a project or portion of a project. *Design intent* is not the project brief (or programme) — it goes beyond the brief to describe the general quality or key attributes that any acceptable solution to the brief must capture. *Design intent* can and should be expressed at various levels of a project, from the project as a whole, to individual spaces, to systems of environmental conditions within spaces. Without an expressed *design intent*, any and all possible solutions to an owner's brief are presumably fully acceptable. There can be no clear direction to design efforts without clear intent.

Owner's briefs typically provide only a minimal statement of needs. A design intent statement converts such owner needs to a verbal description of the design team's vision of a proposed solution. *Design intent* should be developed for all the various elements and systems of a project. For example, workstations for an office area might be intended as highly ergonomic, easily reconfigurable, and using readily available systems components. Lighting for the office might be intended to promote high accuracy and visual comfort, easy maintenance, and low energy costs. A lobby might be intended to convey the corporate philosophy of a company and provide a welcoming environment.

Design intent should describe a clear destination for design efforts, but should not define specific methods. If methods are expressed in intent, then all other possible means of solution are excluded.   (WG)

See also: **Design criteria • Mission statement • Parameters • Rationale**

▌Design rationale

Design rationale is a term used to focus on the underlying reasoning behind a design intention. It concerns the basic structure of thought that brought the design into being. Sometimes referred to as 'intellectual underpinning', the *design rationale* aims to distinguish between the intuitive and the cerebral, and to represent the bedrock on which concepts are structured. However, it must be added that while it is difficult to apply logic to an instinctive approach, the ultimate response may represent a balance between the two.

'Pet idea' is a common type of *design rationale* that typically needs to be aired early on so it can be discarded or be allowed to evolve into a legitimate *design rationale*. When a developed intention is declared in a 'mission statement' or presented as a mini-manifesto and, hopefully, made visible in the proposed design, the *design rationale* flies in the face of whimsical or willy-nilly design attitudes and challenges a 'prima donna' approach.

See also: **Design criteria • Design intent • Mission statement**

▌Determinism

In its broadest sense, *determinism* regards the notion that every event has a cause, that every occurrence is a consequence of some law of nature. It is central to the debate concerning the impact (or lack of impact) of the physical setting on social behaviour. With the concept of *determinism* comes the spectre of the architect being held responsible for built environments that cause contributory factors to a whole range of social ills.

A scale of determinacy and non-determinacy has been identified by Amos Rapoport. *Determinism* is a perception of the physical environment as one that effectively induces or controls human behaviour within it. The opposite of the deterministic environment is one offering 'possibilism', that is, an environment providing options and opportunities through which users can exercise degrees of choice. Between these two polarities lies the physical setting known as 'probabilism'. By providing some degree of choice this environment is not deterministic, but some choices will be more available and therefore more probable than others.

While 'social engineering' is a related term, 'multi-strategic space' and 'indeterminate space' are the non-determinant antitheses of determinism. When heard in architectural criticism, *determinism* is a deadly, accusatory word that is usually reserved for design proposals that exhibit as much freedom of choice to the user as a prison cell.

See also: **Functionalism**

Diachronic   ▮

Natural landscapes may exhibit the beauty of rhyme and contrast simply in their static structure. But people who live in the landscape — as men live in cities — the dynamic structure, the diachronic rhymes, add a new dimension to aesthetic pleasure. They see the same landscape in a state of flux. But, through every change, the landscape retains its identity and each transformation gives them new insight into its essential character. — N. Humphrey

The word *diachronic* refers to comparisons we make through time. This term offers the architect a very direct and meaningful description of an arrangement or treatment of parts or events occurring not at the same time (see Synchronic) but through the variable of time.

Although the word is not in use in everyday conversation, it can capture the transformations in appearance through movement, weather, night and day, and time very clearly. One could conceptualize the comparison from one second to the next or from one season to another. Another example in the field of colour theory is the concept of 'successive colour contrast', where the same colour appears to differ in chromatic strength (saturation) if preceded by its complementary colour. If one walks through a green corridor, for example, prior to moving to a red one, the red appears stronger or more vivid.

In the context of the study of aesthetics, the term 'diachronic rhyme' has been specifically used by Nicholas Humphrey (*Architecture for People* [Mikellides [1980]]) to refer to the pleasure we get when comparing something to its precious self — the rhyme of the flower with the bud, the rhyme of the recurring musical composition. The sense of order gradually emerging as we pass through the streets of a town like Amsterdam is an example of diachronic rhyme according to Professor Peter F. Smith: 'Amsterdam is a case of what Gerard Manley Hopkins called "likeness tempered with difference" extended over the city.'   (BM)

See also: **Mediation • Modulation • Rhyme • Rhythm • Synchronic**

Diagonal

Diagonals introduce powerful directional impulses, a dynamism which is the outcome of the unresolved tendencies toward vertical and horizontal which are held in balanced suspension.
— Maurice de Sausmarez

While the horizontal and the vertical provide basic references for our relationship to the environment, the *diagonal* challenges balance, well-being and manoeuvrability. In a deck of grids, the *diagonal* is the wild card — its slanting dynamic being perceived in direct reference to our concept of stability. Consequently, the *diagonal* is a particularly significant visual element. While its sense of imbalance can be threatening and literally upsetting, the impact of its unpredictability is exciting, it grabs attention and sharpens our perception.

Banned as heretical from Mondrian's Neoplastic grids, the *diagonal* represented a new and revolutionary aesthetic in the paintings, collages installations of the Suprematists and Constructivists. Opposed to the 'passivity' of the horizontal and the 'authoritarianism' of the vertical, El Lissitkzy, inspired by Malevitch's notions of a weightless, flying architecture, experimented with strong pictorial diagonals and gravity-defying slants in his three-dimensional projects. These were later used in full force in the late 1920s by Theo Van Doesburg to destroy the cubic enclosure of his Cafe Aubette conversion.

When introduced to the grid, the *diagonal* represents a short cut. Notable urban diagonals include Barcelona's Diagonale, Washington DC's *diagonal* avenues, carrying important names and terminating in circles, and New York's Broadway — all thoroughfares disruptively cutting through the ordered grid-plan of each city — the latter tracing the memory of a former native American trail.

Broadway cuts diagonally across Manhattan to survive grid lock and to mark an ancient native American track.

See also: **Balance • Constructivism • Dynamic • Focal point • Visual field**

Diagram

A *diagram* is a drawing that, stripped of all superfluous and distracting data, shows the general scheme or outline of an idea or object and its parts. It is a reductive graphic representation of the course or results of an action or process. *Diagrams* are enlisted at the formative moments of design to chart the potential relationship between concept and reality. In functioning as a constructive doodle, and concerned more with idea than appearance, *diagrams* are graphic representations of an idea being structured.

However, the *diagram* is not the idea but a model of it; intended to define its characteristic features. According to the designer Keith Albarn, through appropriate structuring, *diagrams* may generate different notions or states of mind in the viewer. However, these 'different notions or states of mind' are susceptible to three factors that are also rooted in the designer's mind: familiarity with the mode of expression, the amount of information that the drawing supplies and a previous experience of three-dimensional space.

In order to develop an effective design model and to facilitate the evolution of forms in response to this model, a variety of *diagrams*, each with their own potential and conceptual set of rules that aid decision making, may be employed. These include 'schematic' and 'operational diagrams' that are concerned with the relationship and orientation of the parts, and for visualizing changes over time. 'Functional', or 'bubble diagrams', identify the proximity and relative size of the zones of activity, while 'flow diagrams', like their operational counterparts, study possibilities that arise when movement is considered between one point and another. These are all analytical diagrams that investigate the nature of existing conditions and evaluate a completed design in comparison with its original intentions.

See also: **Analytical drawing** • **Diagramming** • **Morphology**

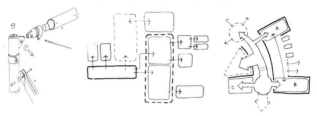

Operational, flow, and functional (bubble) diagrams.

Diagramming   ▮

Diagramming in environmental design fields applies to any effort to visualize situations, requirements, ideas and concepts, such as the study of configurations, relationships and interactions between project elements and aspects. *Diagramming* is a communication tool. It permits the designer to externalize ideas on paper so they can be studied, tested, improved and clarified. It also permits the sharing of ideas with fellow designers, allows them to be confirmed by clients and be understood by bankers, builders and code officials.

Diagramming may take many forms and may appear at any stage in the building delivery process: time graphs and pie charts at feasibility and financing; flow diagrams at project delivery planning; site analysis and bubble diagramming at programming; concept diagrams at early design thinking; and design reasoning diagrams at client presentations.

Diagramming is particularly useful in projects that are large, complex and intricate, and those that are politically sensitive or under intense public scrutiny, or when working with multi-minded querulous clients who have a low error tolerance.

Diagrams can represent physical elements and relationships (spaces, walls, playfields) or abstract principles and ideas (priorities, sequences, intensities).

The art of designing and refining a diagram is an occasion to penetrate, explore and discover. It is an opportunity to carefully study and understand elements, connections and meanings. *Diagramming* is a visual language for appreciating and responding to project requirements; for evaluating proposed schemes and explaining their merits to others.   (ETW)

See also: **Analytical drawing • Diagram • Morphology**

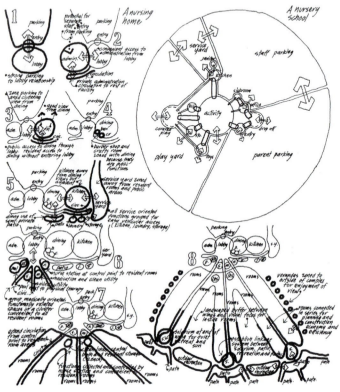

Site analysis diagrams.

Dialogue

Dialogue is a conversation or a discourse between two or more people, such as in the design review or a theatrical performance. In theory, it is possible to have a *dialogue* with oneself. *Dialogue* is information exchange in the search for meaning, and in order for communication to take place there must be a degree of empathy between the transmitter and the receiver.

Dialogue is also interaction between people and things, such as build-ings and spaces. Therefore, dialogue is pure jargon for the recognition that certain elements in a design display a discursive relationship, as if engaged in a 'conversation' that is perceived ('overheard') by the user. In order for a *dialogue* to take place, the interdependency and opposition of various architectural forces, such as solid–void, large–small, horizontal–vertical, etc., have to be in tension either through proximity, contrast, equivalence or superimposition.

An aspect of the ways a building appears to communicate and interact with us is the way that intimate spaces seem attuned to the scale of our bodies, while cavernous spaces — when not articulated with body-sized elements — seem to isolate. Extremes in size and volume can also cause a psychological *dialogue* in which we imagine our bodies as smaller in elevators and larger than life in vast auditoria. *Dialogue* is found in surfaces where smooth finishes invite intimate contact, while excessively textured surfaces can induce a wider berth. Meanwhile, points of textural change usually speak of an architectural special event causing a slowing or speeding up of movement. In this sense, *dialogue* can be seen as our choreographed relationship with architecture. When architectural elements communicate in this way, they contribute to the overall 'narrative' of a design.

See also: **Engage (*dégagements*) • Feedback • Gesture • Interaction • Interface • Kiss • Mediate • Reciprocity • Tension**

Didactic

Buildings that overtly teach can be considered to be *didactic*. The Holocaust Museum, the Arc de Triomphe, the gothic cathedral, as well as the Parthenon, are all clear examples of architectural didacticism. Similar to the Parthenon with its *didactic* friezes, contemporary office buildings and other 'temples' of commerce and industry are being used as armatures for mammoth video plasma screens that usurp the building itself. The medium is the message. The mute and visually abandoned building behind the message is merely the chalkboard on which the daily lesson is scrawled. One need only visit the new and improved Times Square in New York to understand the potential of 'building as billboard'. The most common form of *didactic* architecture is the fast food restaurant. The white castles of the US White Castle hamburger chain and the Burger Kings of this world are both teaching us that we can eat like a king. Other efforts at *didactic* architecture abound. One clear example is Robert Venturi's Baseball Hall of Fame project, which has taken the notion of billboard architecture to its literal extreme.

At another level, *didactic* architecture is subtle. The ubiquitous French Provincial or Georgian mini-mansion, found in suburbia, is teaching the passer-by that the owner is a successful and unimaginative member of middle class society.   (EO)

See also: **Allegory • Narrative**

Diffusion

Diffusion describes the unconcentrated and the inconcise. In archispeak the term can be applied in different ways. One use describes a rambling discursiveness, such as an over-running and long-winded lecture, or, indeed, a design presentation that challenges the attention span of the audience. Such excessive wanderings are a *diffusion* of thought and speech, often characterized as 'verbal diarrhoea'.

Another use of the term describes the blurred edge condition of a shape in the visual field. When this occurs it can cause perceptual ambiguity and tension — the eye finding it difficult to focus on a stimulus that simultaneously appears static and dynamic. Unable to accommodate *diffusion*, the eye, in its attempt to resolve the situation, will continue to scan the stimulus causing a relationship between physical movement and the static shape. Ultimately, our past experience with indistinctness will associate edge *diffusion* with a rapidly moving shape or object.

Carrying a meaning that lies opposite to an additive process, such as absorption and assimilation, *diffusion* therefore describes dispersal, a spreading action like the sprinkling of water through a shower head or the scattering effect of sunlight through a translucent filter. An anthropological use of diffusion describes the influence of one culture as it permeates the religion and people of another. *Diffusion* similarly occurs when the density of architectural form is eroded to become increasingly perforated, segmented or fragmented — when space is released like holes in Swiss cheese to tributarize and interpenetrate the mass.

See also: **Ambiguity • Erosion • Filter • Fragment • Porosity (permeability) • Segment • Scrim • Tension • Translucency**

Dimension

A *dimension* is one of a number of measurements that must be specified to identify a point on a line or a surface, or in a space. A line has one *dimension*, since the distance from a fixed point on the line is sufficient to identify any point on the same line. A surface, on the other hand, is two dimensional. For example, two coordinates, such as longitude and latitude, can fix the position of any geographical location. Space is three dimensional; to fix a position of an aeroplane, longitude, latitude plus height need to be specified. When we need to identify the occurrence of any spatial event, three coordinates need to be stated plus a fourth — the time the event took place.

However, time is not necessarily *the* fourth dimension. This is explained by Thomas F. Banchoff in his book *Beyond the Third Dimension* (1990) in which he relates Edwin Abbott's *Flatland*, a Victorian tale written in 1884 about different dimensional worlds. First, 'Lineland' is a one-dimensional world in which its unseeing occupants, existing as segments, live side by side along a line. 'Flatland' is a two-dimensional world, a plane occupied by geometric shapes who move about like amoebas on the surface of water, and who, with their one eye, see only the lines of others. 'Flatland' is visited by a sphere from the three-dimensional world of 'Spaceland', who, in passing through the plane of 'Flatland', is experienced by Flatlanders first as a dot before expanding to a line and then contracting back to a dot and vanishing. Consequently, Banchoff explains, the Flatlanders' experience of a growing and shrinking segment passing through their world is an experience of time. So, for them, their third dimension is represented by time but, Banchoff continues, this does not mean that the third dimension is time. If 'Spaceland' represents our own three-dimensional word (where time is considered as the fourth dimension) and we were visited by a sphere from the fourth dimension, a similar experience of growth and decline — like the inflation and deflation of a balloon — would be experienced. Banchoff writes that it would be impossible for us to judge whether we were seeing an ordinary sphere changing in time or the three-dimensional slices of a 'hypersphere' from the fourth dimension. Therefore, Banchoff concludes, 'time is a fourth dimension, not the fourth dimension'.

When heard in architectural debate, *dimension* is also popularly used as a jargon term to describe an aspect or facet of a situation or problem. In this sense it refers to its unknown nature, scope or size or its unquantifiable extent. When we refer to a 'new dimension' it usually means that we are measuring a phenomenon along a new direction.

See also: **Flatland**

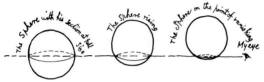

Flatlander's view of a sphere changing in time and space as it passes through his two-dimensional realm.

Disjunction

Disjunction is a term associated with the writings of Bernard Tschumi and his call for a radically new architectural approach. He believes that, when used as a theoretical tool for making architecture, *disjunction*, and its bedfellow 'disruption', are entirely relevant to the current and fragmented breakdown of a Western post-modern culture. *Disjunction* questions the traditional architectural search for accentuation of unity, harmony and synthesis in favour of a 'post-humanist' stance that disrupts coherent architectural form and challenges the principles of its composition. Therefore, *disjunction* is the attempt to deconstruct the traditional components of architecture for their painstaking reassembly into a new kind of architecture.

Demonstrated in Tschumi's theoretical and built projects, strategies of *disjunction* are achieved by a systematic exploration of one or more themes, such as 'superimposition' and 'repetition' — themes that underpin his complex layered design for the Parc de la Villette in Paris. However, while being exercised within the discipline of architecture, his themes are developed at the margins of the discipline, i.e. where the limits of architecture meet the boundaries of other fields of study. Consequently, they are steeped in an awareness of other fields, such as literature, philosophy and film theory, from which techniques, such as deconstruction and montage, are adapted as architectural design tools.

See also: **Ambiguity** • **Deconstructed space** • **Deconstructivism** • **Paradox** • **Transprogramming**

Dualism

Dualism is the theory that reality is composed of only two irreducible substances, for example, matter and spirit. Man has probably been fascinated by duality since he first recognized that he had two arms, legs, eyes and ears. It appears to be a universal cultural concept. Ying-Yang, heaven and earth, humankind and the gods, mind and body, and good and evil are all examples of duality. Zorester (660–583 BCE) can be considered the founder of Western formal *dualism*. His notions of Satan and Jehovah, plus his doctrine of truth versus dishonesty, formed the foundations for Christianity as well as Greek science, including Platonism.

Western philosophical *dualism* is most associated with Cartesian *dualism* (*cognito, ergo sum*). The mind/body 'problem' has kept philosophers busy since Descartes suggested that we are two — our corporeal body and our mind, and that the mind is the seat of our being. On the other hand, John Locke's *dualism* perhaps applies most directly to architectural theory. He contended that the quantitative aspects of a thing are primary. Thus, size and shape are more important than the qualitative features of colour, sound, temperature, pleasure, etc. This conforms to our underlying bias for the objective having greater value than the subjective.

The emergence of Modernism replaced the *dualism* of classical architecture (symmetry, spirit versus matter) with the *dualism* of the Scientific Age (function versus form, objective versus subjective). More recent adventures with holism and phenomenology in architecture are challenging Modernist *dualism* as the spirit of our times. Zoraster may yet take a back seat to Edmund Husserl.   (EO)

See also: **Balance • Cartesian space • Symmetry**

Dymaxion

One could be forgiven for thinking that *Dymaxion* is a name for a new energy drink, but it is a term associated with the technology pioneer, Richard Buckminster Fuller. *Dymaxion* refers to a unique combination of functionalism and prefabrication that converts the Bauhaus epigram 'less is more' into 'more for less'. It is enshrined in the familiar image of Fuller's mast-supported structure called the 'Dymaxion House'.

Although not coined by Fuller (the term *Dymaxion* was devised by a public relations group that sat in on one of his lectures), the term is a compound of 'DYnamic', 'MAXimum' and 'IONs' — words constantly heard on Fuller's lips. A pioneer of prefabricated housing and the inventor of the geodesic dome, Fuller operated outside the mainstream of an accepted design culture. He dreamed of emulating the automotive and aviation achievements of Henry Ford, first producing a revolutionary rear-engined, aircraft-style streamlined car in 1933 called the *Dymaxion*, and also the Dymaxion House. Built of steel, duralumin and plastic, his first prototype for the mass-production dwelling of the future was built in 1929. By 1946, his full-size family dwelling called the 'Wichita' house was designed to be assembled on wartime bomber production lines.

See also: **Ephemeralization • Functionalism • Geodesic • Kit of parts • Tensegrity**

Dynamic   ▮

Being the opposite of stasis and inactivity, *dynamic* is the sign of life. *Dynamic* implies movement, and movement involves energy and time. Seen from fixed points or triggered by our bodily locomotion through the environment, rapid fluctuations in our field of vision will create a kaleidoscope of changing impressions. Whether caused by our bodily drift in space or activity in a static view, the attraction of *dynamic* events is due to the nature of our visual perception which, like other animals, has evolved specifically to detect movement and change in the visual field. Consequently, *dynamic* arrangements of form and space are more likely to attract our attention than static versions.

However, we also project a *dynamic* into the stationary and the inanimate, and there is movement in everything we design. For example, lines, figures, volumes and mass each embody inner forces that exhibit degrees of tension and directional thrust. When two- or three-dimensionally assembled, the result is a fluctuating force-field in which increased *dynamic* occurs when figures and forms depart from the regular, the orthogonal and the symmetrical to challenge gravitational pull, and when the rhythmical timing of their incidence intensifies. A visual *dynamic* resulted from the late nineteenth-century photographic studies by Eadward Muybridge and Etienne-Jules Marey of the attitudes, pulses and flows of running people and animals in motion — an analysis expanded in the early twentieth-century by Futurist artists who distorted and fragmented form in their analysis of speed in movement.

A scale of architectural *dynamic* ranges from the studied coolness of a Meisian rectangularity to the exploded views of the overlapping plates and volumes of the Deconstructivists, and to the all-singing and dancing twists and folds of the curvature of Frank Gehry's free forms.

See also: **Breathe • Contrast • Interaction • Linearity • Rythym • Tension**

Airbrush painting of the twisting *dynamic* in Frank Gehry's The Experience Music Project, Seattle.

Dystopia

The opposite of utopia, *dystopia* describes a nightmarish vision of society, often as one dominated by a totalitarian or technological state. *Dystopias* abound in the literature of science fiction; three of the best known are to be found in George Orwell's *Animal Farm* (1900) and his vision of a 'Big Brother' state in *Nineteen Eighty-Four* (1948), and in Aldous Huxley's *Brave New World* (1932).

A dystopian genre also flourishes in screenplays. Set in the near future, movies like *Brazil*, *Mad Max* and *Blade Runner* make indirect reference to the desolation and placelessness of some contemporary urban settings, such as the high-rise housing block and the shopping mall.

See also: **Disjunction**

Eclecticism   ▮

An eclectic is a person who draws ideas and inspiration from a range of sources. Being eclectic means non-adherence to a single philosophy, that is, being pluralist or 'catholic' in taste and ideas. In archispeak it often refers disparagingly to an architecture of compilation — an architecture which, in the attempt to be progressive, draws from historical pattern-books.

However, despite its common association with a creative redundancy and a sentimentalized borrowing from the past, *eclecticism* does have a reputable history. For instance, in order to forge a new architectural style for the nineteenth century, the École des Beaux-Arts positively encouraged an eclectic design approach — resulting in the neo-Greek style. More recently, Philip Johnson describes having eclectic moments in the early days of the development of his design approach. He describes these as periods of self-doubt when non-revolutionary 'copying moods' take over.

Architects who subscribe to *eclecticism* aim to achieve a synthesis of style founded on the underlying principles of different architectural systems. But this approach rarely rises above the level of imitation and often results in the dreaded pastiche. For example, with its free adaptation and easy assimilation of past styles, the worst of a post-modernist architecture is seen by many of its critics to have produced a kind of Mickey Mouse brand of *eclecticism*. However, all so-called original thinking can be considered eclectic to a degree, as it relies upon past experience, awareness of historical precedent and knowledge of an existing body of work. Indeed, as the design historian Stuart Durant observes, *eclecticism* can be seen as a rational response to an information explosion and the attendant inrush of vast quantities of visual data.

See also: **Bricolage • Post-modernism • Precedent • Vernacular**

Ecological footprint   ▮

Conceptualized statistically, an *ecological footprint* is the area of the earth's surface necessary to provide resources for a number of specific one-time human needs. Seen dynamically, the footprint can grow dramatically when these resources are continually needed on a sustainable basis; and, more importantly, the size of the footprint grows exponentially with increases in population and/or economic well-being. More people, more well-off, use more.

The area of an *ecological footprint* study is within a defined boundary and it does not necessarily contain, nor account for, the vast inputs of the earth's energy and resources that provide support to the harvested and/or mined ecosystems within the footprint boundary. Non-bounded resources, such as climatological systems, fresh and saltwater systems, and possibly other large-scale events such as flooding or fire, can contribute to the maintenance and sustainability of the local resources and are difficult to assess.

Ecological footprinting can help define the consequences of alternative consumer decisions to satisfy human needs. To compare the consequences of alternative buying decisions, all of the areas of the earth needed to support the different systems, and providing the resources for those alternatives would have to be considered.   (LP)

See also: **Arcology • Energy efficiency • Exponential • Sustainability**

Edge condition

Edge condition is important in architecture on many levels from the behavioural to the technical. In all of these senses, and in the natural world, it is a place of tension, of intensification and often of conflict. The edge between two biographical regions, between forest and field or water and land, for example, is a place of heightened activity, of a concentration of numbers of species and individuals, and, hence, of interaction, both beneficial and harmful. These natural edges are also the preferred locations of human habitation, for practical reasons and because their inherent variety and contrast make them especially appealing from a sensory and intellectual perspective.

Edge condition in architectural terms refers to the interface between the natural and built environments, the place where social territories meet, particularly the boundary between public and private, the edge of a space, and where different building materials and assemblies of materials come together. From a practical point of view, the *edge condition* requires special attention because it often mediates between very different social and physical conditions, generating complex and often competing priorities.

Human perceptual characteristics make us especially attuned to visual edge conditions, such as where different materials abut, or where the building or part is perceived as a figure against a background, such as the outline of a roof against the sky. Wall corners and the edges of window and door openings may receive special architectural treatment in recognition of their importance from both a scenographic and social perspective. The aesthetic success of a piece of architecture may depend greatly on how well the architect resolves the various edge conditions.

The zone of space immediately adjacent to the edge of a building or room, both inside and out, is a preferred location for people to occupy. In retail situations it is advantageous to have a lot of edge space adjacent to the public realm for the display of goods. Good daylighting of a building interior dictates maximizing the amount of exterior edge through which light can enter. In their book, *Body, Memory, and Architecture* (1977), Kent Bloomer and Charles Moore identify 'edge' as one of the four key elements, with path, pattern and place, that provide the basis for ordering the physical environment to respond to human needs.   (PDS)

See also: **Boundary • Cutting edge • Gateway • Envelope • Interaction • Interface • Kiss • Parameters • Skin • Symmetry • Transitional space**

Ekistics

Ekistics is a doctrine proposed by Dr Constantinos A. Doxiades for the study and solution of urban problems throughout the world. It was developed by Doxiades in the 1960s and represented an holistic approach to urban planning. Although he did not refer specifically to *ekistics*, his book *Between Dystopia and Utopia* (1966) effectively summed up the underlying philosophy in three lectures delivered at Trinity College, Hartford, Connecticut. Lecture One, 'Towards Dystopia', aims to prove that we live in bad cities and that we are heading towards worse ones ('dystopia' being a term derived from the Greek *dys* + *topos*); Lecture Two, 'Escape to Utopia', sets out to define the history of utopian concepts as being dreams without reason and unable to get us out of the impasse; and Lecture Three, 'Need for Entopia', suggests the need to reconcile dreams with reality to create places that are practicable ('entopia' from the Greek *en* + *topos* = place). In practice, as an urban planner, Doxiades developed the idea proposed in Lecture Three of 'networks on the earth' in the form of 1 km square physical communication grids as the basis of urban areas, each square allocated to particular urban functions and with key communication routes linking with other urban areas. His approach was actually rather rigid and, despite planning such urban areas as the new port of Tema in Ghana and the Pakistan capital Islamabad, his ideas have not had much more practical success or influence than Le Corbusier's Ville Radieuse, to which they bear a close similarity.   (GS)

See also: **Dystopia** • **Utopia**

Elegance   ∎

A strict dictionary definition of the term *elegance* refers to refinement and grace in movement, appearance or manners. The use of this term by architects is similar to its use by scientists and mathematicians, i.e. going beyond appearance to the essence of the thing itself. It generally refers to the solution of a problem or situation that satisfies all the requirements and overcomes the inherent conflicts and limitations with the simplest of means. Writing in his *Elements of Architecture* (1990), Pierre von Meiss defines the elegant solution as 'one (that) carries the complexity of elements through to just one image with extreme economy of means and without compromising nuances'. Voltaire said, 'Elegance always appears easy, everything that is easy is not always elegant.' High aesthetic quality and a high level of craft contribute to creating *elegance* in the architectural sense.

Elegance has often emerged in situations with very demanding technical requirements or where the resources available are very limited, pushing the design beyond obvious solutions. It often involves refinement over a long period of time, or is the result of exploring many design alternatives. Bridges, long-span roof structures and very tall buildings have strict structural requirements that are best met by maximizing strength and minimizing weight. These demands have sometimes led architects and engineers to create forms that not only satisfy technical requirements with great economy of means but also are aesthetically striking. The Salginatobel reinforced-concrete bridge by Robert Maillart and the bridges of the architect and engineer, Santiago Calatrava, have received wide acclaim on both accounts. Indigenous cultures living in harsh climates with limited resources have sometimes developed artefacts of astounding technical merit and functional and aesthetic simplicity. The kayak and the igloo, even in the light of present day technology, are excellent solutions to the problem of survival in the far North. (PDS)

See also: **Balance • Minimalism • Organic • Proportion**

Enclosure

For the same reason as I previously wished to turn your garden into an interior, I now wish to make your hall into an 'open air space'.
— Alvar Aalto

Enclosure refers to containment; a hollow object or defined space that can be occupied either by the body or the mind. Functioning as an artefact of possession, a strong sense of *enclosure* will tend to respond to human scale, but can dramatically vary in degree of containment from complete closure to a most fragile and tenuous definition of place.

However encompassing or elemental the definition of its boundary, enclosure instils a sense of location. For instance, in his *The Concise Townscape* (1961), Gordon Cullen describes *enclosure* in terms of 'here-ness'. He talks of the common experience of the 'outdoor room', a clearly defined urban or rural place in which occupants acquire strong feelings of position and of identity with their surroundings. This sensation, he writes, can be expressed as 'I am in IT, or above IT or below IT, I am outside IT, I am enclosed or I am exposed.'

Whether temporary or permanent, whether abode or outdoor space, *enclosure* is usually coupled with a symbol of congregation — the focal point. Focal points, such as the domestic hearth or television set, urban statue, rural hedge or tree, function to anchor the sense of *enclosure*. However, the 'sense of *enclosure*' is experiential and may not be the result of actual physical *enclosure*.

See also: **Anchoring • Boundary • Focal point • Locus • Place • Skin**

Energy efficiency

Efficiency is the ratio of output/input. Output and input are measured in identical units and efficiency is thus dimensionless (usually expressed as a percentage). Efficiency establishes the cost (in terms of energy, money or materials) to perform a task. Energy-efficient equipment or systems provide high output relative to input — waste is minimized. Efficiency is not equal to effectiveness. It is possible to be very effective very inefficiently, and to be very efficient at being ineffective.

Energy efficiency is the keystone of green design and is fundamental to most design solutions using natural energies (often via passive systems). Many indicators of *energy efficiency* are used in building design. For simple thermal systems (furnaces, water heaters, solar collectors), efficiency (in per cent) is a direct metric. A number of subsidiary metrics are used to quantify the efficiency of other building components — such as the coefficient of performance for refrigeration systems, lumens/Watt for light sources, and solar heat gain coefficient for glazing assemblies. Whole building 'efficiency' is a more complex concept, often described in terms of energy use per unit floor area per year (and normalized for several variables).

Codes and standards provide minimum acceptable values for the efficiency (or equivalent) of many building elements and systems (including whole buildings). It is important to remember that such minimums are not technically acceptable. Designing to meet code-mandated efficiencies is designing to the lowest common denominator — certainly nothing to write home about.   (WG)

See also: **Feedback • Green building • Vital signs**

Enigmatic   ▌

Writing in his Digital Dreams (1998), Neil Spiller suggests that architects — who practice the most public of arts — cannot function without a degree of secrecy. He describes the architect as a double or 'triple' agent who simultaneously operates in a covert and overt manner — disclosing cultural empathy while concealing private objectives. *Enigmatic* concealment allows the designer to be at once poetic and pragmatic, and both scientific and empirical; he or she maintaining a degree of secrecy by experimenting in the 'secret laboratory' of drawing and spinning elaborate narratives around their design concepts.

Indeed, a veil of mystery has long cloaked the design and building processes. It goes back to the time of the medieval guilds when a client could be assassinated for learning its secrets — as happened to the hapless Bishop Conrad who, in 1099, paid the ultimate price after learning of the damp-proofing system for his new Utrecht Cathedral. Enigma also surrounds the birth of linear perspective in 1417 when its inventor, Filippo Brunelleschi, refused to divulge its coordinates to his peers. It occurs again in early nineteenth-century France when physicist Gaspard Monge's coordination of orthographic drawings into a coherent and three-dimensional system of communication, known as 'third angle projection', was immediately classified 'top secret' by the military government.

A fascination with the *enigmatic* is also physically projected into many architectural design approaches. Cloaking devices employed in its manifestation include the scrim and the layering, veiling, filtering and screening of spatial disclosure, the fascination with translucency and the masking of the obvious. It is also accounted for in the need of some architects to tease through paradox, allusion and ambiguity, together with the use of the cryptic and the obscure.

See also: **Ambiguity • Filtering • Ghosting • Layering • Narrative • Paradox • Scrim • Translucency**   .

Engage (*dégagements*)   ▌

A dictionary definition of the architectural usage of *engage* as 'hold fast' and 'attach to a wall' is not strictly true because the term has many archispeak uses. For instance, the architect can engage (come into battle) with a problem, *engage* in dialogue (hold attention), connect elements (interlock), and become deeply committed to, that is, 'engaged in', the business of architecture.

Perhaps its most common use, however, is its function in describing the relationship or coupling of two components or two spaces. For example, two different materials, elements or spaces, or their combination, can be described in archispeak as being 'engaged in a dialogue'. This occurs when tensions or arresting relationships are detected between them. However, from a psychological standpoint, the most profound form of engagement with the environment occurs when we touch the surface of a three-dimensional object. This is when the haptic sense of touch permits us to *engage* feeling and doing simultaneously.

An antonym of *engage* is *dégagements*. If entrances and approaches herald our physical engagement with a building and its circulatory pattern and spaces, then *dégagements* questions the manner in which these spaces are evacuated and the ease by which a building is exited. The term also describes the tension that results when two related forms, components or spaces are deliberately held apart. This can occur when the function of major and minor building forms are physically pulled apart so that each maintains a formal independence while the transition between their spaces is reinforced.

See also: **Coda • Dialogue • Interface • Intervention • Mediate**

Entourage

In order to increase a dimension of reality, orthographic drawings and perspective projections are often embellished with trees, populated with figures, and filled with furniture and vehicles. Known as *entourage*, especially in the US, and supported by an array of dreadful copycat books, these ancillary elements function as graphic props that intend to bring a sense of scale and animation to the drawing.

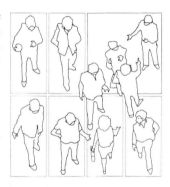

See also: **Animate • Scale**

An array of ready-to-use *entourage* figures await habitation of the space of an axonometric drawing.

Envelope

Envelope refers to the 'wrapper' used to contain the volume of space within a building. The building envelope comprises the stratified membrane of material that exists at the interface between inside and outside in order to provide protection from the elements. Historically, there are two basic types of building *envelope*: those in which the *envelope* is withdrawn within the confines of the structure, such as in a Greek temple and in high-tech structures; and those in which the *envelope*, like a skin, is stretched between or wrapped around the structure, such as in Gothic cathedrals and curtain wall architecture.

However, the notion of envelope as a weather-proofed container of space is turned inside out by 'The Cloud' building designed by Diller & Scofidio for the Swiss Expo '02 at Yverdon-les-Bains. This comprises a saucer-shaped structure hovering above a lake. Its 'envelope' is ephemeral, defined by the shape of an artificial cloud of vapour (shown here) created by 33,000 tiny nozzles spraying jets of water. Expo visitors clad in the personalized protection of disposable plastic raincoats penetrate the cloud to become enveloped by the mist.

See also: **Boundary • Breathe • Edge condition • Enclosure • Interface • Skin**

Scotch mist as *envelope*. Diller & Scofidio's Cloud building for the Swiss Expo 02 in Yverdon-les Bains.

Ephemeralization   ▌

It was Richard Buckminster Fuller who first saw that the process of accelerating technological change was an evolutionary process which he christened *Ephemeralization*, from the Greek *Ephemeros*, meaning 'lasting only a day'. For Fuller the idea that the world faced an intractable crisis of resource exhaustion was totally unacceptable. He believed that the inventive capability of the human mind would always be able to attenuate supplies of crucial resources and would synthesize those that were no longer available. *Ephemeralization* promised to miniaturize demand, not by scarcity but by plenty. He would cite the quartz watch, the ballpoint pen, the mobile phone, the calculator, the camera and the digital camera, the bicycle and the motor car as tamed or untamed species that were progressively being merged into mankind-serving cycles of production and reproduction like the carbon cycle of living things. *Ephemeralization*, he believed, could overcome all anomalies to merge technology into a second organized surface of the earth.   (MP)

See also: **Energy efficiency • Geodesic • Sustainability • Synthesis • Tensegrity**

Ergonomics   ▌

Ergonomics is the scientific study of the working relationship between the human body and its contact points with the hardware of our built environment. To achieve optimum levels of comfort and efficiency, the anatomical workings of the body and its working parts are measured in terms of their movement and are related to the performance of various actions, such as operating a tap or a tool, opening a door, sitting on a chair or working at a desk.

The study of the relationship between the efficiency of persons and their work environment is also called 'human factor engineering' or 'biotechnology'. It attempts to improve the design of machines and equipment so that they match the capacities of the persons operating them, and are thus used more efficiently and without injury to the operator.

In designing a new office or factory, attention is given to worker comfort and their attitude to their surroundings, as well as to the efficiency of their equipment. The effect of environmental stress, such as noise, on people's work is studied. *Ergonomics* involves several disciplines, including engineering, design, psychology, anatomy and physiology.

See also: **Design intent • Functionality**

Erosion

The wearing away of one element due to the abrasion of another provides an attractive architectural analogy. It accounts for a predilection for certain 'sacrificial' materials, such as copper, lead and Cor-Ten steel, i.e. materials that appear to change in quality or surrender their surfaces to the ravages of the elements. A further analogy of *erosion* is also a well-documented technique in architecture. This occurs when we take a solid, often a platonic form, and carve pieces from it to form lungs of air or light.

The original concept often varies from the eventual method of construction. For example, the approach passages and tomb chambers of the Great Pyramids appear to be tunnelled through the limestone as though bored by an insect through fruit. Whereas, in fact, the passages were either cut into the rock below the pyramids or were built within its limestone core — and often lined with granite for preservation. However, the resultant section resembles an eroded whole.

In 1998, Ana Ordas and Richard Rose-Casemore designed a university building in Lleida, Catalunya, Spain, for the UK practice Architecture PLB. Here, the Basque sculptor Eduardo Chellida (1924–2002) was the inspiration. His famous large public works and smaller iron forms were the inspiration for a 'teaching cube', where holes eroded from it form huge foyers and circulation routes buried deep inside the building. The notion of solidity is accentuated through the use of small apertures in the elevation; offering selective views out to the old fortified town while maintaining a cool interior.   (RR-C)

See also: **Diffusion • Porosity • Sacrificial • Segment**

Pyramid tunnelling, and scooped-out library spaces in Architecture PLB's Universitat de Lleida Faculty of Law and Economics, Spain.

Esquisse   ▌

From the French *esquisser*, meaning 'to sketch', the term *esquisse* describes a sketch design that will, almost inevitably, be resolved into the final design solution. Like so much of the French or Frenchified usage, the term is now more popular in Anglophone countries to the west of the Atlantic Ocean than to the east. The term is part of a whole vocabulary derived from the practices and influences of the École des Beaux-Arts in Paris, where architecture was formally taught at least a century before it was in the UK or North America. The oldest university school of architecture in England at Liverpool (predated by the private London Architectural Association school) produced a number of architectural 'Liverpool Sketch Books' in the early decades of the twentieth century. These contained, not sketches from nature, popular with artists since Leonardo and Dürer, and much discussed in the latter part of the eighteenth century (and a part of an artistic practice promoted by John Ruskin in the nineteenth century), but measured drawings of existing buildings and student and staff project design drawings. The use of the term 'sketch' here was not just English understatement; it reflects the ethos of the École des Beaux-Arts in its focus on the Prix de Rome from the early eighteenth-century, when, to ensure that competition was fair, the preparation of the *parti*, or primary massing of the *esquisse*, was conducted in cubicles or loges. The Royal Institute of British Architects continued to offer candidates the opportunity to produce a thesis design to qualify for membership under similar conditions into the second half of the twentieth century. The Liverpool School still had a small studio called 'En loge' well into the 1970s. The elaboration of the designs that followed were invariably variations on classical detailing to enrich and inform the initial 'innovative' massing. In the last quarter and more of the twentieth century, when Germany followed a path of competitions for all public and publicly funded buildings, a similar pattern emerged, with architects identifying their broad intentions for the massing and the wall-to-window ratio and proportion of their proposals, but with little shown in the way of consideration of detail — a costly omission in speculative design terms.   (RH)

See also: **Conceptual drawing • Diagramming • Design genesis • Design intent • *Parti***

Euclidean space   ▌

Nobody Untrained in Geometry May Enter My House. — Plato

Euclid is generally known as the father of geometry due to his publication of a textbook that was used for almost 2,000 years. He did not invent basic geometry, but rather he summarized and popularized the system of geometric logic and axioms of Pythagoras and others that had preceded him. Even today, schools continue to teach Euclidean geometry along with the analytical geometry of René Descartes.

Euclidean space is the space of our rooms. In its simplest terms, it is the space of straight lines and flat surfaces creating rectilinear boxes. Until recently, *Euclidean space* has been the only space pallet of architecture.

Now that we have invented non-Euclidean space — schemas such as Riemannean geometry (curved space) — it is clear that Euclidean geometry is an invention and only one possibility for structuring space. These new spatial paradigms may account for the geometric freedom found in many examples of recent *avant-garde* architecture.   (EO)

See also: Cartesian grid • Matrix • Planar • Platonic solids • Topology • xyz space.

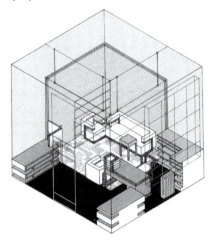

(Herbert Beyer's 1923 isometric of Walter Gropius' Bauhaus office represents a box of *Euclidean space*.

Existential

Existence is a dice game played by an innocent God child. — Heraclitus

Existentialism is the belief in the Self as the Ultimate Reality and the inner struggle of this Self is the basic fact of existence. An individual's reality is understood as complex, ever changing and certainly not predestined.

Phenomenology and existentialism are closely linked, as they are both based upon a belief in subjective immediate sense data as the only reality, and then that reality is only for the particular individual involved. Each experience initiates a new ultimate outcome that did not exist before. In that way, a work of architecture within an existentialist world is similar to a throw of the cosmic dice. Each act of architecture sets up a new chain of future events. Perhaps the highly personal architecture produced by current star architects can be excused as a manifestation of an *existential* world, first postulated by Kierkegaard, where the individual genius is only associated with the pursuit of an individual artistic vision. Mr Fountainhead, Howard Roark, is a poster boy for the architect as the *existential* artist. His struggle and ultimate defeat at the hands of the forces of convention represents the core belief of Nietzsche that the creative individual struggles against a hostile and uncaring world. Nietzsche wrote: '. . . the endless stupid game which the great child, Time, plays before us and with us'.
(EO)

See also: **Phenomenology** • Zen

Experiential

When heard in architectural debate, the term *experiential* is often used to seek further information regarding how a design might touch the senses of its occupants. It relates to the perpetual question heard from tutors at student presentations, 'But what is it really like to be there?'. This is a question that refers to the need to qualify the nature of reaction.

Experiential philosophy is based on the belief that knowledge is acquired purely through empiricism. Experience of architecture falls in two categories of response: sensuality and aesthetics. The sensual experience results from the manner in which we see and touch, while, being concerned less with the sensate, the aesthetic experience is more dependent upon and affected by processes of thought. Therefore, our experience of environment seeks two fundamental responses: delight for our senses and also the need to respond to inherited memories of habitat.

Herman Neuckermans discusses experientiality in the context of vertical and horizontal windows. Horizontal windows, or picture windows, he writes, result in a horizontal stratification of the view. In response to movement, the picture is static. Meanwhile, while emphasizing foreground, middleground and background and allowing more light to penetrate deep into the interior, vertical windows induce a kind of cinematic motion parallax. 'Phenomenology' is a popular *experiential*-related design philosophy.

See also: **Corporeality • Multi-sensory space • Phenomenology • Zen**

Exponential

Any entity that continually increases or decreases, by iterations at a rate determined by multiplying itself with an exponent, is said to experience *exponential* change to the limit set by that exponent. Often used to express *exponential* growth in a population, *exponential* change that is driven by its own feedback without internal limits either crashes spectacularly or soars off the chart and then crashes when a parameter limit is encountered. For example, the growth of duckweed on a pond will increase exponentially until the limits of the surface of the pond are reached. (LP)

See also: **Ecological footprint • Energy efficiency • Fibonacci series • Fractal • Sustainability**

Feedback

Feedback is a link in the chain of information transfer. It is the input–output principle used in self-regulating machines and in biological systems. Information about what is happening is fed back to a controlling device which compares it with what should be happening. If the two are different, the controlling device takes corrective action. In the most sophisticated of self-regulating machines, the controller is a computer — in an animal it is the brain.

Feedback is the mechanism of self-transformation, it is the unpredictable result of dialogue, interaction and choice; it is the sounding board in the cyclical process of design. Generative drawings provide *feedback* concerning the efficacy of a notion; response brings *feedback* to nourish ensuing ideas. The critique (design review) offers academic *feedback* on the degree of success or failure of a design proposal; post-occupancy evaluation provides professional *feedback* on the success or failure of an existing building.

Audio *feedback* is noise that became music to Jimi Hendrix. Similarly, the Deconstructivist notion of superimposition creates an analogous *feedback* of accidental opportunities that are accepted as legitimate design decisions. *Feedback* prompts action; action prompts change; change prompts reaction.

See also: **Dialogue • Interaction • Reciprocity • Transformation**

Fibonacci series

The thirteenth-century Italian mathematician Leonardo Fibonacci devised a number series from calculations concerning the breeding rate of rabbits. Each pair produces one pair of offspring in the breeding season following their own birth, and another pair the following season. Then they stop breeding. From the second generation onwards, the number of pairs born equals the number born in the previous two generations. This yields the series 1, 1, 2, 3, 5, 8, 13 and so on, a sequence in which each number is the sum of the previous two numbers. This notation sequence also occurs in nature in logarithmic spiral growths, such as sea shells, daisy heads and the scales of fir cones.

Besides bearing a curious relationship to botany, Fibonacci numbers also appear to exert a curious influence on art and architecture. The ratio between any two adjacent Fibonacci numbers after 3 is about 1:1.6. This is the so-called golden ratio, or golden section, which has intrigued experts for centuries because of its connection with aesthetics.

See also: **Balance • Exponential • Golden section • Order • Ordering systems • Proportion • Regulating lines**

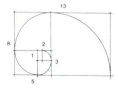

The 1:1.6 ratio between Fibonacci numbers (after 3) in patterns of natural growth approximates the golden ratio or golden section.

Figure-ground

Figure-ground refers to our ability to distinguish or separate an object from its immediate setting. Underlying and controlling any arrangement of objects and spaces in the field of view is a structural framework. In order to detect its pattern we use a perception that simultaneously acknowledges both positive (object in field) and negative (background). Its importance is highlighted in the observation made by the father of modern painting, Henri Matisse. He said that the expressive power in his work lay not in the content but in the control of the 'empty parts around them'.

The interdependency of *figure* and *ground* is demonstrated in the classic reversible *figure* shown here. If we fix our gaze on the central white vase, the surrounding areas — represented by black — appear to define its form spatially. However, if we switch off to a concentration on the outer areas (the two black face profiles), we discover that what was seen as *ground* transforms into a *figure*, now a different entity that takes on a life and meaning of its own. In this second perception, what was at first void has now become tangible — the vase-to-faces alternation causing a graphic experience of *ground* as a dynamic presence, being redefined by the same contours that had previously described the vase. In this optical illusion, however, the fluctuating dominance of both *figure* and *ground* causes the ultimate meaning of the image to remain forever unresolved. Consequently, in order to reduce ambiguity, there has to be a dominance of one element over another.

Dominance of shape, size and value, etc., will determine which bits of information will be perceived as *figure* and which will assume the subordinate status of *ground*. While the *ground*, or 'counter-form', shares in the form of the *figure*, the latter generally has a shape or object quality that seems to visually reside in front of the *ground*.

See also: **Footprint • Interaction • Positive–negative space • Reciprocity**

Alternating vase–faces illusion and a collage that deliberately confuses 'figure' and 'ground'.

Filter

The sunlight did not know what is was before it hit a wall.
— Louis Kahn

A *filter* is an intercepting screen that controls the passage of whatever medium passes through it. Like the *filter* on a cigarette that is intended to remove impurities in the inhaled smoke, it is a device that, in order to achieve the desired outcome, separates out and entraps the unwanted. The term has many 'screening out' uses in archispeak. For example, it can be a controlling device used in people-moving or traffic segregation, a screen for modifying or absorbing light or for controlling views, or a diagrammatic sieve used for flushing out ideas.

Architecture itself can be conceived as a *filter*. Indeed, in his book *Intentions in Architecture* (1963), Christian Norberg-Schultz discussed the idea of the *filter* as a mediator between inside and outside building environments, letting some elements pass and screening out others. When treated as a light box, the envelope can be made translucent like the paper screens of traditional Japanese houses or can be punctured to admit and aim different qualities of illumination. Depending upon the *filter*ing techniques in use, sunlight can be transposed to deflect, diffuse and scatter; it can be mono-tinted or multi-coloured, or split into a multitude of tiny shafts. Aperture configuration and placement in the envelope will also control views from the inside out. However, rather than being explicit, like a panoramic view, the filtered view is an indirect, fragmented and veiled perception. Employing such devices as layering, framing, meshing and scrimming, it is one that screens out the obvious — one in which prospect is revealed by the partially concealed and the glimpsed. Furthermore, the nature of the hollowed out void both within and between buildings can be considered a spatial *filter*. Densely filtered space coincides with an increase in the complexity of the enclosure and closure when, for physical or visual access, small pockets or narrow slots of space are allowed to penetrate the surrounding mass and gush into the space beyond.

Devices for filtering light, space, circulation and visual access are familiar contrivances to those designers who strive to titillate with an architecture of surprise, ambiguity and an air of mystery.

See also: **Closure** • **Enclosure** • *Moiré* • **Scrim** • **Transition** • **Transform** • **Translucency**

Flâneur

> . . . the *flâneur* is not so much a creature of the crowd as someone who remains aloof from the crowd, and observes it from afar. Yet the *flâneur* is also to some extent blasé. The nerves of the modern metropolitan individual are constantly being bombarded with stimuli.
> — Neil Leach

In the *flâneur*, the joy of watching is triumphant. — Walter Benjamin

The *flâneur* is a voyeuristic wanderer who observes the urban scene; a non-participant in the ebb and flow of city life. The term *flâneur* was first used by the nineteenth-century French poet Charles Baudelaire in his critique on modern life in Paris. In the early part of the twentieth century the *flâneur* reappeared in the criticism of German Marxist Walter Benjamin, who studied the origins of modernity as experienced in the city. Benjamin recognized the detached stance of Baudelaire's *flâneur* as one of the means of coping with the shock and discontinuity when experiencing the impact of the modern city.

To be a *flâneur* is essentially to stand back and look objectively at one's surroundings rather than be drawn into the sensory excitement of active participation. Unlike the 'dérive', which is active and engaging (see page 53), the 'flânerie' is a passive walkabout. The domain of the *flâneur* can be found in the bustling street life of the metropolis from which the spectacle of urban life can be quietly consumed.

See also: **Derive** • **Walkability**

Flatland   I

. . . the world portrayed on our information displays is caught up in the two-dimensionality of the endless flatlands of paper and video screen.
— Edward R. Tufte

The term *flatland* was conceived by Edwin A. Abbot, who, in 1884, under the pseudonym 'A. Square', wrote the classic *Flatland: A Romance of Many Dimensions*. This was a remarkable and charming piece of mathematical science-fiction in which polygonal creatures (Flatlanders) inhabit a planar universe where any suggestion of three dimensions is outlawed.

In common use in the US, *flatland* is now used as a euphemism for the picture plane, i.e. the surface flatness of the paper and the monitor screen on which we strive to depict both physical events and to represent abstract ideas not residing in three-dimensional space. All communication between the readers of an image and the originators of an image takes place in *flatland*. In an impossible attempt to break free from the inherent restriction of this featureless terrain, we adopt various techniques and strategies, the most basic of which is, of course, perspective projection.

See also: **Depth cues** • **Dimension** • **Pictorial space** • **Simulacrum**

Focal point   I

A focal point is a position from which the effect of a certain view functions at its optimum, e.g. an axis leading straight to or from an object.— Karel Vollers

A *focal point* is the area of a pictorial composition or a spatial setting to which the eye is drawn and returns most naturally. In terms of painting, possibly one of the most famous *focal point*s is the electrically-charged space between the fingers of God and Adam in Michelangelo's Sistine Chapel ceiling fresco. This is where the eye is drawn; this is the reference point for the entire three-dimensional composition — it is the locus or ultimate centre of attention.

Focal points in the home occur where people gather: the television set, the fireplace (the Latin word for 'hearth' is focus) and the dining table. *Focal points* in towns and cities are key streets and piazzas that create a sense of enclosure, and in which monuments, fountains, sculpture and columns, etc., provide a feature at which the eye and the body may come to rest. When there is no *focal point*, there is no anchor for our sensibilities and we experience the banal sameness of placelessness.

Focal points in both two and three dimensions embody a sense of arrival; of realization that what is sought is found. They signify the message area. They say 'this is the x-spot', 'it is here', 'I have arrived'.

See also: **Anchoring • Axis • Key drawing • Locus • Message area • Punctum • Sight lines • Visual field**

This detail from the 'Creation of Eve' section of Michelangelo's fresco for the Sistine Chapel, Rome, provides a powerful *focal point*.

Footprint

Footprint is a wonderfully descriptive archispeak term that characterizes the evidence, the trace, the stamped impression made by a structure as it is grounded in the earth. Mainly referring to the plan, *footprint* clearly and emblematically defines the drawn figure–ground relationship between solid and void and interior space and exterior space, as though impressed onto the surface of the paper.

Footprint can also refer to the trial primary massing of an idea and its formation as a basic three-dimensional design response known as the '*parti*', or sketch design, whose configuration may remain as a talisman to inform continuing design development.

See also: **Ecological footprint •** *Esquisse* **• Figure–ground •** *Parti* **• Pictorial space • Positive–negative space**

Fractal

Clouds are not spheres, mountains are not cones, coastlines are not circles . . . The number of distinct scales of length of natural patterns is for all practical purposes infinite. — Benoit Mandelbrot

Because of their open-endedness, their complexity in detail, fractals seem to address the paradox of order within apparently chaotic situations. — Rosemarie Bletter

Fractals are a curve or geometric figure, each part of which has the same statistical character as the whole. They are theoretically useful for describing partly random or chaotic natural phenomena, such as crystal growth, fluid turbulence and galaxy formation. Non-uniform structures in which similar patterns recur at progressively smaller scales, such as snowflakes and eroded coastlines, can be realistically and mathematically modelled using *fractals*. Introduced in 1975 by the IBM-employed Polish mathematician Benoit B. Mandelbrot, who also coined the term, the concept of *fractals* became popular in the 1980s through striking computer-graphic images.

We can experience the regular *fractal* in the development of the 'mathematical snowflake'. Its essence is an equilateral triangle, which, after having each side subdivided in equal thirds and replaced with a small copy of the motif, converts the figure into a new generation of itself, i.e. a six-pointed star. After successive generations of this subdivision, the 'snowflake' is realized. But generations can continue ad infinitum. Other basic *fractal* types are known as 'Sierpinksi's gasket' and 'Peano's curve'.

A *fractal* geometry is found on the cladding of the complex of art galleries and cinema's designed by Smart Bates in Federation Square, Melbourne, Australia. It is also famously used on Daniel Libeskind's competition-winning Boiler House project addition for the Victoria & Albert Museum in London. Resulting from cutting edge design engineering, its severely inclined spiral form is covered with three interlocking, similarly shaped, cladding tiles of different sizes. When put together like a jigsaw, they form a larger tile of the same generative shape. Writing in *Building Design*, Richard Bevan reports that the fantastic variety and complexity of form achievable from *fractal* geometry provides an important step toward one design approach of the future. It is one that challenges notions of Classical and Corbusian proportion while operating at the other end of the spectrum to a Miesian Modernism.

See also: **Chaos theory** • **Exponential** • **Fragment** • **Order** • **Transition**

Snowflake *fractal*, 'Sierpinksi's gasket' (fifth generation), and a detail of Daniel Libeskind's proposed extension to the V&A Museum.

Fragment

> So, too, architecture when equated with language can only be read as a series of fragments that make up an architectural reality.
> — Bernard Tschumi

A *fragment* — a piece broken off, a small detached or incomplete portion that survives the whole — can provide a clue. *Fragments* induce an air of mystery and puzzle-solving: the detective pieces together small *fragments* of information in order to resolve a crime, the genetic profiler identifies a host from a miniscule *fragment* of DNA, and the archaeologist interpolates a small excavated *fragment* of an object into a greater understanding of the whole. Designers use grids to structure their concepts into a field of *fragments*.

The *fragment* has a special significance in art, in the photomontages of Dadaism and Surrealism, and especially in the collages of the Cubists where, operating under different agendas, pictorial *fragments* are reassembled and are compressed into the 'mosaic' of a new expression. For instance, the montaged composure of the moving image — from *fragments* of still photographs projected at 24 frames per second — give the illusion of movement. Central to the writings of Charles Baudelaire and Walter Benjamin is the fragmented urban experience as a condition of modernity. This 'channel-surfing' view of the modern world is one in which contemplation is shattered by the fleeting glimpse and the constant disruption of the shock of the new. For Benjamin, the city represents a *fragment* in which the totality of modern life can be discovered.

Functionalist and post-modern architectural approaches can also be considered in terms of bits. While the former used zoning techniques to divide buildings and cities into *fragments*, the latter can be seen as the eclectic 'dolly mixture' assembly of mix 'n' match classical *fragments*. Analysis is the process of breaking down ideas into component parts to be resolved into elements, and concepts into individual factors; fragmentation shatters parameters. Nothing is fixed.

See also: **Collage** • *Flâneur* • **Gestalt** • **Modernity** • **Moment** • **Montage** • **Temporality**

Framing (enframing)

All sequences (of space) are cumulative. Their 'frames' derive significance from juxtaposition. They establish memory — of the preceding frame, of the course of events. — Bernard Tschumi

Our view of the world is defined by frames: door frames, window frames, and surrounding paintings, movie screens and the transmitted lines of television signals. Indeed, our visual perception is, in turn, peripherally 'enframed' by the outer limits of our field of vision. Like the triangle that racks a set of pool balls, frames contain, order and systematize their contents.

Perceptual *framing* has strong links with the technological development of clear glass in the fourteenth century. For example, in his article 'Agents of Mechanization and the Eotechnic Phase', Lewis Mumford describes the paradigm shift between a medieval symbolism and an ensuing Renaissance humanism as coinciding with the dissolving colour of cathedral stained glass windows into the clarity of clear glass. An attendant and naturalistic perception of a sharply focused world then became framed by windows, and also by glass spectacles. By the sixteenth century, the simultaneous invention of the microscope and the improvement of telescopic optics had, on the one hand, rocketed the perspective vanishing point into outer space and towards infinity. On the other hand, it had revealed inner space and, in the words of Mumford, '. . . increased almost infinitely the plane of the foreground from which those lines had their point of origin'.

Like their counterparts in art, media and optics, architectural *framing* devices separate viewer from view, inside from outside, and public from private to crop objects or events from the space beyond. The *framing* wall divides while the window selects and isolates the scene beyond as an apparently flat and static experience. This flatness was highlighted in 1923 in the controversy between Auguste Perret and Le Corbusier concerning *framing* by horizontal and vertical windows — Perret's preference for vertical windows permitting a perspective view that includes foreground and background, while, in removing these depth cues, the horizontal window denies depth and 'wallpapers' the panorama to the glass. Colin Rowe's statement that 'the development of the frame in Chicago was to modern architecture what the column was to classical architecture' (Rowe 1976), takes us to another meaning. This is of an understanding of architecture as 'frames within frames'. In this broader sense, there are the modules of structural space-frames, and the use of walls, floors and roofs to frame volume. In this latter context, *framing* becomes building — representing the container in which human activities are played out.

See also: **Boundary • Interface • Transparency**

Frontality

Frontality is face-to-face confrontation. It describes the orientation of a work of art or architecture to the viewer. However, a head-on confrontation with architecture is attended by underlying anthropomorphic connotations, i.e. when 'building façade' becomes 'face', 'window' becomes 'eye', and 'entrance' becomes 'mouth'. When we come face-to-façade, we recognize and experience *frontality*.

Recognition of the architectural 'face' derives from an understanding of the form of a building and its orientation. Compared with the continuous face of cylinders, the 'fronts' of cubic and rectangular forms and the multi-faceted faces of octagonal buildings quickly provide a recognizable architectural visage. Façades that front onto the public domain receive special treatment, such as ornamentation, to convey wealth, status, value and position. Similarly, in Scandanavia, the face of houses were, and in some areas still are, traditionally 'cosmeticized' with an expensive paint colour while remaining façades were cheaply lime washed.

In Donald Kunze's essay 'Architecture as a Site of Reception' (1994), *frontality* spawns gastronomic notions, such as when we enter a building, 'it eats us', and when we confront a building, we consume it with our eyes ('we eat it'). *Frontality* is when an act of fascination and anticipation takes place. It is a face-off involving perceiving and 'receiving'. In this sense, *frontality* is a dramatic aspect of all art that occurs when we project our imagination through the threshold of the cinema screen, theatre curtain and, indeed, building façade. We confront what confronts us; we receive the image and the sensations that face us — and, conversely, they receive us.

Terming it 'frontalization', Kenneth Frampton writes that, in order to register, frontality demands a degree of spatial volume before it. Moreover, he also describes its extension inside and behind façades — an internal layering of planes continuing the *frontality* theme into the depth of what lies beyond.

See also: **Anthropomorphic • Dialogue • Interaction • Interface • Layering**

Frottage

In its psychological sense, *frottage* is the practice of touching or rubbing against the clothed body of another person as a means of obtaining sexual gratification.

In art and design, *frottage* is the 'brass rubbing' technique of reproducing a given texture or relief by laying a sheet of paper over its surface and transferring its impression with the strokes of a soft crayon or pencil. It was much used by Max Ernst in the development of his collage technique.

The frottaging of environmental surfaces is often termed 'mapping' as, indeed, is any form of physical or visual documentation in architectural projects. For example, through *frottage* one can 'map' a journey via the changing surface textures along a street or through a building.

See also: **Mapping** • **Tactility**

Functionalism

In its search for a new and utilitarian language of architecture as an antidote to classicism, *Functionalism* was at the forefront of early twentieth-century Modernism. Having emerged from the nineteenth-century debate surrounding aesthetic and functional approaches, statements such as Louis Sullivan's 'form follows function' and Le Corbusier's definition of a house as a 'machine for living in' became the mantras of a functionalist design approach. Its doctrine proposed that any designed form — whether building, chair or artefact — should be determined solely by its function, and that anything practically designed would be inherently beautiful.

References to a machine aesthetic and to a form reflecting function provided the primary canons of the functionalist philosophy. This was an approach that sought to express an architecture inspired by machine forms and in which each of its elements were made visible and separately expressed to disclose their function. Both Le Corbusier and Frank Lloyd Wright were active in the formative years of *Functionalism*; both were also inspired by the nineteenth-century doctrines of Viollet-le-Duc and his attempts to rationalize, i.e. functionalize, architecture into a logical system.

However, the initial conceptions of functional space and the new aesthetic later became separated. A narrower doctrine of *Functionalism* then evolved in the mid-twentieth century in which form would result from an advanced technology and a scientific rationalism. Radical criticism of a bleak post-war *Functionalism* came in the 1960s and included the essays and buildings of the leading Dutch architect, Aldo van Eyck. Using a design language that included such terms as 'reciprocity', 'identity' and 'place', he redirected attention to architecture's role as a carrier of meaning. Since then, *Functionalism* deteriorated and went into decline to become vulgarized by what Peter Blake has described as 'literal *Functionalism*' — seen in those ubiquitous city blocks whose forms are shaped by zoning laws and are lined with curtain walls selected from manufacturer's catalogues.

See also: **International Style** • **Functionality**

Functionality

Form follows function, certainly. But who the hell cares? It's the form and the function, not reducing that to some scientific analysis, that will separate it and take it all apart. We want it together. We want the poetry of the thing. — Frank Lloyd Wright

Functionality refers to the first of Sir Henry Wotton's famous seventeenth-century trilogy of architectural attributes; namely, 'commoditie'. In other words, *functionality* engages the utilitarian and quantifiable aspects of form and therefore lies beyond notions of its style or aesthetic content. In the context of modern buildings, Adrian Napper has observed that, unlike the Formula One racing car, which complies rigorously to its functional requirements, they are rarely tested objectively in terms of their degree of efficacy in the relationship of form to function. On the other hand, however, there is an increase in commercial and institutional buildings being tested after occupancy in terms of their conformance to a variety of standards, including physical and psychological comfort.

When Louis Sullivan coined the phrase 'form follows function' near the end of the nineteenth century, there was considerable optimism about what applied science could do to improve the construction and perform-ance of buildings, in terms of human comfort, safety and the efficient employment of materials, particularly iron and steel. In Sullivan's view, function included not only 'commoditie' but also 'firmness'. But, as Frank Lloyd Wright indicated, the more difficult issue was (and still is) what should be the role of 'delight' in relation to the other attributes of Wotton's trilogy. There is much in the built environment that debases Sullivan's dictum by interpreting function in the narrowest terms, satisfying only the most immediate needs of the financier with, at best, token attention to the needs of the user and community at large. Conversely, there are also many examples of architects focusing on poetics to the detriment of workability and durability. Pierre von Meiss argues for an approach that strikes a bal-ance between the various demands of the brief to create buildings that function well in the broader sense. He cites Louis Kahn as such an archi-tect who can create poetry even with the most mundane of functions, such as the utility distribution systems.   (PDS)

See also: **Functionalism • Post-occupancy evaluation (POE)**

Futurism

Futurism was an essentially Italian phenomenon. Founded by the writer F. T. Marinetti, it began as a literary movement that aimed to break the bonds of grammar, syntax and logic in a celebration of sounds of the technological world of the future. In Futurist painting and sculpture, the emphasis was on conveying a sense of speed, on 'simultaneity' (the rep-resentation of successive phases of an object in movement) and on the interpenetration of planes. *Futurism* was skilfully promoted in a series of manifestos, the first published by Marinetti in 1909, and in public performances in which the audience was goaded into uproar.

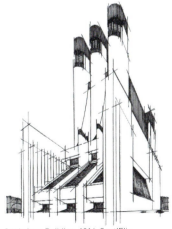

Study for a Building, 1914. Sant'Elia.

The 'Manifesto of Futurist Architecture' was signed by Antonio Sant'Elia in 1914. Identified with the idea of modernity, the dynamic of the city plays an important role in the texts, paintings and sculptures, and, indeed, the architectural drawings of Sant'Elia. While Umberto Boccioni described his sculpture as 'lyrical exaltations and plastic manifestations of a new absolute: speed', Sant'Elia's paper architecture, with its towers, skywalks and high-speed moving pavements, saw the Futurist city as a turbulent machine.

Being extremely receptive to radical foreign imports, it was a post-revolution Russian Constructivism that provided *Futurism's* greatest single descendant.

See also: **Animate • Constructivism • Dynamic • Modernism**

Gateway   ▌

A *gateway* marks boundaries and edges to create psychological transitions between 'conscious' and 'unconscious', 'past' and 'future', and physical transitions between 'inner' and 'outer', 'public and private', and the difference between the sense of 'arriving' and 'arrival'. *Gateways* mark the intersection of pathways and boundaries — where they meet the edges of public spaces, such as towns, parks and neighbourhoods, and the thresholds of the domestic domain of house and garden.

Being an integral part of the boundary, *gateways* are interfaces between two kinds of activity. In order to heighten the sense of transition, they often involve changes of topology, light and surface, and can take on many forms. For instance, the main approach to medieval Oxford was bounded by a wall punctuated with literal gates; meanwhile, the city's expanded and modern counterpart relies upon other less distinguished markers, such as roundabouts and a railway bridge tunnel. In contrast, Christopher Alexander (Alexander et al 1977) writes that gateways should be solid elements and be visible from every line of approach. *Gateways*, they suggest, should enclose the path, punch a hole through a building, form a bridge or a sharp change in level. Above all, he concludes, gateways should be 'things'.

With the coming of the internet and the 'global village', the concept of the virtual *gateway* has shifted to a new kind of portal — through which edges dissolve and boundaries disappear.

See also: **Boundary • Edge condition • Hierarchy • Interface • Framing (enframing) • Threshold**

Generic space   ▌

Ludwig Mies van der Rohe was a great exponent of the value of *generic space*, or universal space, as the answer to the growth and change problem in architecture. If a space is generic, it can more or less accommodate a wide range of uses, without becoming obsolete. Also known as 'multi-strategic space', generic space ideally should offer characteristics that are incomplete and adaptable, offering hints as to how it might be used and made more specific. This is an issue, particularly in relation to housing, that seems to have preoccupied Habraken. However, *generic space* is, typically, often poorly suited to any particular use, owing to the need to compromise on the provision of space features for the sake of the other uses. At one time or another most of us have sat through the painful 'cafetorium' experience of the secondary school theatre or band concert. Another, more common, version of *generic space* is the ubiquitous pre-engineered commercial 'strip' building that can be transformed overnight from a hamburger joint to a shoe store. These structures provide spaces that are so non-committal that they cease to represent anything tangible. No one laments their passing. It is as if they never really existed. (EO)

See also: **Transprogramming • Decorated shed • Serviced shed • Strip**

Gentrification

Gentrification is the process of upgrading usually low-income housing in inner-city areas into the appearance of middle-class residences. Sure signs of *gentrification* include brightly painted brickwork, false shutters, hanging floral baskets, potted geraniums, wrought-iron gates, 'clip-on' conservatories and porches (sometimes supported above fibreglass classical columns), and elaborate house numbers or fancy name plates.

Gentrification can also spread through urban commercial areas like a tidal wave. For instance, the upgrading of Boston's Quincy Market from a down-to-earth open city market to an upscale tourist destination is another breed of *gentrification*. Similar transformations have occurred at Fisherman's Wharf in San Francisco and at New York's South Street Seaport, and, in the same city, along the lower reaches of West Broadway.

See also: **Ornament • Place**

Genius loci

The original meaning of genius is embedded in the Roman concept of every human being having two guardian spirits in the form of fallen angels (*genii*) that give life or spirit to people or places. The development towards the dominant modern meaning of 'extraordinary ability' is complex but seems to have been connected with the idea of 'spirit' through a notion of 'inspiration'. The term *genius loci* as 'spirit of place', however, refers back to the original meaning of genius as 'essence'. Thus, in geography, landscape architecture and architectural design, *genius loci* is now accepted as denoting 'spirit or essence of place'. In his ground-breaking book, *Genius Loci: Towards a Phenomenology of Architecture* (1979), Christian Norberg-Schultz set the stage for this shift from the quantative to the qualitative in architectural theory discourse.

As a consequence of the resurgence of interest in phenomenology during the last two decades, *genius loci* has become a popular and somewhat trite expression in the design studio. It now refers to any quality that defines the experience of a place. Common examples of the *genius loci* tend to describe unique or dramatic natural landscapes. Architecturally inspired *genius loci* is harder to come by; an example of a definitive *genius loci* might be Andrea Palladio's Villa Capra (Villa Rotunda) in Vicenza. (EO)

See also: *Axis mundi* • **Phenomenology • Place • Precedent • Sacred space**

Geodesic

A *geodesic* is the shortest distance between two points on the surface of a solid. For example, the lines of latitude and longitude that encompass the earth are geodesic lines, as is the flight path taken by a Boeing 747 flying the Atlantic by the most direct route. A geodesic dome is one of a classification of domes in which, although not exclusively so, the structural bars of triangulated or triangle-derived forms, such as tetrahedrons and pentagons, come together to form a series of continuous lines over its hemispherical surface.

Albeit a structural failure, the first *geodesic* dome was designed and built by Richard Buckminster Fuller in 1948 using the aluminium slats from a venetian blind. Undeterred, Buckminster Fuller continued building prototype *geodesic* hemispheres in various lightweight materials and of ever-increasing size, forming his company Geodesics Inc. in 1949. His later successes attracted military and commercial interest in the potential of *geodesic* shelters that, delivered whole or in part by helicopter, could be quickly assembled to enclose enormous volumes.

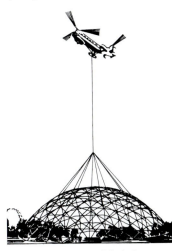

Until his death in 1983, Buckminster Fuller's dream was of producing lighter than air spheres and habitable domes that would umbrella cities. With the more recent development of ETFE (ethyl tetra fluoro ethylene) for its skin, the Buckminster Fuller-inspired biomes of Nicholas Grimshaw's Eden Project in Cornwall bring his dream closer to reality. Indeed, the architects have calculated that using ETFE, the weight of the space-frame is equal to that of the volume of air it encloses; making it is possible to build Buckminster Fuller's vision of a 1 km diameter *geodesic* sphere that could be light enough to float on air.

Dome drop. Buckminster Fuller's air-transportable aluminium dome designed to function as a mobile theatre.

See also: **Crystalline** • **Platonic solids** • **Tensegrity**

Gestalt

Gestalt psychology was a movement initiated at the University of Frankfurt in 1912 by Max Wertheimer and his students Wolfgang Kohler and Kurt Koffka. Formed in response to previous theories of perception that tended to analyse perception and experience by breaking them down into their constituent parts, *gestalt* psychology was an attempt to explain human perception in terms of *gestalts*, i.e. resolved patterns of meaning or constructs. The champion of an aesthetics based on the gestalt approach has been Rudolph Arnheim.

Central to *gestalt* psychology is the study of the act of seeing as a dynamic and creative response system involving both the viewer and the viewed. Their theories have stressed that, in seeking harmony and unity in visual information, our perceptual response first sees a *gestalt* as a unified whole before identifying its constituent parts; furthermore, that our tendency to initially group things into simple units is governed by unit relationships, such as proximity (the relative nearness of elements to one another) and similarity (the relative sameness of elements). It proposed that, although the interacting parts of a pictorial array can be perceived as independent, their visual reassembly brings a whole, the sum of which is greater than the parts. Moreover, it also aimed to show how the mind can perceive organized wholes by understanding relationships between otherwise unconnected physical stimuli, a commonly given example being that of the illusion of the moving picture created from a series of photographic stills.

Consequently, *gestalt* criticism is opposed to the idea of empathy, and holds that we do not ourselves project aesthetic and emotional qualities into the work of art, but that we find them out there waiting for us.

See also: **Figure-ground** • *Moiré* • **Proximity** • **Resolved** • **Visual field**

Two arrangements of the same collection of elements. A *gestalt* occurs when their configuration causes recognition.

Gesture

In human discourse, *gesture* involves movement of face, hands and body as a non-lexical reinforcement in the communication of thought and emotion. Architectural *gesture* is a similar form of mime which conveys motion or action, and to understand it we have to invest its body and limbs with the capacity for expressive movement. We then appreciate how a building can 'hug' the landscape, 'embrace' the visitor or 'blow kisses' of acknowledgement to nearby surfaces and forms.

Like the stylized *gestures* in ballet, buildings and their components can also strike physical attitudes. Their forms can 'lean', 'arch', 'point' and 'pirouette', and, like the facial 'nod and wink' of recognition, façades can, through their reciprocity of materials, proportion and scale, transmit awareness of others in close company. *Gesture*, therefore, is the language of human presence embodied in the dimensions and stance of a building. Like the need to achieve human scale in a building, it is a body metaphor that reveals the human origins of architecture. There are no dictionaries of architectural body language and *gestures*, but whether flamboyant and 'arm-waving' or discreet, like a nudge, a recognition of *gesture* will result from a particular and physical action that is sensed and interpreted by the viewer.

Popularized in Kimon Nicolaides' book *The Natural Way to Draw* (1941), the gesture sketch is a tool used by some designers to capture the essence of a design. Like the one shown here, Frank Gehry famously uses the quick *gesture* delineation as the soul of his creative process.

See also: **Anthropomorphic** • **Corporeality** • **Dialogue** • **Metaphor**

Frank Gehry's sinuous gesture of an emerging concept for the Stata Center at MIT.

Ghosting ▮

Ghosting is a term usually applied to the hidden line or invisible line convention in architectural drawings. It refers to a broken, dashed or dotted line used to ghost the outlines of important forms or planes that are concealed from the line of view — either within the space of the drawing itself or occupying a point forward of the picture plane. Within the convention, dotted lines signify hidden contours, while broken lines signify shapes that appear in front of the drawing. Broken lines are also enlisted as 'stretch lines' in exploded drawings when the fragmented parts of a graphic are ghosted.

Ghosting can sometimes appear as a kind of architectural 'doppelganger' — a secondary apparition of itself as in the duplicate images produced by defective television reception. Stanley Tigerman's work for the 'The Little House in the Clouds' project is just such a case in which a handed version of the main building is ghosted in topiary. Another form of architectural *ghosting* is found in Venturi and Rauch's full-scale three-dimensional delineation in stainless steel of the memory of the form of Benjamin Franklin's Philadelphia home.

See also: **Convention • Dualism •** *Moiré* **• Trace**

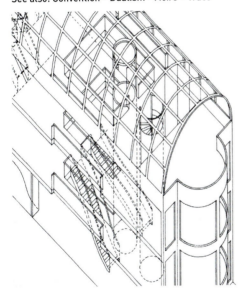
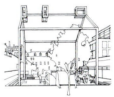

Ghosted internal circulation in a Peter Pran axonometric, and Robert Venturi's traced apparition of Benjamin Franklin's Philadelphia house.

Golden section ▮

The *golden section*, or 'golden rectangle', is said to be one of the most visually satisfying of all geometrical forms. This calculable formula for beauty perceived in a ratio of perfect proportion was known to the Greeks who, as early as the fifth century BCE, had already applied its harmonious balance to the Athenian Parthenon. It was also much used by Renaissance architects and artists in their triumph over matter. Through mathematics,

---

they believed, beauty and harmony could be calculated. Consequently, geometrical and arithmetical plans pervaded their exterior and interior architectural compositions.

A particular distinction of the *golden section* lies in the fact that it produces a number of integrally related areas; its character is such that the ratio between the bigger and the smaller measurable quantity is equal to the ratio between the sum of the two and the bigger one. The geometric construction of a golden rectangle (shown here) begins with a square which is then divided into two equal parts by the dotted line EF. Point E now serves as the centre of a circle whose radius is the diagonal ED. An arc of the circle is drawn (DG) and the base line BA is extended out to intersect it. This becomes the base of the rectangle. The new side HG is now drawn at right angles to the new base, with the line CD brought out to meet it. The resultant rectangle is a *golden section*. However, this rectangle embodies

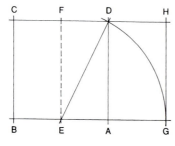

an unusual property: if the original square is removed, what remains will still be a golden rectangle.

Golden ratios can be found in the work of many leading architects, including Le Corbusier, who felt that life was 'comforted' by mathematics, and Louis Kahn, Tadeo Ando, Mario Botta and so on. However, a favourite pastime of some historians is to impose the *golden section* on historic buildings — many of which were not designed in that way.

The *golden section*. If the original square is removed after construction, what remains will still be a golden rectangle.

See also: **Fibonacci series • Ken • Modular • Ordering systems • Proportion • Regulating lines**

Green building

Designers and clients alike readily employ the term *green building* (or 'green design', 'green architecture'). *Green buildings* are perceived as good buildings. There is no detailed agreement among users of this term as to what specifically constitutes a green building. There is a general consensus, however, as to the broad character of such a building. A *green building* is usually expected to pass two key litmus tests: (1) the construction and operation of the building minimizes negative impacts upon surrounding and distant environments; (2) the building provides excellent indoor environmental quality for its occupants and users.

Two major procedures for evaluating *green building* claims are currently in widespread use: the US-based LEED (Leadership in Energy and Environmental Design) programme and the international Green Building Challenge. Both of these rating systems outline elements and decisions that will minimize a building's negative impacts and, to some extent, maximize its positive impacts. Either rating/evaluation system can be used as a guide to green design strategies.

Green buildings are usually undertaken as a response to the serious negative impacts (global warming, air pollution, storm water pollution, loss of energy reserves, deforestation) that a building may impose on diverse and often unseen constituencies in today's global energy, materials and labour markets. Concern for the interior environments of such buildings ensures that they do not do distant good while imposing local harm.

Green building should not be confused with sustainable building. *Green building* is simply one tool toward a larger goal of sustainability. (WG)

See also: **Ecological footprint • Energy efficiency • Sustainability**

Greenfield site

A *greenfield site* is a previously undeveloped, virgin landscape setting. When not protected by 'Green Belt' restrictions, *greenfield sites* hold the potential for development. *Greenfield sites* are also associated with a latitude of design freedom that allows the 'object building' — the classic example being located in a field in Poissy, near Paris. This is Le Corbusier's starkly-placed Villa Savoye — often described as a 'grounded spaceship'.

Greenfield sites join a mini-spectrum of redevelopment locations. For example, a 'brownfield site' describes the potential reuse of previously developed sites, such as abandoned industrial sites, usually contaminated, while a 'greyfield site', much used in the US, refers to the redevelopment of asphalted or 'blacktopped' sites, usually car parks.

See also: **Figure-ground**

Grid

And then the startling grid; urban chaos contained
in mathematics; a city mapping itself. New York,
New York! On the ground the order's less visible.
— Clare Pollard

Organizing space according to an x and y axis, the *grid* is one of the oldest tools for ordering data and collectively sequencing elements and composing their negative space. The *grid* is the underlying structure that lurks behind the chart and graph. Like woven fabric and wire mesh, concepts structured as *grids* provide a net of fragments, each fragment of a gridded net invoking the extended field. The *grid* acts as an adaptive scaffolding, a skeleton on which the stuff of content is scaled and hung. Theo van Doesburg saw the *grid* as the fundamental origin of art and promoted it from its role as background design armature to a primary foreground-framing device. Employing a system of equidistant and intersecting axial lines that set centre lines to denote spatial pathways, *grids* have been used to plan cities on virgin sites — from the ancient Hellenistic city of Miletus to Manhattan, New York.

The *grid* is a powerfully ambiguous system, simultaneously relentless and yet egalitarian in that its pieces are interchangeable. For the ancient Greeks, it provided an organizing principle without direct aesthetic intentions. More recently, Piet Mondrian, Frank Lloyd Wright and the design group known as Superstudio all envisioned a world mantled with a *grid* — its uneven terrain draped with the predictability of its Cartesian net. However, although *grids* can be easily draped on virgin terrain, they are difficult to imprint on the footprint of existing freehold settlements. For instance, when replanning London after the Great Fire of 1666, Sir Christopher Wren's initial gridiron proposal, complete with sightlines through to the River Thames, was quickly shelved due to the intractability of an irregular patchwork of medieval private ownership.

When reduced to its intersections we isolate the abstract anchor points of the 'point grid' — a means by which, to paraphrase Bernard Tschumi, we can introduce a diagram of order into the disorder of reality. When two *grids* are superimposed, each with a different locus, their layered confrontation provides new fields of opportunity to increase design negotiability — the resultant tension or electrical interface caused by their play-off realizes the 'displaced *grid*'.

See also: **Cartesian grid • Euclidean space • Matrix • Order • Ordering systems • xyz space**

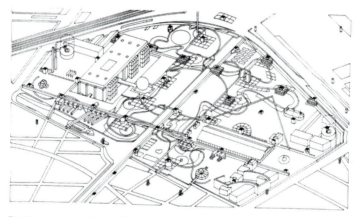

The lines and forms of Bernard Tschumi's plan for the Parc de la Villette in Paris (1983–93) is braced by the nodes of a point *grid*.

Heroic   ▮

The term *heroic* refers to the celebratory architecture of antiquity when huge monuments were erected to symbolize national or religious sentiment. They also commemorate deities, epic bravery on the battlefield, or the florid pomposity of great dead leaders. For example, the Egyptian pyramids, the Imperial Roman Trajan Column, the Arch of Titus, and the Victor-Emmanuelle in Rome, are all examples of a so-called *heroic* architecture. Consequently, at the core of the meaning is that of monumental scale. Generally speaking, an epic architecture stands diametrically opposed to one that responds to human scale and, when misplaced, can affront the more sensitive critic.

However, the archispeak version of *heroic* can act as a double-edged sword. On the one hand, it can be used as a positive response to the scale of thought or the boldness or breadth of an undertaking. On the other hand, it can disguise derogatory connotations — sending a veiled accusation that the designer has bitten off more than he or she can chew. At its worst, the term is used as a polite substitute for a negative reaction. In order to discover if such comment is fit for a hero or a heroine, the recipient has to be sensitive to the tone of the reviewer.

See also: **Allegory** • **Celebrate** • **Monumentality** • **Scale**

Hierarchy   ▮

Architecturally speaking, *hierarchy* is an ordering device that clearly arranges form, space, function, etc., according to a ranked degree of importance or capacity. By establishing priority scales in a structure in which some sets of elements will occupy a more dominant position than the others, the architect instils a sense of order, sequence and stability.

It was during the Renaissance that the concept of hierarchy came to be employed as means of ordering space and material. This came as a new compositional principle that became more important than the concentration, hitherto, on number and pleasing aesthetic relationships. *Hierarchy* meant that the elements of a building had to be differentiated against priority scales in terms of primary, secondary and tertiary components. For example, the enhancement of 'entrance' is the most fundamental hierarchical exercise — achieved by a change of scale, an increase of detail or the addition of a feature.

The term is similarly used in architectural drawing where a *hierarchy* of line-weight is used to designate the spatial zones: darker lines signifying 'foreground'; medium thickness lines signifying 'middleground', and fine lines signifying 'background'. Similarly, in design, the clear ranking of formal and spatial elements into a classification of primacy provides a framework of understanding between building and user. Indeed, in the words of Robert Adam, without *hierarchy*, '. . . creativity can be squandered in incomprehension and obscurity'.

See also: **Balance** • **Collage** • **Composition** • **Context** • **Gestalt** • **Order** • **Ordering principles**

Heterarchy

Heterarchy is a term found in a branch of metaphysics dealing with the nature of being. It is much used in the writings of Lebbeus Woods where he employs it to describe an alternative state of existence — an idealized, graphical setting in which to locate his visionary architectural drawings. As opposed to hierarchy that infers a predetermined and vertical chain of authority that operates downward from elevated positions of power, *heterarchy* is a spontaneous and self-motivating lateral network of people who do their own thing — a system of authority that is centred on individual invention and one responsive to their evolving actions.

In this Woodsian utopia, *heterarchy* is made up of 'freespace', a world in which architectural construction is free from preconceived value, function or meaning. A network of freespace constitutes a 'free-zone' — a system devoid of a mass culture (which Woods sees as diminishing the autonomy of the individual). 'Freespace' embodies patterns of urban order realized by knowledge, innovation and performance. In Woodsian archispeak we also find 'ontology'. This is the theory as to what exists and the study of the static and hierarchical state of being, while 'ontogenetics' is the study of *heterarchy*, the dynamic state of 'becoming'.

Heterarchy also describes a non-hierarchical organization with organizational diversity. Some progressive architectural firms in the 1970s experimented with heterarchical matrix organizational structures. Even SOM (Skidmore, Owens & Merril), with their studio or team-based structure, attempted to be a heterarchy.

See also: **Hierarchy • Utopia**

High-tech (low-tech)

High-tech is the high classicism of post-modernity, and the airport is its temple. — Michael Sorkin

The continuous cycling and recycling of architectural styles seems to reflect the mood and the spirit of a time. Peaks in the rotation of this fashion carousel can almost be measured in decades: Deconstruction in the 1990s, post-modernism in the 1980s, and *high-tech* in the 1970s — the latter recycling the earlier Modernist glorification of the machine and of machined products. During its short-lived fashion, several *high-tech* architects associated with this particularly English technology-based architecture leapt to prominence, with the wittier members of this group surviving; namely, Norman Foster, Nicholas Grimshaw and Richard Rogers.

The seeds for a *high-tech* fashion were possibly sown in the early 1960s; in the quasi-scientific study of optical illusions, a fascination for metallics and a science-fiction fantasy for man–machine environments that coincided with Gagarin's first orbit around the earth. This fantasy was rekindled in the 1970s but this time expressed in an exposed technology. This psychological need to confront a complex technology saw mechanisms made visible; an exposed 'wristwatch' architecture where the hitherto hidden parts of buildings became exposed — their mechanical guts being spilled directly into the street for all to see. But this 1970s excursion into high technology had to be clarified. In order to make it legible and more digestible at a human scale, bold colours were enlisted to symbolically diagram, i.e. colour code, individual elements. The *high-tech* flagship is Piano & Rogers' Centre Pompidou in Paris, and the later adoption of the style by almost every new airport — from Kansai to Denver. According to Michael Sorkin, there is a good argument for this. After all, an airport is the extension of an aircraft by other means, and there is a logic to looking at the formal language of aerodynamics as a point of departure.

Critics of *high-tech* describe it as useless technology and as elevating logic to a system of rules. However, by the late 1990s and coinciding with the rise of interest in green architecture, the term *low-tech*, with all its ramifications, became fashionable.

See also: **Archigram • Metabolism • Module • Servant/served • Transparency**

Histororsity

Sometimes referred to as 'historonics', *historosity* is the point of reference for a structure, especially as it pertains to the historic precedent on which an architectural typology is based. This is often referred to as the 'subconscious memory' of a typology or styling that is prevalent in hybrid or mixed-use structures.

Applied to urban, suburban and rural settings, it is common in infill projects where buildings are designed to fit into an existing context or environment. An example is the new apartment building or hotel that is carefully placed in a sensitive context, such as the fabric of an historic district. For example, it could apply to the siting of replacement structures or new buildings in settings such as Savannah, Georgia, Charleston, South Carolina, and Alexandria, Virginia, where new building is generally required to embody *histority* or historonic characteristics in order to fit into its surrounding context.   (MAT)

See also: **Context • Memory • Palimpsest • Site specific • Typology**

Hyperrealism

It is our only architecture today; great screens on which are reflected atoms, particles, molecules in motion. Not a public scene or true public space but gigantic spaces of circulation, ventilation and ephemeral connections. — Jean Baudrillard

We are increasingly becoming comfortable with the post-modern condition of existence as outlined by Baudrillard in the above quotation. Described as *hyperrealism*, the world of electronic images is bolstered by a supporting cast of physical environments that are jazzed up reality. In his essay 'Travels in Hyperreality' (1986), Umberto Eco describes these places as not just Disney World but virtually the entire State of Florida and most of California. The most audacious hyperreal world is Las Vegas. In *Learning from Las Vegas* (1972), Robert Venturi lauded the ordinary and the ugly of the Las Vegas of the 1960s. With the addition of casinos such as New

York New York, Paris and the Luxor, today's lesson from Las Vegas is that hyperreality sells, as long as it is neither ugly nor ordinary, and more ominously that we are slipping away from an architecture of substance, truth, depth and profound meaning towards an architecture of cheap gratification.   (EO)

See also: **Cyberspace • Decorated shed • Simulacrum • Strip • Virtual reality**

Hypothesis

As used in science, *hypothesis* is a speculative claim, a conjecture that is not yet supported by evidence. In a research project, the 'research hypothesis' is usually part of a larger theory, seeking to explain hitherto unexplained observations. If proven or corroborated, these observations would become part of that theory's set of mutually supporting statements. Because observed evidence cannot logically prove a hypothesis, but its absence can disprove it, research proceeds by establishing a 'null hypothesis' — the 'hypothesis of no difference' — and tries to disprove it.   (TM)

See also: **Design intent • Mission statement • Thesis**

Icon(ic)   I

If the term 'typology' describes the distillation of a formal body of architecture into categories of type, then *iconic* describes the pictorial or mental
picture of an architectural example that is quintessential of the type.

Features which make a building architecture can be represented by
a graphic image. The chosen image can then become a symbol or an
identifying mark. An *icon* has no fixed scale; it may represent an entire
city or just a detail of a building. The piece of concentrated architecture
functions like a 'jingle' in a song. A 'jingle' is the characteristic sequence
of just a few notes which, when played with specific timbre, loudness and
interval, evokes the complete work. Occasionally, such 'keynotes' grow
into a unified symbol, such as the opening notes of Beethoven's Fifth
Symphony which became interpreted as the morse-coded letter 'V' (for
victory) during the Second World War.

Similarly, an *icon* is an extract, denoted by just a few lines. It referen-
tially marks an important and representative point in the evolution of an
architectural style, type or genre. *Iconic* forms often stem from tradition,
like the shape of an igloo. They can also be invented. For example, the
columns of the Alvorada Palace in Brasilia (1957) were designed by Oscar
Niemeyer to represent the then modernistic identity of Brazil, but the two-
dimensional depiction of their clearly defined contours is still widely
adopted as an *icon* in that country and is used on everyday tokens like
cinema tickets, bank notes and stamps.

An *icon* may also reflect a complex three-dimensional shape which, as
a whole, is not clearly defined. For example, the Guggenheim Museum in
Bilbao, Spain, designed by Frank Gehry is an *icon* of modern architecture.
Its highly complex form demands numerous and different perspectives in
order to convey its overall impression. The inability to express this complexity by one fixed and definitive representation merely emphasizes the
complicated nature of this image building. In contrast, Oscar Niemeyer's
Museum of Contemporary Art in Niteroi, Brazil, is a rotational volume and
its contour remains the same when seen from any direction. Perched on a
promontory, the building's minimal width at ground level allows open and
unimpeded views over the sea. The line of rotation, from which the volume
is composed, typifies Niemeyer's fascination for the sensual curve; a free
and weightless line escaping from the harsh right-angle. In the mind, the
drawing and the building fuse into an *iconic* image.   (KV)

See also: **Allegory • Analogue • Key drawing • Paradigm • Precedent • Typology,
Zeitgeist**

Icon in a spin. Oscar
Niemeyer's Museum
of Contemporary Art,
Niteroi, Brazil, and
his iconic columns
of the Alvorado
Palace, Brasilia.

Interaction

Whenever we engage in an abstract or a physical sense, we interact. *Interaction* is dialogue and interchange; it refers to the input–output alternation of cause and effect. It is a two-way action or influence between two parties when information is exchanged.

Interaction is an all-embracing archispeak term that finds widespread currency across the entire design process. For instance, the architect interacts with the client, with the site context and with the design idea, as each in turn interacts with all the others. Form interacts with space, materials interact with the solid and the void, while different materials interact with each other, and so forth. In archispeak, all is in *interaction*. A common use of the term is also found in the context of the reciprocal flow of information in our interactive relationship with the machine. But the machine also functions as a result of an *interaction* of its parts — each working within a whole system, like the elements of a painting or the components of a building.

An extension of our *interaction* with buildings is the current interest in the kinaesthetic aspect of the architectural experience, a preoccupation that finds an echo in the elasticated walls in Roman Polanski's movie *Repulsion*. With its roots in the ubiquitous digital screened façade and the plethora of student projects that explore 'talking walls', 'pulsing walls', 'breathing walls' and 'living walls', emerges the truly 'interactive wall'. The animated version shown here was developed by the Royal College of Art research student Socrates Yiannoudes. Made of a flexible elastic membrane, the wall physically transforms in real time when sensing a moving human presence. Driven by pneumatic pistons equipped with sensors aided by a motion-tracking technology and three-dimensional modelling software, this prototype interactive wall functions as a 'living' entity with which the user relates and communicates.

See also: **Dialogue** • **Didactic** • **Engage (dégagements)** • **Gesture** • **Juxtaposition** • **Kinetic** • **Mediate** • **Reciprocity**

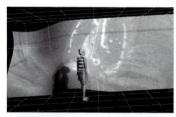
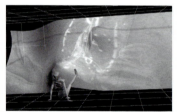

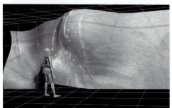
The project explores the kinaesthetic experience of a pneumatic wall equipped with motion-tracking technology that activates in response to human movement.

Interface   **I**

The secret of form is that it is a boundary, it is the thing itself and, at the same time, the cessation of the thing, the circumscribed territory in which the Being and the non-Being of the thing are only one thing.
— Georg Simmel

Interface is a point of contact where interaction takes place between two forces, processes or subjects. *Interface* is a surface lying between two spaces. We interface when we enter into dialogue with others.

A conceptual drawing provides an *interface* between creative thought and its visible manifestation; a building envelope functions as the *interface* between inside and outside, and a monitor screen acts as the *interface* between corporeal and virtual worlds. Lebbeus Woods describes the 'Alice in Wonderland' ease with which we can oscillate between the *interface* dividing the physical and abstract worlds when he talks of his relationship with a drawing of an interior he made as part of his 'Centricity' series entitled 'Neomechanical Tower (Upper) Chamber'. He writes: 'I am standing now outside the drawing, an onlooker. Once I was inside, on the other side of the paper's surface. Then, in the space and time of the drawing's making, I moved with such ease back and forth through the now impenetrable barrier, the boundary between seeing and making — I remember that. I moved so easily in the space between the mind and the hand, between the eye and the extension of the hand pressed into the paper's surface.' (Woods 1997) Interestingly, the paper *interface* of this particular drawing by Woods was to find a new *interface* in the celluloid and silver screen of the cinema. This occurred when a version of it reappeared to inspire the set for the interrogation chamber in Terry Gilliam's movie *Twelve Monkeys*.

See also: **Boundary** • **Dialogue** • **Interaction** • **Intersection** • **Juxtapose** • **Kiss** • **Reciprocity** • **Transition**

International Style   **I**

Initially championed in the work of Le Corbusier, Mies van der Rohe, Walter Gropius and J. J. P. Oud, the term was originally used to label a plethora of diverse and radical design approaches which were spawned in Europe in the 1920s and which laid the foundations for Modernism. However, propogandized by the book title *The International Style* written in 1932 by Henry-Russell Hitchcock and Philip Johnson (the latter being a disciple of Mies van der Rohe) to accompany the 'Modern Architecture: International Exhibition' at New York's Museum of Modern Art, the term became rigidly exclusionistic. It was now casually used to describe a functionalist restraint and a clear technological aesthetic as applied to architecture and industrial design.

Beatriz Colomina has described the Hitchcock–Johnson publication and accompanying exhibition as a political weapon in the promotion of modern architecture in America, but the moment the term was coined, the style came under attack and died. Its demise was due to its varied design expression in different parts of the world and, especially the degenerative

Modernist variants spawned particularly in the UK in the ensuing decades, the *International Style* quickly detached from its original use as an umbrella term for Modernism. It now loosely refers to a particular breed of architecture which, at its best, describes a machine-influenced and early stripped-back minimalism and, at its worst, conjures up drab images of 1950s style concrete and glass curtain-wall office blocks, schools and hospitals. Also, the spread of the *International Style* into major cities around the world, together with its apparent disregard of culture or context, is also blamed for neutralizing and replacing an architectural diversity and ethnicity with bland and faceless buildings.

See also: **Context • Functionalism • Minimalism • Modernism**

Interpenetrating space

Interpenetrating space is anti-cellular space. It coincides with the blurring of edges and boundaries, i.e. when a sense of continuity is created between one space and another. Degrees of spatial interpenetration correspond to an increasing breakdown of the architectural envelope when openings allow space to flow and become as one with adjacent or surrounding space. For instance, when large apertures are cut into the envelope, their framing elements appear to be a part of both the inside and outside — the larger the openings, the more the envelope dissolves into transparency and the greater the sense of inside out and outside in. A similar transparency can result when the corners of floor and wall planes are deconstructed, literally pulled apart to release the flow of space and light as expressed in the 'architectural kiss', or when wall, ceiling or floorscape planes are projected through a plane of glass with a continuity that connects interior to exterior.

A past master of *interpenetrating space* was Alvar Aalto. When designing 'outside' he would employ architectonic devices to create the impression of an outdoor room; when designing 'inside' he would approach it as a landscape in miniature. His techniques of spatial interpenetration included exaggerated or reversed perspective applied to emphasize distance and also to embrace the outdoors in his buildings by funnelling exterior space into its interior.

Possibly its greatest exponent was Mies van der Rohe. His German Pavilion for the Barcelona International Exhibition in 1929 poetically exemplifies the liberation of free-flowing space in which mass gives way to

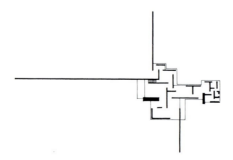

Project for Brick Country House, 1923. Plan of Mies van der Rohe's first design, which dissolves enclosure to allow space to flow.

floating, independent planes, and enclosure dissolves into openness and a spatial cohesion to provide a microcosmic extension of infinite space. However, *interpenetrating space* is given definitive expression in his ultimate Modernist glass box — the Farnsworth House completed in 1950.

See also: **Closure • Co-mingling space •** *Plan libre* **(free space) • Superimpose • Transparency**

Intervention ▮

Each of us is a kind of crossroads, where things happen.
— Claude Levi-Strauss

The *intersection* of horizontal and vertical lines forms the archetypal cross, or the primary axis. This represented the ancient concept of space and the cosmos; the *intersection* of its two lines denoting the centre of perceived location. From this recognition, and the attendant ability to distinguish up, down, left and right, came our entire understanding of space. When the primary axis cross is further subdivided by more intersecting lines, we achieve an elementary navigational aid. The point of intersection not only locates the navigator but their lines subdivide space into parts — horizontal space being defined by points of the compass and a fixed vertical axis.

Therefore, 'X' marks the hot spot; the crossing-point of pathways, drawn lines, planes or lines of thought. When different lines of thought intersect they can result in agreement or argument. Intersecting routes are intercepting nodes that mark moments of choice and the opportunity to change direction, or to meet others travelling from other directions. The *intersection* of routes and river crossings mark the sites on which settlements are historically founded.

In architectural drawing, the *intersection* of two or more lines is traditionally emphasized to denote an important moment of measure. Sometimes *intersections* are marked with a dot, such as in a 'point grid', to indicate with precise certainty the locality of a junction, a point of crossing or a point of friction.

See also: **Balance • Composition • Contrast • Edge condition • Grid • Kiss • Ley lines • Node • Planar • Time line**

Intervention ▮

Similar to the widespread use of the word 'installation' in art circles, *intervention* is popular archispeak jargon for describing an architectural design intention. It is one of those common four syllable terms like 'frontality' and 'articulate' that seem to roll off the tongue to sound impressive. Its meaning substitutes more common terms, such as 'design statement' and 'project proposal', to imply artistic connotation and a sense of control in the act of design interference.

Intervention also refers to the impact architecture has upon its context, i.e. it 'intervenes' between conflicting site conditions. 'Urban intervention' is the phrase used most to describe architecture that has an impact upon its milieu. Therefore, *intervention* is the in-between; the mediation of an idea and the impact on its environmental destination. Its consequence, of course, is change.

See also: **Context • Dialogue • Dynamic • Mediate • Synthesis • Transformation**

Issue

Issue is the fashionable buzzword for 'problem'. An issue is a point in question, an important subject for consideration or debate. People get passionate about issues. In the world of architectural design education, everything and anything of import becomes an *issue*: urban issues, site issues, spatial issues, psychological issues, and so forth.

The act of design is surrounded by *issues*. Once identified in a project, issues are to be 'confronted', 'addressed' and 'resolved'. Consequently, a good strategy is to first determine all the *issues* relevant to a design project and incorporate them in a mission statement, i.e. a platform from which to advance and, indeed, communicate the outcome. Many reviewers and designers will carry 'pet issues' and promote them in debate.

See also: **Mission statement • Parameters • Problem solving**

Journey   ▐

In archispeak, *journey* describes the course of a concept — the passage of a design idea from genesis to realization. Some architects, such as Michael Hopkins, have described the design process as a *journey* through a dense forest. The expedition is either preconceived, i.e. charted by a series of pre-positioned signposts that point the way toward the destination, or open ended. The latter is a much more exciting excursion — the design process representing an adventure into the unknown; one filled with risks but offering the exhilaration of the unexpected.

See also: **Design intent • Problem-solving**

Juxtaposition   ▐

Juxtaposition describes the placing of elements side by side in order to invite their interaction and the activation of a comparison of relationships. The adjacent positioning of two or more contrasting shapes, surfaces, forms, materials or spaces heightens visual interest, especially when the character or quality of each element is maintained. In two-dimensional arrangements, or in film when rapid sequences of paradoxical pictorial events are disclosed, juxtapositioning holds the power to attract the attention of the viewer. This engagement, through shock and surprise, is a technique fully exploited at the birth of Modern Art — in Dadaist photomontage and Surrealist collages, and in the early Russian movies of Dzija Vertov and Sergei Eisenstein.

Similarly, spatial *juxtaposition* in architecture depends upon the autonomy of space — a cellular condition that, in turn, relies on the degree of enclosure of each constituent space by the planes that define its configuration. When this integrity of this containment breaks down, the condition of *juxtaposition* becomes compromised and is dissolved into a new and more ambiguous condition. This is when spatial interpenetration takes over. Using historical reference, Pierre von Meiss develops the two conditions of spatial *juxtaposition* and interpenetration. He cites the Modern Movement introduction of the '*plan libre*' as the catalyst that released architectural space from its hitherto juxtaposed configurations and into the continuity and dynamic of spatial interpenetration.

See also: **Collage • Contrast • Edge condition • Interaction • Kiss • Layering • Montage • Parallax •** *Plan libre* **(free space) • Superimpose**

Ken

The *Ken* is the Japanese module traditionally used in the planning and arrangement of architecture. The *Ken's* ratio of 1:2 is based upon the proportions of the tatami mat, a traditional floor covering made from woven rushes and dimensioned to comfortably accommodate two seated people or one person sleeping. As such, the tatami mat module became adopted as a standardized unit in room measurement, its length (1 *Ken*) determining the centres of the interval between columns, its width (1/2 *Ken*) providing the dimension of the *Ken* grid. Used against the *Ken* grid, a veritable 'origami' of different mat arrangements aid the plotting of room sizes and their relationship with others. Furthermore, as an ordering device, the *Ken* is used three dimensionally, i.e. both horizontally in planning and vertically in elevating.

Any analysis of the work of Tadeo Ando will, apart from his concern for 'place' and 'nature', reveal his deep interest in geometrical ordering, and it is here that one can find the *Ken* module in action. However, as the merging of Japanese and Western architectural traditions are also a major preoccupation of his work, this analysis will also discover, particularly in his Koshino House, the *Ken* working in conjunction with the golden section. Also in Japan, the advent in the late 1970s of the 'capsule hotel', which evolved in the face of increases in population density and business commuters, are fitted out with person-sized sleeping compartments with a plan dimension that exactly matches that of the tatami mat.

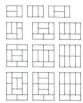

Variation in arrangement and number of tatami floor mats achieve an increasing room size.

See also: **Grid • Matrix • Metabolism • Module • Order • Ordering systems • Proportion • Regulating lines**

Key drawing

The *key drawing* functions as a central communication vehicle in a design presentation. It usually emerges as a recycled drawing that has already proven its worth in summarizing the concept earlier in the design process. In other words, knowledge of this image stems directly from the designer's experience of visualizing architectural form during the act of design. The importance of the *key drawing* is illustrated in our attitude to many signature buildings that tend to be visualized in our mind's eye more by the associated published drawings than any actual visit to the site. Indeed, the extensively published drawings of many widely known buildings, such as the classic plan of the Farnsworth House, or James Stirling's axonometric of Oxford's Florey Building, are more widely known than their physical counterparts — the *key drawing* often capturing the essence of an architectural intent. Through media exposure this becomes a mental icon that is 'visited' and 'revisited' in the mind's eye.

Key drawings also play an important role in design competitions when, during the initial cull, judges will quickly form a shortlist of entries for a later and more deliberated selection of winners. Seen in this context, the *key drawing* provides an eye-catching and potent 'first impression' that is seen over a greater distance than smaller drawings and, hopefully, is one that cannot be easily ignored nor rejected.

See also: **Focal point • Icon(ic) • Message area**

Kinaesthesia   ▮

Kinaesthesia is a subtle aspect of our sensorial appreciation of space; it is a kind of sixth sense. It concerns space that is primarily experienced through the skin and muscles in response to our position within it or movement through it, such as when we detect an oncoming subway train from the rush of the plug of air that precedes it. Japanese landscape designers are particularly aware of the subtle relationship between visual and kinaesthetic space for, in a culture where living space is at a premium, they can stretch its experience through a masterly manipulation of irregularly positioned textures and objects, which necessitates an increased and correspondingly irregular number of muscular sensations.

Other exponents of *kinaesthesia* include Steven Holl, who develops the experiential aspect of moving through a building in his work, and Hiroshi Naito, who designed Gallery Tom in Tokyo — a gallery for the partially sighted filled with objects that offer delight to the sense of touch. Gallery Tom provides an architectural essay on the way we all experience buildings through temperature, texture and acoustics. Naito explains that the users '. . . experience the building by the number of steps, by feeling the light on their skin, they touch the volume of space by sound'. A notable feature is the roof above the upper sculpture gallery. This is pierced by a row of diagonal strips of clerestory ceiling lights. These create shafts of alternating cool and warm air which are sensed kinaesthetically when visitors move about the space.

See also: **Dynamic • Corporeality • Experiential • Interact • Kinetic • Multi-sensory space • Tactility**

Kinetic   ▮

Thinking in movement phases trains our sense of movement on flat surfaces and in space and is indispensable for the creative work of our time. — Emile Ruder

Kinetic concerns the dynamics of movement. 'Kinetic art' is a term that was first used by Naum Gabo and his brother Antoine Pevsner in 1920 to describe an art form, usually sculpture, that incorporates real or apparent movement, such as the orbits made by the mobiles of Alexander Calder. Awareness of *kinetics* is a theme picked up in the deliberations of the German painter Paul Klee who compared the *kinetic* understanding of ancient and modern man. Klee wrote in *Typography* (1981): 'A man of the ancient world sailing in a boat, taking proper enjoyment in it and appreciating the ingenious comfort of the device. And that was how the ancient man portrayed things. And now consider what a modern man experiences walking over the deck of a steamer: first his own movement, second the movement of the ship which may be in the opposite direction, third the direction and speed of the river's movement, fourth the rotation of the earth, fifth its orbit, sixth the orbits of moons and stars round about.'

The moment we begin to physically and perceptually move through a built environment will animate this awareness; and as designers we have infinite scope for introducing and increasing this dynamic into its design. Sequences of movement can, for example, embody increase and decrease of size and value, run from inside out, and vice-versa, and be spaced out in time. Indeed, the components of architecture can be linked in different ways to be projected at an appropriate speed.

Apart from the telescopic action of gasometers and the dynamics of moving structures in theme parks and fairgrounds, physical examples of a *kinetic* architecture include the sliding façade wall in SITE's showroom for the Best Products Company Inc., Wilkinson Eyre's award-winning 'blinking eye' bridge in Gateshead and Hiroshi Hara's Sapporo stadium in Japan which, using hovercraft technology, opens up to receive its soccer pitch brought into play from a greenhouse situated outside its envelope.

See also: **Dynamic • Interaction • Kinaesthesia**

Kiss

We talk of the *kiss* in architecture when one element comes deliberately close to another — without ever quite touching — so that the poignancy of the moment is not lost on the observer or user. We are not talking wet and sloppy kisses here, or those soft and fumbling misplaced pecks from an ageing aunt. Rather, we refer to a peck, a precisely placed air-kiss, which, showing mutual respect through restraint immediately before the point of contact, holds both parties in perfect tension for a moment in time and space.

In the most elegant of skyscraper designs, we talk of the buildings 'kissing the sky'. One thinks of the art deco Chrysler and Empire State buildings in New York (1930 and 1931, respectively), but certainly not the Seagram and AT&T buildings (1958 and 1984, respectively).

Likewise, buildings can embrace the ground; again with the analogy of an air-kiss. The Farnsworth House, Illinois (1951), by Mies van der Rohe, hovers over the ground and comes to land only with a soft staircase landing and 12 slender columns. Compare this with Philip Johnson's later House in New Canaan, Connecticut (1949), which, while sharing the Farnsworth's glass envelope, comes to ground with a thud.   (RR-C)

See also: **Articulate • Engage (** *dégagements* **) • Interaction • Juxtapose • Proximity • Tension**

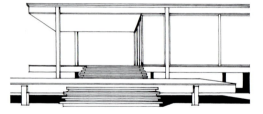

Kissing the ground.
Mies van der Rohe's
hovering Farnsworth
House, 1946–50,
Fox River, Illinois
(© DACS 2003).

Kit of parts   █

A *kit of parts* is usually associated with the industrialization or prefabrication of the components of a building. In his article 'Systems Generating Systems', written in 1968, Christopher Alexander explains: '. . . a generating system is not a view of a single theory. It is a *kit of parts* with rules about the way these parts may be combined'.

Promoters of the early examples of building systems, such as cast-iron churches, houses for early colonial development and hospitals for the Crimea War, were keen to stress that these structures were sound and durable, and the equal of those made on site. This need to promote may be explained by the contemptuous association of the word 'kit' at that time. For example, when used in conjunction with the adjective 'whole', it meant the entire lot — the whole 'kit and kaboodle'. However, the catalogue approach to housing design of Charles and Ray Eames in the 1950s changed all that. They became the darlings of the architectural world and thus spawned a whole generation of consortia building systems in the US, UK and elsewhere. This new generation of designers were proud to call their systems *kits of parts*.

Interestingly enough, the word 'kit' derives from the Dutch word 'kitte' — a tub or 'kit' — a wooden flat-bottomed, usually round, container. This may explain Gerrit Reitveld's interest in adaptability and the present Dutch architects' obsession with prefabricated systems.   (AB)

See also: **Bespoke • Module • Serviced shed**

Lateral thinking

Lateral thinking is a complementary and deliberate process of thinking that enlists insight, creativity and humour to break free from logical avenues of problem solving. Logical patterns of thinking are called 'vertical thinking'. Vertical thinking is a process that follows established patterns of deduction, but once recognized and reacted to, these patterns can become consolidated and resistant to change. By contrast, to escape these traditional patterns in order to explore new avenues of thought, lateral thinking, initially at least, follows the least likely paths of thinking.

The techniques of *lateral thinking* are described in Edward de Bono's classic book of the same title published in 1970. These techniques include alternative ways of restructuring and rearranging given information, challenging assumptions, and the deliberate generation of as many different approaches to problem solving as possible. Brainstorming is the group setting for the use of *lateral thinking*; it is a creative activity involving the provocation of new concepts cross-stimulated by others. The brainstorming session provides a formal but uninhibited environment in which no idea is too ridiculous to be tabled. Here, ideas can be turned upside down, back to front and sideways. Analogies, words and random forms of stimulation may be enlisted to trigger new directions of thought.

While vertical thinking is described as thinking emanating from 'inside the box', *lateral thinking* is thinking 'outside the box'.

See also: **Black box** • **Problem solving**

Layering

Layering is an architectural buzzword that was in common currency long before computer imaging. Indeed, the idea of a building as the conscious expression of a series of layers of space or materials seems to have begun with the early Modernists' development of the free plan. In buildings such as the Barcelona Pavilion designed by Mies van der Rohe or Le Corbusier's Villa Savoye, rooms were only partially separated from each other, or from exterior space, allowing one to experience the building as a series of overlapping layers of space and opaque planes whose relationship changed as the viewer moved. This dynamism was one of the important characteristics that separated Modernism from the static approach of most earlier architectural approaches.

A more recent influence has been the search for means to capture the chiaroscuro often found in traditional masonry load-bearing construction, but decidedly lacking in the thin-wall interior and exterior enclosure of many twentieth-century column-framed buildings. The rise of post-modernism and the energy crises of the 1970s helped to free architects, even those with a continuing commitment to Modernism, to look for ways to visually enrich and technically improve the performance of a building's exterior envelope. Even though contemporary enclosure systems are highly differentiated, consisting of a *layering* of different materials and services, each with its own distinct image and role, underlying layers are usually completely hidden. Architects have tried various strategies to suggest, or actually reveal, those underlying layers. One is the use of transparent cladding to protect, but not hide, selected underlying layers, including structure. Another is to remove or displace portions of the exterior cladding. High-tech buildings often reverse conventional *layering* orders by placing structure and services outside the building envelope. Architects have added space, sometimes even habitable space, between these layers. (PDS)

See also: **Parallax** • *Moiré* • **Order** • **Scrim** • **Servant/served** • **Transparency**

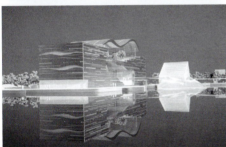

Vertical glass sandwich of space fronting Jean Nouvel's Fondation Cartier in Paris and the horizontal layers of Terry Farrell & Partners' National Aquarium in London.

Ley lines

Ley lines refer to the notion that our prehistoric predecessors, presumably using a sixth sense, could tune into magnetic force-fields which enabled them to undertake extended journeys into the wild for salt and flint. Set against this is the theory of ley lines first proposed by Alfred Watkin in 1925 and expounded in his book *The Old Straight Track*. Although his theory was rejected by the scientific community, Watkin suggested that a landscape systematically littered and marked with notched hillsides and strategically positioned copses and stones showed that humankind moved with the aid of a full-scale 'map' of the environment. Indeed, with trade occurring at their intersection, he believed that *ley lines* provided the initial template for the later establishment of settlements and road systems.

Also, within any primitive organic society, the person who could create a straight line was seen to posses extraordinary prowess. Watkin proposes that this person was, in effect, the first 'environmental draughtsperson' who, when aligning two wooden staves with the eye, could determine a dead straight line in the wilderness. He suggests that the stave became the precursor of the 'magic wand', its user assuming the status of magician.

Therefore, when heard in architectural debate, *ley lines* usually refers to rather special axial lines or lines of force, i.e. lines of vision or movement that connect important points or denote paths of sacred or mystical significance.

See also: **Axis • Linearity • Mapping • Sight lines • Regulating lines • Tension**

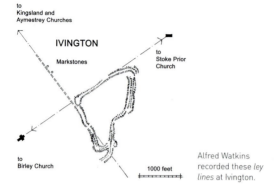

Alfred Watkins recorded these *ley lines* at Ivington.

Linearity

Linearity describes the dominating directional dynamic. As this dynamic can be expressed both by individual and multiple lines of force, this has particular relevance to architecture both in terms of its making and the resultant form. The designer perceiving lines of force originating from elements in the physical context, such as the horizon, topography, the direction of the wind or sun and the location or form of man-made objects, present or past, may incorporate these lines when creating a two- or three-dimensional compositional design arrangement. However, whether straight or curved, these lines may or may not be evident in the final built form. Where evident, they may be visible as lines or implied by the directionality of the resulting two- or three-dimensional forms. For example, when a plane or volume assumes width and length it also assumes *linearity*; its dominant axis implying direction. The longer the axis, the more dynamic the impression of its orientational thrust. Linear elements can contribute to either a dynamic feeling or a sense of repose. Converging lines, vertical lines and lines that are irregular in form or alignment are more dynamic. *Linearity* can both dominate a landscape topology, as in the curve of an amphitheatre, or be subservient to its contours and its dominant lines of demarcation. A curving or broken *linearity* can be seen as being more humane than one unbroken and straight. While strings of waterfront buildings tracing a meandering coastline can appear to celebrate the land–water interface, a relentless and unbroken *linearity*, such as a seemingly endless line-up of mono-directional terrace houses, can smack of a Cartesian determinism.

Linearity is particularly evident in the exterior appearance of buildings grounded in Modernism, with its aversion to ornament and its appreciation of the bold colours and simple patterns of contemporaneous painters, particularly Mondrian. In classic modern buildings, such as those designed by Mies van der Rohe at the height of his career, the absence of ornament, the emphasis on flat surfaces, and the repetition of simple forms gives prominence to the edges of planes and the expression of linear structural and glazing elements. More recently, buildings by architects such as Zaha Hadid and Thom Mayne, utilize converging planes and linear structural elements to create an architecture that is as spatially dynamic as their two-dimensional representations.   (PDS)

See also: **Axis** • **Diagonal** • **Dynamic** • **Ley lines** • **Sight lines**

Locus

Locus is an exact place, the point that generates a line or the line that generates a plane moving according to specified conditions. *Locus* describes connection, intersection and centre of gravity. *Locus* is the focal point. Therefore, *locus* refers to the central location, the heart of an abstract or physical condition. It is a defining moment, a fixed position, a recognized place or position of intervention. For example, Nelson's Column occupies the *locus* of Trafalgar Square; Trafalgar Square is the *locus* of London's New Year's Eve celebrations. While Martin Pawley describes the home-based computer as the *locus* of the notion of the global village, Aldo Rossi describes the city as the site, the *locus* of the 'collective memory'.

See also: **Context** • **Intersection** • **Focal point** • **Message area** • **Place** • **Punctum** • **Site specific**

Lung

The term *lung* is one of a series of body-related metaphors, such as 'heart', 'breathe' and circulation', that entered the architectural vocabulary during the eighteenth century via a more enlightened approach to city design. Influenced by discoveries about the human circulation system made by William Harvey in 1628 and the ensuing advances in the body sciences which promoted the importance of personal hygiene and healthy exercise, *lung* was adopted as part of a medical image that approached the built environment as a living organism. This saw the city as functioning like a healthy body with free-flowing 'arteries' and offering its citizens the ability to 'breathe'. Consequently, the concept of the urban *lung* as contributing to the 'healthy' anatomy of a dense built environment led to tree-lined boulevards and greater public access to existing city gardens and parks, such as those in Paris, and the planned incorporation of green 'breathing space' in the metropolis, like Washington DC's Great Mall and New York's Central Park.

   Lung is also used in archispeak to describe a volume where light and air combine to give an invigorating sense of space. For example, we talk of a *lung* of space, where occupants and users can find respite from the conventions of mean circulation routes and working environments. Here, natural daylight, views and natural ventilation systems combine to encourage a general feeling of well-being.   (RR-C)

See also: **Breathe** • **Decision-making space**

Mapping

As systems of information and communication 'shrink the world', so, too, the definition and subjects aligned to *mapping* expand. Formerly, map-making was viewed as an act of recording and translating the three-dimensional landscape into a two-dimensional system of codified representations to aid instruction and orientation. While these surface topographical readings of the terrain had many cultural variations, which reflected and expressed the common interests of their time and place, their purpose tended towards objective readings based on necessity and survival. However, maps are never benign, they are tools of highly edited and focused information that frame a set of prescriptive criteria. It is equally rare that maps are purely synoptic and the history of representational drawing and map-making reveals an intrinsic relationship to its maker's cultural and political predilections.

In ancient societies the relationship between the measurements of the natural world, the cosmos and divinity were inseparable. The development of the basic map-making tools of mathematics, numerical proportion and geometry were a construct of a belief in a world of sacred, ordered natural beauty.

The new social and cultural freedom of post-Second World War Western civilization propelled the notion of *mapping* into a new orbit. This period of experimentation gave rise to the cross-fertilization and hybridization of ideas across many disciplines: art, architecture, psychology, politics, science, literature, etc. The hard world of numbers and scientific fact collided with the soft world of sensation, memory, illusion and aspiration. This spirit of analysis with attitude engendered *mappings* of a whole range of diverse subjects — cognitive maps (Kevin Lynch), *mappings* of the everyday (Robert Venturi), psychogeographical maps (the Situationists) — resulting in the visualization of information previously thought of as either intangible or irrelevant.

The perceptual shift from objective map-making to a combination of both subjective and objective *mapping*, mirrors the change in focus of our cultural direction. That is to say the shift in the control of information from institutional power bases to the self interests of the individual. Now 'everyone' is *mapping*: artists, architects, anthropologists, genealogists, geographers, writers — from the empirical to the ephemeral, from necessity to narrative.   (SB)

See also: **Ley lines • Order • Topology**

Materiality

We were concerned with seeing materials for what they were: the woodiness of wood; the sandiness of sand.
— Peter and Alison Smithson

If there existed a hit parade of archispeak terms, *materiality* would vie for pole position. Representing a hot architectural topic, the term has been around for less than a decade and is constantly heard in architectural debate. Indeed, it seems coined just for use by architectural critics.

Its meaning, of course, refers to the touchy-feely nature of material used in a building design — what a building is made of and what it feels like. According to the critic Hugh Pearman, *materiality* is a slightly fetishistic preoccupation, its widespread currency possibly a reaction to the virtual world created on paper and video screens by today's software as used by all architects.

Writing in *Building Design* (2003), Adrian Forty cites the American historian, Sarah Williams Goldhagen, as offering clues to our current pre-occupation with 'thingliness' and its attendant concern for palpability and substance. She sees *materiality* as seeded in the existentialist philosophy of Jean-Paul Sartre and the search for a heightened state of mind. That is, its meaning is less concerned with materials and more with how people are, or can be, affected by materials.

See also: **Corporeality • Experiential • Multi-sensory space • Tactility**

Matrix   ▋

Like a mother's womb, *matrix* is a place of conception, (re)generation or formation. It is a hollowed-out template that will reproduce or replicate an image of itself. Like the intercellular receptacle in which typeface or a die is cast, like footprints in the sand, or the geological impression left behind in the rock once a fossil or a mineral is removed, *matrix* is a mould. When we fashion architecture using Cartesian grids, we similarly employ a *matrix* that shapes and conditions the nature of the architectural end-product. But in so doing we also create an architectural 'mould' that, in turn, shapes and conditions a profound impression on those who inhabit it.

This 'impression' is evidenced by anthropological studies that have compared difference in the perceptions of those who live in environments dominated by the corner and the straight line and those who do not. So-called 'primitive' and agrarian societies who are more exposed to the rawness of the natural landscape do not share our conditioning to rectan-gularity and the perceptual side-effects of constancy scaling and optical illusion. Theirs is a curvilinear world in which the circle dominates the square, where rounded forms prevail and where the land is ploughed not in straight lines but in curves. In this perception an environment filled with corners is one filled with mysterious and useless adjuncts of space.

Also used to describe the location of atoms in a crystal or a molecule, *matrix* joins the terms 'net' and 'web' to express cyberspace. But cyber-space does not follow a Cartesian logic; its geometries occupy higher spatial dimensions. For instance, the movie trilogy *The Matrix* featured the use of a *matrix* to generate the 'reality' of a virtual world. Meanwhile, the jury is still out regarding the full implications of this technology on human sensibilities.

See also: **Cartesian grid • Chora • Constancy scaling • Euclidean space • Grid • Order • Ordering systems • Typology**

Mediate

Mediate is yet another top ten archispeak term. Derived from the adjective 'median' (situated in the middle, the in-between), *mediate* means to intervene between hostile factions or conflicting ideas or principles.

Mediation between conflicting design demands and limitations is the essence of designing. Resolving programmatic conflict by transforming 'problems' into design opportunities is what constitutes the act of design as a creative process. Essentially, all architecture mediates at some level. The executed building becomes a mediator between climate and comfort, between the incarcerated and the general public, or between restrictive codes and regulations and the unbridled desires of a client. At a more esoteric level, the deliberate user discomfort imposed by Peter Eisenman in projects such as House 6 or the Wexner Centre is a mediation between the complacency supported by orthodox architectural practice and yesterday's *avant-garde*.

Particularly interesting is the architect as amateur mediator between spouses during the design of their first custom home. Divorce is a common outcome of failure to successfully accomplish this delicate task.   (EO)

See also: **Articulate • Dialogue • Edge condition • Engage (** *dégagements***) • Interface • Intervention • Reciprocity**

Memory

Memory is the present's mode of access to the past. The past is preserved in time, while the memory image, one of the past's images or elements, can be selected according to present interests.
— Elizabeth Grosz

When I turn to memory, I ask it bring forth what I want: and some things are produced immediately, some take longer as if they had to be brought out from some more secret place of storage; some pour out in a heap . . . — St Augustine

In archispeak, *memory* concerns the architectural embodiment of past objects and events. For example, in *Body, Memory and Architecture* (1977) Kent Bloomer and Charles Moore discuss the house as a repository of distant memories: potted plants guarding the front door recalling sentinels at the city gate; the garden as microcosm of our vague recollections of primordial beginnings, the hearth recalling the communal hub with its mantelpiece carrying a 'treasure house' of important possessions.

Using the metaphor of archaeological excavation, Walter Benjamin describes *memory* as city-like; labyrinthine networks of passages and streets representing the convoluted and intertwined threads of *memory*; open squares and spaces representing the voids of forgotten things. In his Berlin essays (1932), Benjamin describes the city as heaped-up ruins of the past. A corollary to Benjamin's metaphor is a mnemonic technique of *memory* recall practiced since the fifteenth century. This mentally stores information in the buildings of an imaginary city or the compartments of a building. Rather than keywords or numbers, this use of 'place' for *memory* is based on the premise that images and spatial relationships act more quickly on the mind. However, Benjamin's concern is the redemption of lost objects and events — their sites endangered by an urban amnesia. When expressed, urban *memory* is marked by monuments that, by celebrating their own permanence, allow the past and present to coexist. Paradoxically, in *Words and Buildings* (2000) Adrian Forty cites Paul Connerton when he distinguishes 'inscribing' *memory* on objects and 'incorporating' *memory* through ceremonial practices. In other words, war memorials are less significant than the rituals that take place around them.

   All awareness of the past is founded in *memory*, remembering the past being crucial for our sense of identity. As the manifestation of architecture can itself provide a kind of knowledge through which the past remains accessible, this accounts for the significance of *memory* in design. For example, memories of times past can be woven into the fabric of buildings through materials and architectural and historical references. Among the most poignant expressions of an inscribed *memory* in recent times are the cuts made in the envelope of Daniel Libeskind's Holocaust Museum in Berlin. While its form metaphorically alludes to the dislocation of the Jewish experience, the trajectory of cuts respond to axial lines drawn from the surrounding sites of the razed houses of holocaust victims. These act both to connect the building to the city and to the *memory* of those it memorializes. Although alienated by Modernism and dismissed by some critics as poetic hype — and sometimes cynically expressed as 'the plausible plastered over the forgotten' — *memory* remains an important dimension in architectural thinking.

See also: **Anchoring • Metaphor • Moment • Temporality**

Message area   ▎

The term *message area* refers to the central import of a graphic work, i.e. that zone of a picture, drawing or photograph from which the meaning of the image is communicated. In other words, *message area* represents its pictorial *raison d'être*. For instance, ads are meticulously designed and tested using an Eye Movement Recorder, i.e. a sophisticated apparatus that surreptitiously tracks and monitors the eye as it views and reviews the compositional format of a pictorial image. Advertising images are rejected when their meaning, or message, is not quickly detected — a successful image being one that rapidly and efficiently communicates its central information. If we apply the findings of this research from the adman's world to that of architectural image-making, several important principles arise. First, a bland or boring image will quickly be rejected by the eye; time spent in its viewing often being much less than that spent in its creation. Second, in our digital world of instant communication, the *message area* of an image must be immediately apparent. If not, it quickly becomes rejected to become a redundant part of a presentation display. This is significant in design presentations when a photograph, orthographic or, particularly, a perspective drawing is questioned in terms of the message it attempts to impart.

   Architectural images have to be carefully designed. For instance, the *message area* usually coincides with that part of the image exhibiting the highest value, colour and optical texture contrast, or the area involving the highest incidence of drawing medium variation. In order to determine the *message area* of a drawing, the central reason for creating the image must first be determined. Once identified, this should then be retained as the guiding principle throughout its compositional and pictorial development.

See also: **Contrast • Focal point • Key drawing • Locus • Punctum**

Metabolism

Metabolism first appeared in the 1960s. Its proponents sought to bring the newly expanded urbanized city into harmony with nature. Small, prefabricated capsules that could be added to, or subtracted from, receptive parent structures made the city more responsive to rapid change. The first realization of these concepts was architect Kisho Kurokawa's Nagakin Capsule Building of 1972 in Tokyo, which featured fully outfitted, prefabricated small (8 x 12 feet) living units. The emergence of Metabolist concepts simply continued the Japanese tradition of modular construction and building parts.

Tatami mat-sized overnight sleeping capsules for Japanese commuters who miss the last bullet train home.

However, *Metabolism* was not just about harmony with nature, it also concerned architecture as a natural organism that could adjust to shifting environment (homeostasis) or context. Among others, Kenzo Tange and Arata Isozaki (unlike their Archigram contemporaries, whose ideas remained on paper only) produced a built body of Metabolist work.

See also: **Archigram • High-tech (low-tech) • Ken • Module**

Metaphor

Similar to the way we talk of 'transparency' to denote unimpeded access and 'layering' to describe degrees of complexity, *metaphor* is the process of using language to understand one thing in terms of other things. However, *metaphor* is not itself a language but an idea expressed by language that can both enrich our experience of architecture and, tapping conscious and unconscious motivations, reinforce our ties with the phenomenal world. Because of its complex and paradoxical nature, the language *metaphor* has proved a useful device for expanding creative imagination. For instance, the concept of the labyrinth has served as a *metaphor* for human existence while machine *metaphors* were particularly popular early in the twentieth century. When Frank Lloyd Wright said 'my god is machinery' he reaffirmed the traditional American faith in technology. Similarly, recurring *metaphors* for the city include the 'city as a living organism' and the 'city as a machine'.

More significant is the body *metaphor*, i.e. the association through which we humanize built form. For example, anatomical references such as 'circulation', 'skin' and 'skeleton', expressions of architectural gesture, rhythm and proportion, together with the way in which human scale is projected into the built environment, are all examples of a metaphorical association used to create an architecture that discloses its human origins. Drawn from the vocabulary of archispeak, metaphorical word concepts can form before ideas about the building itself. Sometimes referred to as 'pre-conceptual thoughts' or 'word precedents', they tend to touch on the more poetic aspects of an idea. Once formed about an embryonic architecture, *metaphors* can spring from physical or symbolic sources or from disassociated but parallel lines of thought.

We all carry in our heads a personal library of memorable word-pictures drawn from a plethora of the everyday, but in a true sense these words are metaphors and, as such, they are detached from their basis of sense. Therefore, *metaphor* is essentially ephemeral but it can hold immense power and can induce a profound influence upon us and others.

See also: **Allegory** • **Analogue** • **Design intent** • **Gesture** • **Rhythm**

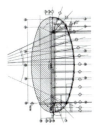

Leaf *metaphor* for the auditorium roof plan of Architecture PLB's Jersey College for Girls.

Methodology

Methodology means the science or lore of methods. Since it is longer and sounds more sophisticated, it is often used by architects to enhance their explanation of their design process in place of 'method', in order to make it sound more profound and grandiose than it actually is. This misuse is then compounded by not even describing the method used to arrive at a certain design, but simply describing the solution. On the principle that you can fool some of the people some of the time, this sometimes works. It can also backfire, if the audience happens to know the proper meaning and use of the word.

Its root, 'method' (from the Greek *meta* (through) and *odos* (road)), means a way to get through a problem or task. This neutral understanding is often laced by the sense it derives from being coupled with the word 'systematic', as in 'systematic method' or 'systematic procedure', i.e. a well ordered, step-by-step manner of doing things. Thus, by now, the term 'methodical' almost exclusively means doing things according to a systematic, well-organized method.

These terms have been part of the vicious controversy about 'design methods' following attempts in 1960s and 1970s to adapt the approaches (methods, techniques, procedures) that proved so successful in the space programme to design. This coincided with the effort to use computers for this work — which required that it be described as 'systematic procedures', i.e. sequences of well-described actions leading from a well-described initial situation to a clear end result.   (TM)

See also: **Functionalism**

Minimalism

The difference between a good architect and a poor architect is that the poor architect succumbs to every temptation and the good one resists it. — Ludwig Wiggenstein

Blithely tripping from the lips from presenters of those prime-time television interior-design programmes, the term 'minimalist aesthetic' can so easily be considered a fashionable design approach. But, to paraphrase John Pawson in his book *Minimum* (1996), the concept of *minimalism* is far more profound than any reference to style. Indeed, the recurring ideal of simplicity has a moral dimension, implying selflessness and unworldliness in the quest to purify the spirit and to achieve inner tranquillity. The culture of simplicity is shared and represented by many societies with belief systems that seek a way of life free from the encumbrance of worldly trappings and the distraction of the trivial in order to be in touch with the essence of existence. Involving ordering systems comprising repetition and pure geometry, the cult of unadornment has been advocated by almost every kind of religious and spiritual sect from Buddhism to the Shakers and Quakers, the Japanese concepts of Zen to the essayist Henry Thoreau and his 'back to nature' quest for elementariness. Minimal living has always offered a sense of emancipation; it can be seen as the reflection of some innate, inner quality, or the pursuit of philosophical insight into the nature of harmony, reason and truth.

Pawson is one of the great exponents of *minimalism* in architectural design. He cites Mies van der Rohe and Luis Barragan as architects who have, using as little design as possible, achieved the 'excitement of empty space' in great designs. However, *minimalism* goes far beyond the Modernist maxim 'less is more'. Indeed, according to Pawson (and those television presenters should take note), beyond the sparseness that is attributed to an ornament-stripped, machine aesthetic Modernism, lies a simplicity that results from a considered reduction or condensation to the essentials. It is accomplished only by the most complex of means and dedicated design work.

See also: **Elegance • Modernism • Zen**

Mission statement

Not an edict from a religious sect but a term popular during the 1990s in the world of business. *Mission statements* are a publicity tool through which corporate hierarchies declare their aims and aspirations in order to project a sense of responsibility to their clients and to induce motivation in their employees. However, their transfer, along with other corporate jargon, such as 'upsizing' and 'downscaling', from a vehicle of corporate vision to architectural design sees them both as a personal design talisman and as a marketing tool for design proposals.

Mission statements function as a declaration of intent that accompanies and charts the design journey. Appearing in the form of words and images at the opening of a design presentation or review, *mission statements* function to bullet-point critical issues and to prioritize the aims and objectives of a project. Apart from appearing business-like and acting as a prompt in student presentations, their usefulness is in quickly establishing with the client or the reviewer the direction of a design process. *Mission statements* can also function as a benchmark against which the success or failure of the scheme can be measured — which, after all, is one of the core purposes of the design review. In this context, therefore, it is crucial that the ensuing presentation of work appears to address and engage the central issues that have been flagged in the *mission statement*.

See also: **Crit • Design intent • Design rationale**

Modernism

That which is modern stands in opposition to the ancient, the new in opposition to the ever-same. — Walter Benjamin

Modernism is a state of mind. Being modern means being up to the minute, contemporary and part of the present, but being a Modernist is an assertion of belief in the tradition of the new. According to Perry Anderson, the emergence of *Modernism* is an antiplural, cultural force that occurred both before and after World War One. It responded to three decisive co-ordinates: reaction against the official art of the ruling classes; the impact of new technologies; and the expectation of social revolution.

Modernism is the umbrella name for a vast array of movements with ideologies including formalism, functionalism and rationalism, its mainstream representing an intellectual approach through abstraction and idealization. It affected all the arts and, as film-makers, artists, architects and poets struggled to come to terms with the 'new times', it blossomed in many different fields. *Modernism* came to maturity in the 1920s. It first flourished in the liberal atmosphere of Weimar Germany, where many of the ideas that transformed architecture and design, and in due course the appearance of the everyday world around us, developed.

Concerned less with the senses and emotion, *Modernism* is constantly being re-evaluated. Critics of the spatially and socially ordered and segmented world of Modernist architecture and town planning — which compartmentalizes people from traffic, the rich from the poor, and home from work — suggest that the tragic irony of Modernist urbanism is that its triumph has helped destroy the very urban life it hoped to set free.

See also: **Cubism • Constructivism • Fragment • Futurism • Functionalism • Modernity • Montage • Transparency**

Modernity

Bramante in our own age preserved what Brunelleschi did, adapting it to the uses of modern life. — Giorgio Vasari

Vasari felt Bramante was practising *modernity* in the sixteenth century. Unlike Modernism, which flourished in the twentieth century, *modernity* began as early as the ninth century. Christian theological history regards the start of *modernity* to be marked by the start of a coexistence between ecclesiastical and civil authority, or when the Papacy proclaimed Charlemagne emperor.

For the rest of us, the predominant meaning of the term *modernity* is the state of affairs after the Industrial Revolution. Architectural *modernity* perhaps began with Philip Webb's 'Red House' for William Morris, while, in a wider context, the essential characteristics of a *modernity* of high capitalism was first identified by Charles Baudelaire in nineteenth-century Paris. He characterized the experience of *modernity* as being the contingent (dependent on an uncertain event or circumstance), the fugitive and the ephemeral combined with the immutable and the eternal. Baudelaire's concept of the experience of *modernity* was later brought to prominence in the 1930s in the writings of the German philosopher, Walter Benjamin. In his 'Arcades Project', the Parisian glass shopping arcades of the time represented the site of the spectacle of consumerism and consumption.

Recently, many academics thought architectural modernity had been replaced by post-modernity, but it now appears that *modernity* never left. (EO)

See also: **Fragment • Modernism**

Modulate

Variety is not just the spice of life, it is the very stuff of it. — J. Vernon

Modulate is a design move that employs a measured irregularity to work against the plain and the predictable. It is a controlling device that, being anti-regimentation, brings variegation to the standardized and variety to the ordinary and the commonplace. Like the term 'articulate' and its synonyms 'rhythm' and 'tempo', *modulate* comes from the world of speech and sound. We *modulate* speech when we inflect the tone and pitch of the voice in order to denote emphasis or to make a point; similarly, when making music we change pitch from one key to another. Therefore, *modulate* refers to the way we increase interest levels in a system by introducing frequency changes in patterns of form and volume. Rather than be bland and monotonous, like the drone of a boring monologue, a modulated architecture is one that is subtly or dramatically modified through shifts and changes of register. Modulation results when we articulate height, angle, level and interval in the compositional arrangement of mass, silhouette or fenestration.

A poetic example of modulation occurs in the stratified façade of Le

Stratified modulations between upper cell apertures, lower library window mullions and columns on Le Corbusier's monastery at La Tourette near Lyons (© FLC/ADAGP, Paris and DACS, London, 2003).

Corbusier's monastery at La Tourette, shown below, where each layer of its fenestration is horizontally and vertically varied to reflect different rhythmic categories of experience. For example, the upper repetitive bands of openings dramatize through uniformity the solitude and silence of individual cells, while immediately below the playful rhythms of screen and column celebrate those parts of the building where the monks come together in order to dine or to study.

See also: **Articulate • Breathe • Rhyme • Rhythm • Transition**

Module

A *module* is a unit used in construction; it is an element that expresses the proportions of the entire structure. A *module* can range from a brick to a space *module* — the self-contained pod of a spacecraft. It is also a unit of length used for measuring a period of educational study and for expressing proportion.

In the construction industry a *module* is a prefabricated, factory-made, standardized component. Modular components can include walls, windows, or whole rooms or blocks of rooms complete with built-in service systems, such as electrical wiring, water and drainage. Using the techniques of modular construction, components can be later assembled on site in a variety of ways to produce buildings of different configuration.

Aside from Le Corbusier's development of his 'Modulor' proportional system, the term 'modular' is also used by other industries, such as the flat-pack furniture industry, to describe any product made in separate sections and marketed as a kit that can be assembled in a variety of ways to produce different systems. In the computer industry, for example, the various components of a computer can be interchanged and connected in different ways to produce custom-made systems for specific tasks.

See also: **Archigram • Kit of parts • Metabolism • Modulor**

Modulor

A work of art should provide a sensation of mathematical order . . . and the means by which the order is achieved should be sought in universal means. — Le Corbusier

Of all the early Modernists, Le Corbusier was the only architect to construct a design philosophy around a personal theory of harmony and proportion. Based upon his discovery of the six-foot height requirement of a British bobby, his 'Modulor man' related to a complete proportioning system. Derived from the golden section and the Fibonacci series, it was conceived to give proportion to everything from a door handle to heights of buildings, to ceiling heights and room widths. However, by forcing the Vitruvian 'golden rectangle' into the Fibonacci series to create his proportional system, Le Corbusier's man, shown overleaf, is anatomically impossible.

However, a key feature of the *modulor* is that it incorporates two related proportional systems: one a single series of measure, dubbed 'red'; the other a double series of measure, dubbed 'blue'. The result is a geometric series that, using fewer coordinated dimensions than is possible with an arithmetic series composed of the same number of different dimensions, creates a much richer and more complex patterning.

See also: **Anthropomorphic** • **Fibonacci series** • **Golden section** • **Ken** • **Order** • **Ordering system** • **Proportion** • **Regulating lines**

Le Corbusier conceived of his Modulor man to govern lengths, surfaces and volumes, and to maintain human scale (© FLC/ADAGP, Paris and DACS, London, 2003).

Moiré

Moiré is a visual effect that occurs when the periodic units of two or more grids or mesh screens are overlapped and superimposed. The resulting optical illusion is one of a shimmering dazzle, which is particularly pronounced when the intersections of the two grids are equal and when their grid patterns are small in scale. According to the physicist, Gerald Oster, the illusion is thought to be caused by the inability of our eye to resolve all the overlapping points of intersection. The result of this lack of visual resolution is a pattern of perceived interference, a ghosting effect that, like the shimmering colours of 'Newton's rings' often seen on slick black surfaces in bright sunlight and in the laminations of glass, provide a trace of emphemerality and allusion that seems to fascinate architects.

See also: **Diffusion** • **Layering** • **Scrim** • **Superimpose**

Moment

Practically we perceive only the past, the pure present being the invisible progress of the past gnawing into the future. — Henri Bergson

Sensing the presence of the *moment* is a particularly modern aspiration. Owing to its potential to represent a split second of intense sensual experience within the ephemerality of the modern world, the category of the *moment* became important to such influential writers as Walter Benjamin and Martin Heidegger. However, they saw its transient experience as one in which awareness and sensation are divorced. In other words, in the instant of its actuality we can only sense the *moment* — recognition of its presence being realized only later in its immediate aftermath.

In physics, *moment* is related to the movement of a force as, for example, in the 'moment of inertia' or the 'bending *moment*'. In everyday language it is often associated with opportunism, as in 'seize the *moment*'. Some would say that this *moment* of impulse represents free will. The term is also often used to describe the instant when revelation occurs of the intended meaning in the experience of a building or in the thinking behind the design proposals of others. Such revelations result when the intentions of the designer and the understanding of the user coincide. This is the *moment* that represents a heightened state of consciousness, an instant of vision and insight or, in some cases, a *moment* of shock.

Similarly, design is sometimes realized as a *moment* of truth as in the flash of inspiration, usually while in the bath. But, in reality, it is more likely to be the outcome of a process of decision-making at times of crisis or test, and the consequence of such considerations, as in Shakespeare's 'matters of great *moment*' (Richard III). As such, the *moment* can become the essential element or an important factor of the design process. Some students of architecture would deem the testing *moment* as the time they present their work to tutors, but then it is usually anticlimactic and over in an instant.   (AB)

See also: **Fragment • Memory • Modernity • Temporality • Thereness (thisness)**

Monolithic   ∎

Monolithic describes an upward thrusting mass or object that breaks the horizon line to reflect the pull of gravity and demand attention. *Monolithic* forms include the large upturned stones erected by our ancestors, the enigmatic black slab in Stanley Kubrick's movie 2001: *A Space Odyssey*, the monumental columns and obelisks that occupy the locus of countless city squares, and the deterministic silhouettes of residential tower blocks. However, the latter example is far away from the common perception of the monolith as a mediator between heaven and earth.

One does not argue with *monolithic* structures; they are massive, seemingly immoveable, solidly uniform and, more often than not, uniformly dull. When heard in archispeak, *monolithic* can sometimes refer to 'oneness' but generally describes an architectural one-liner, a take-it-or-leave-it environmental statement, or a stand alone edifice usually of large proportion and often without significance.

See also: **Monumentality • Scale**

Montage   ∎

Montage — the connecting of dissimilars to shock an audience into insight . . . — Bill Nichols

Montage multiplies the potential of collage to couple two realities on a single plane that apparently does not suit them into the juxtaposition of an infinite series of realities. — Bill Nichols

Montage is one of the important keywords of Modernism. Derived from cinematic editing and from collage, the technique is notably exploited in

photomontage when two photographs of irreconcilable images are juxtaposed, their joint presence requiring adjustment in the viewing. The
presence of one image disrupts the understanding of the other; the second
image confounding whatever reflection the first may itself have provoked.

Developed in 1919 in the World War One propaganda photomontages
of artists like John Heartfield and George Grosz, in which different photographic stills are collapsed into one to disrupt chronological time, the
concept of *montage* was initially applied to film by the Russian film director
Sergei Eisenstein. Used in such movies as *Battleship Potemkin*, his
cinematic *montage* was a filmic method of structuring narrative ideas in a
juxtaposed and carefully edited sequence of separate pieces or images.
Eisenstein explains: 'Through montage, associations in the viewer are
aroused by separate visual elements — montaged pieces of the analysed
fact. Only in the sum of their experiences do these produce an emotional
effect similar to and often stronger than the effect of the fact itself.'
Eisenstein's cutting, editing and piecing together of selected fragments of
audio-visual material not only anticipated a modern sensibility, epitomized
in the fragmented experience of 'channel surfing', it introduced a form of
communication that challenges a functionalist concept of the order in
which we experience architecture.

Indeed, influenced by cinematic *montage*, architects like Bernard
Tschumi and Rem Koolhaas (the latter having studied, directed and acted
in films) have enlisted *montage* as a tool for ordering space. Driven by the
need to disrupt normal response patterns, movement through space and
the ritual of everyday functions are architecturally 'spliced' and juxtaposed
to be experienced as a succession of isolated and often contradictory
events. The impact of such *montages* stems from the fact that the excerpts
from life they contain at first seem quite unrelated, imbuing them with a
new and dramatic meaning.

See also: **Collage • Fragment • Juxtaposition • Layering • Storyboard • Zoning**

Monumental

Big boxes not always the best gift. — John Handley

Monumental describes objects, events or achievements in works of art
and architecture that assume epic proportion or noble significance. A
Gulliverian bigness can impose an automatic respect but it can also repel.
For example, in an experiment in which architectural drawings were
presented as much 'larger than life' representations, viewers' first
impressions displayed a certain wonderment and reverence, despite
ensuing and critical reactions to the quality of the graphic content. Like
it or not, a *monumental* architecture — from Egyptian pyramids to corporate skyscrapers, together with civic and religious buildings — assumes
awesome proportions in order to induce a deferential reverence.

Although the term may be properly applied to the pyramids, it is not
always necessarily a synonym for 'large'. *Monumental* can also be applied
to a work elevated in idea and simple in conception and execution, and
having something of the timeless nature of great architecture. However,
when the size of an object is described in this way, it relates to the scale of

the setting and the context of its perception. For instance, the monumentality of the Eiffel Tower is assumed by comparison to that of a known body of tall structures. However, compare this with the monumentality of Mount Everest.

See also: **Monolithic • Scale**

Mood board

Mood boards are employed by many designers to communicate the planned ambience or theme of an intended project. They are also enlisted for the orchestration of colours, effects, finishes and fittings in a proposed building design. Usually comprising images culled from magazines, the *mood board* can function both as a personal design generator and as a device for communicating the nuances of a design approach to others.

Another version of the *mood board* is also known as a 'feelie board'. These present to the client the range of colour and materials and small-scale fittings destined for use in the interior architecture. As it provides a point of physical contact for the user, the presentation of such information brings a more engaging dimension to the understanding of the design proposal. Using combinations of photographs and real samples, a basic *mood board* can comprise proposed colour schemes, examples of finishes, ironmongery and light fittings, etc.

See also: **Conceptual drawing • Context • Design genesis • Design intent • Mission statement • Narrative • Tactility**

Morphing (metamorphosis)

The advent of new computer software in the 1990s not only provided film-makers with a new animation tool but also gave architects the means to take them beyond the mere juxtaposing and contrasting of form. This software allowed forms to be stretched and to simulate flowing transitions between one form and another. *Morphing* refers to the special effect of digital transformation in which parts of one image are gradually manipulated frame by frame to correspond with comparable parts of a second image, so that an apparently seamless *metamorphosis* occurs.

The term *morphing* is derived from *metamorphosis*, which describes a dramatic transition. Metamorphosis is a natural phenomenon that also features in mythology and popular imagination. For example, hair into serpent, pumpkin into coach, and frog into prince. Meanwhile, Kafkaesque human-to-insect transformations occur in literature and horror movies. A zoological *metamorphosis* — transformations such as the larva into pupa, egg into chick or bud into flower — are often metaphorically used in architectural design thinking.

Morphing has also become a popular term in student ranks. It accounts for many design *parti* that seem to imply movement from one form to another.

See also: **Transformation • Transition • Zoomorphic**

Morphology

Borrowed from the disciplines of biology and philosophy, where it refers respectively to the study of the basic form of an organism and the science of the form of words, the term *morphology* is used in archispeak to describe the study of the changing structure of an architectural form and its formation in response to different conditions, such as time or function, or to the relationship of a form to existing typologies.

Therefore, morphological research is a reductive mapping process conducted with the aim of disclosing the basic spatial structure of a building or of an urban footprint. This necessitates the analytical break-down of the whole into its parts and, in order to lay bare the architectural 'mechanism', the clear figure–ground distinction between solid and void. Consequently, morphological drawings are purely mechanistic diagrams that can be employed to study spatial structure from a whole range of aspects. For instance, the *morphology* of a building can be disclosed via a diagrammatic distillation of its plan such as the reductive diagrams of Gerrit Reitveld's Schröder House shown here. The plan is repeated using different emphases to show, in this case, circulation, room function, structural footprint, spatial primacy, etc.

The *morphology* of a town, city or a region is illustrated in the common use of a succession of maps in a site survey, each shown identical in scale and size to communicate points of change over time in the history of its evolution.

See also: **Analytical drawings** • **Diagram** • **Diagramming** • **Mapping** • **Typology**

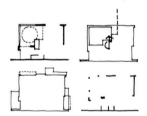

Morphological plans of Gerrit Reitveld's Schröder House (1924) showing its main space, approach, unification of the whole and structural footprint. (redrawn from Hideaki Haraguchi's book *Comparative Analysis of 20th-Century Houses* (1989)).

Multi-sensory space

Perhaps the most glaring fallacy in much of the neo-Platonic architecture of the past half-century has been the dangerous belief that a humanly satisfying building need not take more into consideration than proportional perfection or compositional purity. Many such buildings have attained their diagrammatic climax much more effectively in two dimensions than they ever have in three; but a house for real people with real bodies must account for much more. — Martin Filler

When critically used in design reviews, the term *multi-sensory space* is usually heard in a challenge that counters a purely visual or graphical appearing architecture, i.e. an architecture that seemingly pays little or no heed to the potential tactile qualities of mass and surface texture. In other words, it signals the need to design for all the senses. A *multi-sensory* design approach recognizes that we experience through more than one sense: the sensing of temperature change and air movement (kinaesthetics); the aroma of different materials and the fragrances of plants (olfaction); the sounds of reverberant space (acoustics); and the touch of surfaces through fingers, hands and feet (tactility).

Exponents of a *multi-sensory* architecture include Oriental landscape designers, Stanley Tigerman, Charles Moore and Richard Oliver, and Hirisho Naito. Moore and Oliver's New York residence for a partially-sighted client includes locational signals using texture, sound and smell. For instance, variously sized rooms act as 'sounding chambers', and a snaking handrail runs through the house with a profile found pleasurable to the grip of the client. Although this house was designed for a visually challenged client, the issue remains that a purely 'pictorial' environment designed by 'visual animals' for visual consumption misses the point that we experience our setting through all five of our senses! This term refers to what is seen by some as one of the most significant omissions of contemporary architecture; namely, the need to move away from a singularly visual architecture in favour of a design approach that experientially accommodates all the senses.

See also: **Corporeality • Kinaesthesia • Syneasthesia • Tactility**

Narrative

Myth is the infancy of narrative. — Carl Jung

Narrative is a spoken or visual commentary, account or story of unfolding, connected events or experiences. *Narrative* is a form of communication. It is also a transaction in that its exchange relies upon an initial 'contract' formed between the narrator and the recipient. *Narrative* also concerns transformation — a story unfolding until its meaning brings revelation.

An architecture can be formed around *narrative*; *narrative* can be spun around an architecture. For instance, the architectural competition — perhaps, the most prominent way in which society chooses the built form of the future — is a setting in which, more often than not, the architect is absent when designs are reviewed and judgements are made. Using increasingly diverse media, architects must convince both the jury and the public of the potential of their vision *in absentia*, which necessitates emphasis on the 'process' of thinking and the 'intellectual underpinning' of the design as much as the end product. One approach involves developing a *narrative* disclosure that, using precedents and influences drawn from inside and outside the building culture, tells the story of the process of design. The design proposal is therefore wrapped in relevant, yet diverse, reference that gives it credence and helps to bridge the gap between established thinking, analogy and innovation. This is a communication tactic that induces the viewer to comprehend a design proposal in terms of a 'plot' and to judge its efficacy against the processes that created it. This strategy is designed to build-up revelatory expectation in the viewer–listener; consequently, it is important that the narrator–designer satisfies those expectations.

Rem Koolhaas has described the sequential experience of his buildings in terms of an unfolding *narrative*. An ex-movie maker, Koolhaas sees the approach and entrance as 'introduction', movement into and about the building as unfolding 'plot', and, as in the structure of movies, the journey peppered with measured 'mini-climaxes' leading to an ultimate 'climax' or denouement.

See also: **Storyboard • Transformation**

New Brutalism

New Brutalism is a label emanating from the mid-1950s that was coined to describe the late work of Le Corbusier and his contemporary British disciples who specialized in an undisguised, functional, raw concrete architecture.

The term is also associated with a related series of 'B' words. 'Beton Brut', for example, refers to concrete left in a raw state after the removal of its formwork or shuttering. Often shuttering with a marked grain is used, as this prints a decorative finish on the exposed surface. 'Bush-hammered' or 'battered' concrete refers to the technique first used by Paul Rudolph of breaking off by hammer the edges or 'noses' of exposed corrugated concrete forms to create a coarse texture of light and shadow. 'Bunkers' and 'barracks' join *Brutalism* in the common admonishment of such architecture by a disenchanted lay public who know the buildings they love to hate, and who see their perpetrators as insensitive environmental bullies. However, one soft spot in the hard world of a post-war British Brutalist architecture is Sir Hugh Casson's celebrated Elephant House at London Zoo.

See also: **Functionalism • Modernism**

Node

Node is one of the five elements of a city described by Kevin Lynch in his *Image of the City* (1960). He determined five recurring elements: 'paths', 'edges', 'districts', 'landmarks' and 'nodes'. *Nodes* are usually parts of transportation systems and are often located at the crossing or the intersection of 'paths'. Train and bus stations, town centres, and complex intersections where a number of different roads come together are all examples of *nodes*. They can also simply be concentrations, such as a street corner hangout or one of the small parks and plazas. Landmarks often work in conjunction with *nodes* as points of reference — navigational aids when locomoting through the city. They are usually rather simply defined objects, buildings or features of the natural landscape that have been given great symbolic significance.

According to Louis Hellman, the term *node* is one of the machine-image euphemisms imported into the language of modern architecture, such as 'kit-of-parts', 'module', 'deck' and 'duct'. An architectural *node* is simply an intersection, a crossing point, a point where forces meet. For instance, at a small scale, Reitveld's three-way connection (shown here) for his Red, Yellow, Blue chair expresses in microcosm his de Stijl philosophy of a *node* creating an intersection with lines of infinity. In a house, the stairs and landings would be *nodes*, as would the clear articulation of a coupling device that connects one element to another in a high-tech building.

See also: **Gateway • Edge condition • Interface • Intersection • Kiss**

Gerrit Reitveld's nodal intersection used on his Red, Yellow, Blue chair (1917) expresses the infinite extension of an object beyond its boundaries.

Order

Order without diversity can result in monotony and boredom; diversity without order can produce chaos.— Francis D. K. Ching

Every design is based on *order*. Ordering is what we do to make the world around us appear more intelligible. It is an intellectual construct that enlists abstract concepts of arrangement, sequence and classification as a means of exerting a degree of control over our concrete reality. When events are 'out of order' we become confused. *Order* brings clarity through organization and helps us to gain a better understanding of ourselves in relation to our setting. For instance, perspective projection drawing is a means, but not the only means, of two-dimensionally codifying the way that we see; landscape design is a way of exerting control over the wilderness.

A common value system in architectural and urban design is the hierarchical ordering of elements, i.e. the articulation of a scale of significance in form and space expressed through size, shape and disposition. Such value systems result from a selective perception and are dominated by the culture or ideology of those who impose it. However, established concepts of *order* can be subverted and superseded. Some designs now appear to be based upon anti-order. *Order* was the bane of the Deconstructivists. They decried conventional architectural *order* as a sham, a fiction. However, even chaos has *order*, therefore *order* may be an inescapable result of designing architecture.

There have been many attempts to produce a workable definition of this term. It seems that Louis Kahn wrote extensively on the subject: '. . . I wrote many, many words on what *order* is', he said, before giving up and simply stating '*order* is'. However, one elegant definition comes from the sculptor, Donald Judd, who describes *order* as 'reason made visible'.

See also: **Composition** • **Fibonacci series** • **Golden section** • **Ken** • **Modulor** • **Ordering systems** • **Proportion**

Ordering principles

The devices we employ to describe the ordering of a design can be traced back to the set of tools inherited from Euclidean geometry. These comprise instruments such as the axis, regulating lines and zoning, etc., and can involve the organizational use of grids and systems of measure and proportion. The result of any mathematical theory of proportion is the provision of a system or set of rules from which to determine lengths and widths of the forms and spaces that make up a building so that there is an intelligible relationship between the parts. Such rules first appear in Vitruvius, were used by the Greeks, the Medievals and were re-expressed by many Renaissance artists and designers. The most famous descendant of these ordering principles was still in use in the early part of the twentieth century. This was Le Corbusier's proportional theory called the Modulor — a means of controlling human scale based upon the relation between the golden section and the Fibonacci series.

However, when imposing order, designers will also use other value systems to dictate the arrangement of form. For instance, course of action, movement, principles of pictorial composition and narrative, etc., can also function as frameworks for inventing the order of relationships. In his book *Architecture: Form, Space & Order* (1979), Frank Ching outlines a basic series of building footprint ordering strategies, including 'linear', 'clustered', 'radial', 'grid' and 'centred', but, of course, these can involve two or more of these organizational systems in the same design.

Varying from person to person and from place to place, these systems are prompted by our general desire to arrange the world so as to make it easier to understand and navigate. They provide a rich range of methods that have evolved over time.

See also: **Composition • Fibonacci series • Golden section • Ken • Modulor • Order • Proportion**

Organic   ▮

An architecture that responds to cultural, organic, and existential experiences can be a psychic bulwark against the misuses of technology and the trend toward mechanization. — Herb Greene

Associated with the writings of Henry James and Henri Bergson, and the architecture of Louis Sullivan, Antonio Gaudí and the early work of Frank Lloyd Wright, an *organic* design tradition concerns the representation of patterns of biological growth or the display of properties associated with living organisms. *Organic* architecture embodies references to the kinds of living things that supply shapes, gestures and relationships that speak of the natural world, while, simultaneously, creating links with human empathy and understanding.

Opposed to a Cartesian design tradition and a machine imagery, the *organic* approach draws upon the evolutionary nature of life. It uses as form determinants the specifics of the site, climate, building function and the social and psychological needs of the users. Physical attributes of *organic* design tend to include the curve and the undulate, expressed in the plasticity of surface, rhythmical progression, textural interface and an association with ornament. However, here ornament is not associated with the superficial and the trite, but, in the words of Louis Sullivan writing in his *Kindergarten Chats* (1900), is evidence of 'the ten-fingered grasp of reality'.

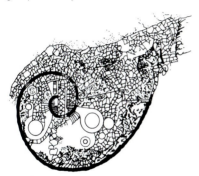

Rather than creating a new form using the geometry of abstraction, Bruce Goff's Bavanger House, Oklahoma, is inspired by a natural form.

Another understanding of *organic* design is as total design — a 'from soup to nuts' approach, in which all the elements of a designed system are brought together through contrast and harmony: part to whole and part to part.

See also: **Exponential** • **Modulate** • **Rhythm** • **Synchronic** • **Telos**

Ornament

No excess. — Ancient Greek proverb

Rather like its synonym 'decoration', the term *ornament* has, for the past 80 years, evoked negative attitudes in design circles. In his book *Ornament* (1986), Stuart Durant describes its decline in contemporary architecture as coinciding with the ascendancy of the Modern Movement and a Reductionist approach that rejects the patterned adornment of objects and buildings as not being critical to their form or function. There is also the belief that an 'add on' layer of decoration, using motifs based on natural or geometric patterns, will adulterate the purity of the form, plus an attendant misgiving that such an embellishment can camouflage a multitude of design sins. Indeed, while Louis Sullivan championed its use, Adolph Loos went so far as to describe the use of *ornament* as wasteful and tantamount to a criminal act. Conversely, Sullivan saw *ornament* as a requirement for a fully-developed architecture, and approached the form of his buildings as a host for allusion and ornamentation. For him, *ornament* was a means of expressing the spiritual intent of a building in ways not always accomplished by its main lines and masses.

While modern architects regarded the form itself as *ornament* (something they would never admit), *ornament* at its best does have the power to bring layers of complexity and a rich visual density to the perception of form. Moreover, as the architectural use of a variegated colour and texture is often associated with ornamentation — and has been subdued if not prohibited in the recent past — its eradication by a Purist aesthetic has, as did the Puritans before them who 'Tippex'd' away the medieval colours from Gothic cathedrals, tended to jettison the baby with the bath water.

See also: **Celebrate** • **Decorated shed** • **Tactile**

Palimpsest   ▌

The term *palimpsest* is derived from the Greek *Epalimpsestos*, meaning 'scraped again'. Along with other disciplines, such as art, music and literature, architecture uses the term as a metaphor to describe the partial erasing and constant overworking of sites and buildings over time. This can involve building over, within, above or alongside the previous or existing structure and can generically (and often inaccurately) be regarded as 'remodelling'. Thus, the 'memory' of the site and its traces of the past are respected and complemented by the new.

A distinction should be made between wholesale site clearance and new build, a common phenomenon, from a respectful understanding of the past and considered insertion of the new. For example, the twelfth-century church of St Clemente in Rome was built over a (circa) fourth-century Constantine basilica, which, in turn, was built on earlier remains — facts that were not known until the mid-nineteenth century. A more current illustration can be found in the debate that raged over what should be built over Ground Zero, the site of the Twin Towers in New York. The site had a history prior to the towers' construction, but it now has a more poignant 'memory' that will forever be embodied in the evolution of that setting.

In *Landscape Archaeology*, written by M. Aston and T. Rowley in 1974, the 'landscape' is described as a *palimpsest* 'on to which each generation inscribes its own impressions and removes some of the marks of earlier generations. Constructions of one age are often overlain, modified or erased by the work of another'. Aerial photography, such as that recorded in the run up to the Millennium, can clearly identify such 'marks', offering clues to the patterns of use over time. (R R-C)

See also: **Context • Memory • Metaphor • Trace**

Paradigm   ▌

The success of Frank Gehry's Guggenheim Museum in Bilbao, with its significant influence upon that city's domestic economy, has marked a paradigm shift in the relationship of landmark architecture to the role it plays in marketing a city. — Martha LaGess/Michael McNamara

The concept of *paradigm* emanates from the work of scientist Thomas S. Kuhn who used the term in the early 1960s to describe the means by which certain theories, such as Einstein's relativity theory, achieve dominance. When a consensus of viewpoints and practice cluster around a particular theory, a 'world view' is formed to consolidate a set of game rules. This consolidation has been described by Michel Foucault as a 'discursive formation'. When such theories are challenged, i.e. when accepted theoretical systems become outmoded, then a '*paradigm* shift' occurs. Another wrinkle on *paradigm* shift is Charles Jencks' idea of a 'Jumping Universe'. He takes the position that our world undergoes a rapid *paradigm* shift every few millennia — and suggests that we are currently in the midst of one of those 'jumps'.

The concept of *paradigm* has been successfully adapted into archispeak to describe theoretical patterns of thought represented by the cyclical 'isms' — the emergence of a new and dominant aesthetic representing the *paradigm* shift. The function of *paradigm* to allow a more focused study of the condition of architecture and the social context in which it was created explains the ubiquitous '*Paradigm* project' in first-year architectural programmes. These projects study a representative example of a paradigmatic structure from which to clone a design response.

See also: **Icon(ic)** • **Precedent**

Paradox

Successful architects are immediately caught in a paradox. Architecture is itself a mixture of bifurcating aspirations, by necessity both poetic and pragmatic. — Neil Spiller

If one has a passion for the absolute that cannot be healed, there is no other way out than to constantly contradict oneself and to reconcile opposite extremes. — Freidrich Schlegel

Paradox is a self-contradictory or seemingly absurd statement. *Paradox* reveals inconsistency and ambiguity by its contrariness; it is the simultaneous occupation of a single notion by two opposing concepts. *Paradox* occurs when absurdity or contradiction is brought together, the friction of their polarity causing sparks of new and heightened meaning.

In architecture, *paradox* disrupts assumptions about systems; it places conflict before synthesis and fragmentation before unity. When *paradox* is involved there is no single coherent outcome. It can arise from metaphoric relationships, contradiction and ambiguity. But the consequence is not necessarily chaotic — one part of a paradoxical equation ultimately requiring connection with its opposite to reach fullness of meaning. Indeed, in his book *Radical Reconstruction* (1997), Lebbeus Woods argues for a paradoxical design approach in favour of Cartesian logic, which reduces complexity to a universally applied mathematical system. Architectural *paradox*, he proposes, is a more fitting design language for the fragmentation and dynamism of our modern existence. The simultaneous realization of mutually exclusive qualities and ideas, he claims, transcends former categories of knowledge and takes us towards a more developed, more complex form of order.

See also: **Ambiguity** • **Complexity** • **Contrast** • **Disjunction** • **Dualism** • **Order**

Parallax

The movement of the body as it crosses through overlapping perspectives formed within space is the elemental connection between ourselves and architecture. The 'apparent horizon' is a determining factor in the moving body's interpretation of space. — Steven Holl

Parallax results from a difference in the location, or direction, of two objects or surfaces when viewed from different positions, such as the difference between the images in a viewfinder and the camera lens. Movement of the viewer causes motion *parallax* — one of the primary cues to our perception of a three-dimensional event. For example, while two-dimensional pictures do not change with different viewing positions, the reality of a three-dimensional view, say from a moving train, would involve motion *parallax*. This is when objects in the foreground and background of the field of vision appear to travel at progressively decreasing speeds — the dynamic of 'slippage' or interference occurring when they overlap and this signals a heightened sense of depth.

Steven Holl describes *parallax* as 'perspective warp' — movement through overlapping spaces defined by solid and cavity, causing the multiplicity of experience when movement axes leave the horizontal dimension. Vertical movement, causing vertical and oblique 'slippages', questions the historical notion of perspective as enclosed volumetrics based on horizontal space. He proposes that the transformation of this horizontal view is the key to new spatial perceptions.

See also: **Depth cues • Juxtaposition • Layering • Superimpose**

Parameters   ▮

The process of searching, grappling, and pushing the boundaries of any medium is important to the creative process because it separates ideas caught in the conventions from ideas that have been set free. — Sophia A. Gruzdys

The dictionary defines *parameter* as a constant in an equation, as one of a set of measurable factors that define a system and determine its behaviour, a factor that restricts what is possible, determines a range of variations, a boundary.

In archispeak, the concern is not with equations nor with precisely what is measured, but with the boundary aspect: limitations or constraints on the range of possible design solutions. Constraints are imposed by laws of nature, human laws and regulations, client expectation and our own (lack of) imagination, in decreasing order of rigour.

Accepting such limitations is often comfortable because it narrows the range of possibilities; exploring how far they can be stretched expands that range. The danger arises because it is perceived to be adventurous and heroic to do this, there is a tendency to confuse the quality and appropriateness of a solution with its extent of 'pushing the envelope'; the latter is often accepted as the deciding criterion. But it is considered as uncool, stodgy and worse to point this out, as it is to suggest that the use of the term *parameter* is part of an archispeak culture of using obscure words to aggrandize simple design moves.

A truly rigorous questioning of the restrictions and challenges of a given project is known as 'interrogating the brief' — a process in which the given might be challenged and, possibly, augmented by a modified set of rules. This might include questions concerning materials, size, cost or many other factors — some visual, others functional.   (TM)

See also: *Avant-garde* • **Boundary • Closure • Composition • Convention • Cutting edge • Design intent • Problem solving • Zoning**

Parasitic architecture

The definition of the term 'parasite' refers to an organism living in or on another and benefiting at the expense of the host. This biological term has been borrowed by designers to describe an architecture that opportunistically 'piggy-backs' existing structures or cannibalizes waste or leftover space found around, between, in or on existing structures or buildings. *Parasitic architecture* projects are the stuff of sketch designs and ideas competitions that encourage lateral thinking and aim to sharpen design skills. The classic habitable bridge, habitable billboard, habitable wall, together with the ubiquitous roof addition, all come to mind.

Albeit confined to drawings on paper, the 'freespace' interventions of Lebbeus Woods invade the Cartesian matrix of 'idealized space' in existing cities, such as Berlin and Zagreb. His parasitic structures hang from or burst through the fabric of existing buildings. Intentionally confrontational, they are intended to prod a re-evaluation of our occupancy of traditionally constructed space in terms of use and meaning.

See also: **Arcology**

Parti

Not to be confused with its cousin — the developmental conceptual drawing — the *parti* of a design represents a reductive abstraction in two or three dimensions that reflects the subjectivity of the design solution. Derived from the French expression *prendre parti*, meaning to make a choice, *parti* was adopted in the École des Beaux-Arts in Paris in the nineteenth century as a key element of its architectural programme. The term refers to the central and salient motif of a project; the primary massing of a proposal in sketch design form which, defined at its inception, remains as a referential talisman throughout the design sequence. It is the *parti* that encapsulates in a simple drawing or a model the quintessential and formal expression of the core idea; it is the spirit of a design which reduces the main shape for overall form of a scheme to a simple diagram. The economy involved in making such a diagram is referred to in Louis Kahn's famous statement that any architectural intention worth its salt should be capable of being described using a minimum of just 10 lines and be so robust that nothing will destroy the concept or 'seed'.

The *parti* can appear in many forms: perspective sketches, projection drawings, or as simplified schematics that depict the basic spatio-formal working parts of the architectural 'mechanism'. The *parti* can also function as a valuable and insightful presentation device through which a focused and magnified view is revealed of the characterizing or organizational themes of the design.

See also: **Analytical drawing** • *Esquisse* • **Key drawing** • **Robust**

Pattern-making

When heard on the lips of more purist and minimalist designers, *pattern-making* tends to be a pejorative term used to negatively describe an activity associated with 'decoration' and 'wallpapering'. In this context, *pattern-*

making refers to the superficiality of a decorative approach that exclusively makes arrangements of shapes for their own sake.

However, there is another and profound version of making patterns that is copiously documented by Christopher Alexander *et al.* in their ground-breaking book trilogy of which *A Pattern Language* (1977) is the most celebrated. Its publication in the 1970s provided a working document for applying patterns, units of the architectural language, to an alternative approach to *pattern-making* — from city scale down to the smallest construction details.

See also: **Footprint • Ornament**

Personal space   ▮

Don't stand so close to me. — Sting

The pioneering work in proxemics in the 1960s by Richard Sommer and Edward T. Hall has re-evaluated our relationship with our spatial setting and demonstrated that our conception of space is by no means confined to the volume occupied by our bodies. We exhibit similarities with animals in that we carry with us various territories or 'bubbles' of *personal space* that emanate from zealously guarded intimate zones that extend out across private sectors to wider and less personal frontiers. Not only does this psychological space shrink and expand between personal and less exclusive parameters, but the concept of our own physical size can fluctuate in response to a psychological spatial relationship — our body seemingly growing in stature when confined in small spaces, such as elevators, and, conversely, diminishing within vast spaces, such as cathedrals or auditoria.

The concept of non-physical space is moved to broader spectra with K. Lewin's theory of 'psychological life-space' and the notion of 'action space' proposed by Horton and Reynolds. Lewin's 'life-space' refers to the perceptual map in which we live out our lifespan that embraces the spatial corridors connecting home, work, recreation and social contact — this perceptual map being electronically extended by telephone, television and the internet. Meanwhile, the theory of action space relates behaviour, perception and sociocultural attitudes. We place self-imposed limits on our location and movement through space by decisions made within socio-economic frameworks; decisions that dictate the location of home, workplace and mode of travel, with additional factors such as length of residence influencing our perception of the urban environment.

See also: **Defensible space • Mapping • Place • Proxemics**

Phenomenology   ▮

Enough of science and of art:
Close up those barren leaves;
Come forth, and bring with you a heart
That watches and receives.
  — William Wordsworth

Feeling is all. — Goethe

The French term *bourrage de crane*, or 'brain stuffing', is the antithesis of *phenomenology*. Science, in particular, is the anathema to the phenomenologist, for whom the unfettered direct experience 'free of scientific and other constructs' is the only true reality. *Phenomenology* is the antidote for the extreme Cartesian Rationalism of the Newtonian Universe. 'I think, therefore I am' is replaced with 'I don't think, I feel, therefore I am.'

In the tight circles of the architectural academia of the late twentieth-century, *phenomenology* was briefly the answer for those who dared to penetrate Heidegger and Foucault. As part of a larger sustained attack on logical positivism, *phenomenology* became the justification for any work of architecture that moved the architect. Christian Norberg-Schultz, the most influential architectural writer on the subject, uses vernacular Norwegian farm sheds to illustrate phenomenal architecture. In a similar vein, Michael Benedikt, in his book 'For an Architecture of Reality' (1987), describes the qualities of 'Presence, Emptiness, Materiality and Significance' as necessary for a building to exhibit phenomenological power. His examples also tend to be simple vernacular sheds.

Ultimately, the basic tenet of phenomenological design — that is based upon highly subjective personal experience — has doomed it to the scrap heap of architecture's search for a useable and sustainable theoretical base. After all, Christopher Alexander has described it as a 'quality without a name'. Since architecture is unavoidably a public art that is seldom simply serving the pleasure of its creation, it must inevitably provide an appropriate shared experience. (EO)

See also: **Existential** • **Materiality** • **Vernacular**

Pictorial space

Impressions on the eye from the real world comprise a visual cocktail of signals that are superimposed over a less obvious underlay of structural information. In order to understand how these signals are simulated in order to depict a pictorial illusion of space, we have to isolate the components of the visual experience. Our visual perception involves the detection of a network of positive and negative areas divided into three basic pictorial zones: foreground, middleground and background. The network is represented by patterns of perceptual 'patches'; each patch in the network representing a specific shape, tonal value, hue and surface quality, such as glossy or matte, that, to a lesser or greater degree, differs from that of its neighbours.

Close scrutiny of the nature of this pattern finds a fascinating and unpredictable structure of interlocking shapes that takes us to the very heart of *pictorial space*, for this is the essential diagram that is perceived by the eye (and the camera) and is translated by the brain into the illusion of space on the two-dimensional plane.

Pictorial space created as graphic displays via drawing and photography, etc., has to rely upon the secondary clues to depth, which include light and shade, aerial perspective (atmospheric perspective), overlap and convergence.

Linear mapping
exercise showing the
patches of colour and
value change seen in
a photograph.

See also: **Constancy scaling** • **Depth cues** • **Figure–ground** • **Positive–negative
space** • **Visual field**

Picturesque

With regard to the term picturesque, I have always myself used it
merely to denote such objects, as are proper subjects for painting:
so that according to my definition, one of the cartoons (of Raphael),
and a flower piece are equally picturesque. — John Gilpin

A valuable coin in the currency of the tourism industry, *picturesque* means
'like a picture'. It is a term derived from pictorial composition and is used
to describe the dramatizing of nature by creating stage-like settings and
landscape set-pieces that are animated by pedestrian movement.

Mainly influencing landscape garden and park design, the cult of the
Picturesque and ideas of the sublime came to a head in the eighteenth
century and were revived in the nineteenth century. The *picturesque* movement was an important aspect of Romanticism, which was to make nature
conform to an ideal. The idea was to create a landscape or a building, or a
combination of the two, to look like a picture. To do so, they turned to the
great seventeenth-century masters of landscape painting for inspiration
— artists such as Claude Lorraine and Salvador Rosa — to create vividly
striking landscape settings involving artificial temples, grottos, follies,
ruins and fanciful rock formations.

However, if heard as an adjective in reviews, *picturesque* can be used
in a derogatory manner, as in 'pretty as a postcard'. It is often used as a
euphemism for 'cute'.

See also: **Composition** • **Serial vision**

Place

> . . . spaces receive their being from locations and not from 'space'.
> — Martin Heidegger

When we awaken from a dream, descend from a journey in the air, or arise from illness, our first necessity is to locate ourselves in time and place. — Roger G. Kennedy

Place is a geographical point that has its roots in history and in the future — the space where you come from and go to; *place* is where you are at. 'Where' is the operative word. *Place* is that particular location or portion of space occupied by an object or a person. *Place* provides a setting for containment and appropriation; *place* is a reference for our existence, it is a form of possession, an occupied territory, it is lived-in space.

Therefore, *place* is a body-centred context that provides a point of view and a reference point for our existence. When we territorialize our setting, this is called 'place-making'; when we reinforce occupancy, we create a 'sense of *place*'. When in *place* we gain identity and become aware of our surroundings. However, whenever the natural position of objects or our body are disrupted, they seem 'out of *place*'. When there is no anchor for our sensibilities, we experience the banal sameness of placelessness.

The site for a building is a *place* in the making but many regard the essential role of architecture as that of making '*Place*' in a spiritual sense versus creating a physical *place*.

See also: **Anchoring** • *Axis mundi* • *Genius loci* • **Intersection** • **Locus** • **Memory** • **Personal space** • **Proxemics** • **Thereness (thisness)**

Planar

The polyhedral forms, which have been labelled 'geometric' in a mindless exclusivism, are hardly abundant in nature. Even those which man constructs as a plane (doors, tables, boards) tend, with time, to warp into parabolic forms. — Antonio Gaudí

Planar is a term mainly used in the US to describe the abstract nature of flat or level surface. *Planar* is more an idealized concept that assumes a monochromatic flatness and an orthogonal assembly. This assumption is based upon the Euclidean, Platonic and Cartesian notion that ideal forms exist as independent of nature and that the pure geometries embodied within objects should be exalted in all endeavours. In this perception, a plane is the record left by a moving line and architecture is envisaged as being composed Meisian fashion and involving primary *planar* elements — from a topographical flatness of the ground plane on which a building is grounded to the sheltering planes of its orthographic walls, floors and ceilings.

However, despite this idealized conception as a cubic, volumetric enclosure, *planar* elements can be bent, folded, warped, twisted and otherwise distorted. Further differentiation of *planar* characteristics is achieved with the colour and texture of their material. Indeed, the morphology and potential articulation of the plane is limitless — a potential famously characterized in the work of many architects who break with the Cartesian tradition, such as Frank Gehry, Ron Arad and Zaha Hadid.

See also: **Cartesian grid** • **Datum** • **Euclidean space** • **Topology**

Plan libre (free space)   ▌

The concept of the *plan libre*, often termed 'free space', was first developed by Le Corbusier in his Dom-ino House and later incarnated in his radical Cook House (1926) and the Villa Savoye (1931), i.e. framed structures in which internal dividing walls could be freely positioned when and where required. The *plan libre* was the most important of his five tenets of a 'new architecture', which also included pilotis (columns), roof garden (the site reclaimed on the roof), the horizontal strip window (*la fenêtre en longueur*) and the free façade. The *plan libre* was made possible by the innovation of a service-integrated reinforced-concrete frame on to which clients could build their traditional houses or prefabricated components. By divorcing the 'supporting' and the 'separating' (or 'space defining') as two discrete functions, this technique would hold massive repercussions for modern architecture. The *plan libre* heralded the 'open plan' and 'burolandschaft'; floors could now be planned as uncluttered and individualized spaces on separate levels. Indeed, European architects now worked in a new Cubist-inspired conception of space as essentially many sided.

   However, the free space of the *plan libre* is not to be confused with the term 'freespace', mentioned in the essays of Lebbeus Woods. Here, he refers to an opportunistic commandeering of leftover urban space.

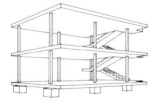

See also: **Continuum** • **Cubism** • **Diffusion** • **Framing (enframing)** • **Interpenetrating space** • **Transparency**

Plan libre: Le Corbusier's space-liberating Dom-ino concrete frame (© FLC/ADAGP, Paris and DACS, London, 2003).

Platonic solids   ▌

. . . cubes, cones, spheres, cylinders, or pyramids are the great primary forms that light reveals to advantage; the image of these is distinct and tangible within us and without ambiguity. It is for this reason that these are beautiful forms, the most beautiful forms.
   — Le Corbusier

Pure mathematics — mathematics for its own sake, without any practical goal in mind — began in the seventh century BCE in Greece, together with the deductive techniques of abstraction and proof. Proof is the art of flawlessly arguing from premise to conclusion; abstraction is the art of perceiving a universal quality or qualities in different things and forming a general idea as to their common origin. With reasoning came reduction and the invention of abstract shapes and solid pure forms whose Greek-derived names — cube, cone, pyramid, cylinder, etc. — we still use and which came to lay the foundation for Euclid's geometry.

Associated with Plato and his ideas, the *Platonic solids* refer to the five specific abstract forms shown below: the cube, regular tetrahedron, regular octahedron, regular dodecahedron and regular icosahedron. A polyhedron is termed 'regular' if it has as its faces just one type of regular polygon, and all its vertices are congruent. However, polyhedra are merely termed 'Platonic' by tradition because, according to Euclid's *Elements* (300 BCE), these figures do not belong to Plato as they can be ascribed to others, such as the Pythagoreans.

See also: **Cartesian space • Euclidean space • Topology**

The five *Platonic solids*: tetrahedron, cube, octahedron, dodecahedron and icosahedron.

Poché

From the French for 'pocket', and mainly used by American architects, *poché* refers to a graphic treatment applied to the solid portions in orthographic design drawings in order to heighten their spatial legibility. When not left as a pure line drawing the delineated thickness of sliced walls and other solid masses, including the earth on which they stand, particularly in plans and sections, they are more often than not shaded or filled-in with a dark tone or solid black. This is known as '*poché* work'. At the larger drawing scales, alternative *poché* treatments of the cut include colour shading and diagonal hatching.

Poché has also become an opportunity for inhabited 'found space', i.e. under the stairs and within the cavity of walls.

See also: **Figure–ground • Positive–negative space • Footprint • Working wall**

Poetic

There is something mystical about the term 'poetics'. From Plato and Aristotle to Gaston Bachelard and Igor Stravinsky, the word has been employed to address the aesthetics of genesis, the qualitative ingredients of space, the making of music. — Anthony C. Antoniades

Poetry and architecture have been frequently regarded as twinned arts — Thomas Hardy notably pursued a career in both. The phrase 'the poetry of architecture', coined by John Ruskin in his 1873 pamphlet of the same name, has since been picked up by architects such as John Soane and Louis Sullivan, and can usefully refer to buildings with one of two qualities associated with poetry: depth of meaning, or sublime and elevated effects.

In the first sense, *poetic* is a keyword when discussion moves to conceptual architecture. Bachelard, for example, seeks a *poetic* architecture where the building connects with a deeply held experience for those who witness it. In the latter, it refers to effects moving in their beauty — Luis Barragan's use of colour, the light of Venice.

Poetry itself often has a kind of 'architecture' that holds the work together — whether this means stanzas or a rhyme scheme. *Poetic* therefore also occurs when a building is in some way like a poem; in its structure or vocabulary of devices. If poetry is a way of moving through language in which repetitions, juxtapositions and rhythms are used to create emotion, then buildings can create similar effects. The Berlin Jewish Museum by Daniel Libeskind, with its entrance from the underground, its diminishing corridors and intolerably long central staircase, uses allusion, resonance and rhythm, and is often labelled *poetic* by enthusiastic critics.

(CP)

See also: **Breathe • Metaphor • Modulation • Rhyme • Rhythm**

Porosity   ▌

Space is permeable. Flows go both ways, in and out of it, space is permeated and permeating. — Michael Menser

Porosity is one of the key concepts of the urban experience discussed by Walter Benjamin when describing city characteristics, such as social, spatial and temporal organization. Using Naples as the model, Benjamin saw this city as an unplanned, chaotic conurbation in which spaces and buildings meld and interpenetrate. Therefore, *porosity* refers to the absence of spatial boundaries and divisions between phenomena, one thing permeating another, the merging of old and new, interior and exterior, and the diffusion of public and private.

Urban indeterminacy offers choice of movement, making navigation of the metropolitan labyrinth difficult and the chance of losing oneself — an adventure that is echoed by Will Alsop who, writing in the catalogue accompanying the John Soane Museum exhibition of his work, criticizes the predictability of the gridiron and applauds the unexpected and the attendant ability to lose one's way in the complexity of the porous city.

'Permeability', i.e. providing optional means of spatial penetration, is often used as a substitute term for *porosity*. In the writings of Steven Holl, the lateral penetration of a building becomes 'horizontal *porosity*'.

See also: **Co-mingling space • Diffusion • Erosion • Interpenetrating space •** *Plan libre* (free space) • *Promenade architecturale* • **Transparency**

Positive–negative space   ▌

In three-dimensional work, 'positive' refers to the space that is materially occupied as distinct from the areas of unoccupied space that are shaped by the positive areas. Albeit marketed as a small confection in its own right, the hole in a Polo mint or a Lifesaver is an example of negative space, while in pictorial design, where the term is more commonly used, 'negative space' refers to the empty space surrounding and defining positive elements. The concept that positive elements dominate and appear nearer the eye, while negative elements appear passive and receding, seems to emanate from a notion of space as the negative of form.

However, just as 'positive' can become 'negative' in two-dimensional displays — as exemplified in the alternating pictorial ambiguity of figure–ground illusions (see page 77) — so, too, three-dimensional 'negative space' can be made 'positive'. This transformation regularly occurs in the sculpture of Rachel Whiteread where surrounding or contained space is made concrete. Her work plays games with our sensory perception of what is solid and what is void, and is, perhaps, best illustrated by her series of full-sized casts made of the volumes of room spaces within the three storeys of a town house (shown here). There is also her celebrated sculpture that was temporarily displayed on the empty plinth in London's Trafalgar Square. Made in clear resin, this rhetorical piece represents an inverted, transparent version of the stone plinth — the corporeality of its form being upturned into a seemingly ephemeral and 'negative' version of itself.

Whiteread's work emphasizes that to perceive 'negative space' as mere emptiness is a mistake; its presence is as perceptually supercharged as are the so-called positive visual elements.

Rachael Whiteread's untitled (1993) concrete sculpture celebrating 'negative' as 'positive' in her full-scale cast of a house interior.

See also: **Figure–ground • Interaction**

Post-modernism (po-mo)

As an architect, I try to be guided not by habit but by a conscious sense of the past, by precedent thoughtfully considered . . . I am for richness of meaning rather than clarity of meaning, for the implicit function as well as the explicit function. — Robert Venturi

It [post-modernism] rejects the idea of a single style in favor of a view that acknowledges the existence of many styles . . . each with its own meaning. — Robert A. M. Stern

According to one of the main advocates of *post-modernism*, Charles Jencks, Modernism went out with a bang on 15 July 1972, with the dynamiting of the Pruitt-Igoe housing complex in St Louis. While it is something of an oversimplification to attempt to precisely pinpoint the beginning or end of any complex trend, it definitely is the case that the social programme and aesthetic of Modern architecture came under increasing criticism in the early 1970s. Mies van der Rohe's maxim of 'less is more' became replaced by Robert Venturi's rejoinder 'less is a bore'. Such scepticism towards belief systems led to the rise of *post-modernism* during the period 1978–81.

Post-modernism is a portmanteau term covering those architects who reintroduced decorative elements, historical references and context as important features in their buildings. They argued that in their reformist zeal modern architects had filled the cities of the world with sterile glass boxes that in no way met people's emotional needs. However, richness rather than clarity, a conscious sense of the past, physical and associational experience, and the acknowledgment of the existence and the indiscriminate use of many styles has characterized post-modern architecture, and now sees this term often used in a disparaging manner.

Apart from the ubiquitous shopping malls and supermarkets that exemplify the pluralism and baseness of the movement, classic examples include Philip Johnson's AT&T building (1984) in New York and Michael Graves' Portland Public Services Building (1982) in Portland, Oregon. Both buildings make abundant use of historical details and decorative elements in contrast to the Modernists for whom' history' and 'decoration' were taboo.

See also: **Eclectic**

Post-occupancy evaluation (POE)   ▌

We all evaluate the performance of buildings, although not necessarily in a self-conscious and explicit way. In a hotel room, for example, conversations taking place next door may be overheard. In this case, the acoustical performance of the building is being assessed. The room temperature, quality of lighting, storage, finishes, and even the aesthetic quality of the view from the hotel window, are also informally evaluated. Similarly, those waiting for an elevator may judge the waiting time to be excessive. The evaluation criteria used in this case comes from expectations that are based on previous experiences with elevators.

Post-occupancy evaluation (POE) is the systematic feedback phase in the building process that formally tracks the sequence of planning, briefing, design, construction and occupancy of a building. *POEs* can involve troubleshooting during the move-in period, thereby correcting unforeseen problems, balancing and fine-tuning of the building, auditing space utilization, and documenting the successes and failures in building performance. Early research work conducted in the late 1960s, together with influential publications in the 1970s, including Oscar Newman's *Defensible Space* (1972), pioneered *POE* as a process of evaluating buildings in a methodical and rigorous manner after they have been built and occupied for some time. *POEs* focus on building occupants and their needs, and thus they provide insights into the consequences of past design decisions and the resulting building programme. This knowledge forms a sound basis for creating better buildings in the future.   (ETW)

See also: **Defensible space • Design criteria • Vital signs**

Post-structuralism   ▌

Although it sounds like it should be something that comes after structuralism, *post-structuralism* is really just another form of structuralism. Structuralism, (the belief that the structure of a thing, especially linguistic structure, is more important than the thing itself), eventually turned on itself in a 'serpent devouring its own tail' fashion. *Post-structuralism* contends that there is nothing but structure and all meaning is contingent upon the reader. Thus, there is no relevancy to the author's intent regarding content.

The architectural significance of this revelation is that now anything goes. The architect is no longer responsible to his or her audience, only in creating a disembodied structure that people can respond to however they wish. Ironically, this has resulted in highly personal and idiosyncratic architecture. It has become a perverse type of individualistic formalism without any agreement about the rules of the game.   (EO)

See also: **Semiology** • **Sign** • **Phenomenology**

Praxis

Praxis describes the act or practice of an art or skill as distinct from the theory that underpins its application. *Praxis* also refers to a collection of examples or techniques that may be used as models for practice.

In the original Greek sense, *praxis* referred to any action or doing. The study of *praxis*, or 'praxiology', has become an increasingly popular academic topic, with the publication of well-received texts by Dana Cuff and Spiro Kostoff, among others. Of particular interest is the relationship between the academy and practice, and the role that gender and race play in the profession.

See also: **Typology**

Precedent

It has always been my view that good design depends on precedents, and I have always encouraged my students to seek previous examples of their design problem and seek to build on or expand the ideas of others. Isaac Newton has said: 'We stand on the shoulders of giants'.
— Alan J. Brookes

During the initial phase of design, the nature of an evolving idea may be strongly influenced by an existing architectural example, an architectural feature, or, indeed, the credo of an architectural movement. A *precedent* is used when an example is found to coincide with the spirit of the design intention. The *precedent* then becomes a model that may be followed or adapted for use. Many architects freely acknowledge this debt, such as the respective tributes to Classical architecture, Russian Suprematism and early science-fiction comics by Michael Graves, Zaha Hadid and the members of Archigram — the concepts of the latter, in turn, providing a popular and recurrent *precedent*.

Aside from such popular 'non-architectural' sources as yacht technology and fairground structures, there is also the widespread interest in movies as a means of exploring and communicating spatial, perceptual and temporal qualities in architectural design; architects like Steven Holl, Rem Koolhaas and Jean Nouvel acknowledging this source. *Precedent* models can draw from a wide range of cinematic sources, such as sets for movies with architectural attitude: Ridley Scott's *Blade Runner* and *Alien*, Fritz Lang's *Metropolis* and Terry Gilliam's *Brazil* providing perennial sources of inspiration.

While some students reject any disclosure of outside influence from existing buildings on the grounds of plagiarism, the inclusion of *precedents* in presentations is good practice as no new architecture is, in itself, original but a composite of innovation, past experience and knowledge, and sometimes subliminal awareness, of a relevant and significant body of existing work. Indeed, as Geoffrey Broadbent observes: 'All iconic processes of design employ precedence.'

See also: **Icon(ic)** • **Morphology** • **Typology**

Problem solving

Art is solving problems that cannot be formulated before they have been solved. The shaping of the question is part of the answer.
— Piet Hein

Writing in *Companion to Architectural Thought* (1993), Mark Gelernter discusses two extremes of *modus operandi* in the *problem-solving* process. At one extreme lies a Functionalist approach that sees the design solution already 'formed' and awaiting discovery. Solutions are fashioned from an objective study of external constraints, i.e. the various functions proposed for the building. It is a *problem-solving* route that avoids preconception, individuality and personal values. The other extreme sees the architect as a romantic and creative genius. Design solutions result from a subjective route that draws its inspiration from preconception, special insight and inner creativity. The aim is originality of form, the process being subject to few external constraints. However, Gelertner documents a *problem-solving* model proposed by Bill Hillier, Professor Pat O'Sullivan and others that draws on the work of Karl Popper and Jean Piaget. Described as the 'conjecture-test' model, this *problem-solving* approach accommodates both external constraints and inner creativity.

The model proposes that when faced with a blank sheet of paper and a design problem, the architect very often sets out with a set of preconceptions fuelled by the designer's personal repertoire of 'solution types', i.e. workable solutions for different typologies banked from a previous experience in *problem solving*. Once a preconception is formed, it becomes tested against the external parameters of the problem — the proposed form being evaluated against an array of factors including function. As the preliminary proposal rarely satisfactorily answers all the factors, the designer then moves into an alternating cycle of modification and evaluation until the problem is resolved or the project deadline is reached. If successful, the designer will add this solution type to a personal and expanding bank of preconceptions for future reference. A successful solution type may be adopted as a starting point for *problem solving* by other architects. In this case, it becomes absorbed into the cultural tradition.

Gelernter concludes that, as part of this *problem-solving* model, architectural form is neither exclusively fashioned from outside constraints nor simply 'cooked up' from the creative imagination. It does offer a more satisfactory explanation of the 'analysis–synthesis model', which is what actually takes place in design.

See also: **Black box** • **Charette** • **Concept** • **Design genesis** • **Journey** • **Lateral thinking** • **Parameters** • **Resolved** • **Synthesis** • **Tabula rasa**

▎ Processional space

Processional space responds to the movement of groups of people who, being involved in some ritualistic ceremony, pageant or demonstration, move forward in orderly succession while accompanied by a formal chain of architectural events. Found in many cultures, processing is an ancient phenomenon in which both processor and spectator have roles to play. The formality of processing takes place between two fixed points and is usually observed by a strict geometrical symmetry. For instance, buildings and cities that involve processing are designed around a processional axis. Sacred buildings like Gothic cathedrals were formed around a spine along which the ritual and rhythm of an orderly progression of linear movement can take place and be observed; sacred cities like ancient Rome and Peking were entirely planned around broad processional routes — the latter connecting the Imperial Palace and the Temple of Heaven.

Another form of *processional space* is the *promenade architecturale*. Those involving a vertical movement through space range from monumental staircases like the Spanish Steps in Rome, those seen in Busby Berkley's Hollywood musicals to Le Corbusier's programmed walk through and up to the roof of the Villa Savoye and Frank Lloyd Wright's graceful spiral descent down the ramps of his Guggenheim Museum in New York. However, when connecting one point or place of devotion to another, *processional space* involves continuity of movement and visibility. It is a place to see and be seen.

See also: **Axis** • **Linearity** • *Promenade architecturale* • **Sacred space** • **Sight lines** • **Symmetry**

▎ *Promenade architecturale*

The *promenade architecturale* is more than a preferred route of circulation; it . . . provides a rigorously orchestrated tour through the themes, images, and ordering systems deployed in a given project.
— Deborah Gans

Derived from the concept of the picturesque revived in nineteenth-century theory, the term *promenade architecturale* was invented by Le Corbusier to describe the journey through a building. Based upon his sketchbook study tours to Italy and Greece, Le Corbusier firmly believed that forms directly affect our senses and that, through their arrangement, architects can play upon our emotions. In responding to the structural and organizational needs, and to the way we move through buildings, these arrangements, by defining the *promenade architecturale*, may provide a rich sequence of visual experience.

Le Corbusier's design for the Villa Savoye at Poissy near Paris provides an almost filmic sequence of perambulatory space beginning with a central, ceremonial entrance positioned at the bull-nose of a curve responding to the turning circle of a car. Facing the entrance is a gently sloping internal ramp that threads the three levels of the house. As the ramp unfolds, and with it the *promenade architecturale*, vistas, glimpses and veiled and filtered views of both the interior and out to the limits beyond its edge are sequentially encountered. Treated as a discrete design element, the promenade concludes on the roof and, on leaving the enclosure of a curving screen that acts as a final arabesque to the sequence, the climactic release of terrace views.

Similar 'promenades' are also carefully embodied in the early designs of Richard Meier, Rem Koolhaas and the late James Stirling — the latter using the up-view axonometric, a drawing type first promoted by August Choisy at the end of the nineteenth century, to illustrate the spatial and structural organization in a recognition of the 'rubber-necking' gaze of the perambulating stroller. Frank Lloyd Wright also exploited the *promenade architecturale* at Taliesen West, and ritualistic promenades that intensify awareness of earth and sky are designed into the approaches to Tadeo Ando's churches. Steven Holl's buildings reflect a similar spatial experience as if in a progression of cinematic stills. He suggests that our perambulatory experience of architecture is made up of an infinite number of perspectives projected from an infinite number of viewpoints. This implies a need to create architecture that not only gives priority to the bodily experience, but also serves to bind the intention of the architecture to the perception of the viewer.

See also: **Corporeality** • **Experiential** • **Linearity** • **Processional space** • **Serial vision** • **Sight lines** • **Transparency**

Proportion   ▮

. . . every part is disposed to unite with the whole, that it may thereby escape from its incompleteness.— Leonardo da Vinci

The classical theory of proportion consists in an attempt to transfer to architecture the quasi-musical notion of a 'harmonious order', by giving specific rules and principles for the proportionate combination of parts. — Roger Scruton

Proportion refers to dimensional size, and also to an ordering process involving the correct or pleasing relationships of things to each other or the parts of a thing in relation to the whole. The ancient notion that the cosmos is a harmonious mathematical creation and that, to engage in its order, the things we create must obey the same mathematical laws has been an enduring principle. For centuries, from the mysticism of number in ancient Greece to the Middle Ages, through the proportional systems of the Renaissance to Le Corbusier's Modulor Theory, there has been endeavour to subject objects of different dimensions and musical harmony to certain rules and fixed numerical systems. Much of this stems from an understanding of the harmonious relationship between the parts of the human body and — when outstretched — its relatedness to the square and the circle. Reviving the proportional ratios of the Pythagoreans and Vitruvius, Renaissance masters, including Leon Battista Alberti, Leonardo da Vinci and Albrecht Dürer, reawakened the doctrine that art, music and architecture could be structured on the analogy of the well-formed human physique.

While some architects are attracted to proportional systems in the belief that their intrinsic ratios makes them appropriate for all kinds of design solutions, such an approach is not without its critics. For instance, Emile Ruder writes that proportional systems based on calculation have barred the way to creative design; they have become crutches on which to support the incompetent. Moreover, writing in his *Mind and Image* (1976), Herb Greene argues that, like cultural experiences that have programmed us to see only a part of the world, the effectiveness of, for example, the golden section and the Modulor, is quickly shattered. This occurs the moment we perceptually move off the axis and change our angle of view. As if in agreement with David Hume's T*reatise on Human Nature* (1739–40), which proposed that while served by reason, creative judgement should be led by passion, Greene suggests that the designer can never be free of his or her personal design codes of 'valued *proportion*', and can invent strategies to accommodate proportional sets arising from each design circumstance. Greene concludes: 'As an architect I would treat *proportion* as a spatial adjustment within a composition. In buildings the adjustment should provide human scale and a unifying sense of purpose and, above all, should express some experiential value for the user.'

See also: Composition • Golden section • Order • Ordering systems • Regulating lines • Scale • Symmetry

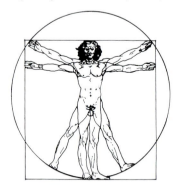

Squaring the circle. Leonardo da Vinci's interpretation of Vitruvius' analogy of the well-shaped human body as a model for harmonious design.

Proxemics

**Some thirty inches from my nose the frontier of my Person goes . . .
Beware of rudely crossing it I have no gun but I can spit.** — W. H. Auden

Deciding exactly where performers will stand on a stage in theatrical productions is called 'blocking out a scene'. In social science, the word *proxemics* is used to designate the study of how people utilize the small spaces around them. *Proxemics* can be thought of as similar to choreography and the cultural 'dance' that members of different social and ethnic groups get into when they interact.

Coined in the 1930s and popularized in the mid-1960s in Edward T. Hall's studies of inter-personal space, published in his classic *The Hidden Dimension* (1966), *proxemics* refers to the term 'personal space' (see page 140). Personal space refers to a psychological bubble of space around people which they consider extensions of themselves. Invitations, often involving ritual gestures, are usually required before these spaces can be entered. Subdivisions of personal space include 'intimate distance', i.e. six to eight inches, 'personal distance', i.e. 18 to 30 inches, and 'social distance', i.e. four to seven feet.

However, it was in the 1980s and 1990s that the concept of having 'one's own space' has really developed in the architectural vocabulary, with particular stress on the degree to which others may try to intrude on this essential freedom. Contextually, the space needed by a person or special interest group is often defined in terms of those who might be expected to encroach upon it.

See also: **Boundary • Collage • Figure–ground • Gestalt • Intersection • Juxtaposition • Personal space**

Punctum

Punctum is one of the two terms distinguishing themes of presence and absence in the viewing of photography that has entered the archispeak vocabulary. These refer to states of recognition, i.e. levels of human interest when viewing a scene, and stem from the writings of the French socioliogist, Roland Barthes. The other term, 'studium', refers to the spectators' casual, take it or leave it, broad field of interest; it is a kind of knowledge, a 'contract' of understanding in the meaning of a scene between its creator and viewer. To recognize the 'studium' is to engage with the intentions of the photographer.

Meanwhile, *punctum* is the dot, spot or minute speck of colour that punctuates the 'studium'. Not to be confused with the message area or focal point of an image, the *punctum* leaps out of the scene to engage and distract the viewer. According to Barthes, a *punctum* results from what the viewer brings to the viewing and, therefore, lies beyond the control of the creator of the image. Sometimes, he suggests, a *punctum* may not be realized at the time of viewing but recollected later.

Architecturally speaking, *punctum* is a cut or a point of incision into an existing formal condition which brings new and often unintended meaning and reorientation in the viewer.

See also: **Contrast • Focal point • Locus • Visual field**

Reciprocity

An eye for an eye, a tooth for a tooth. — Book of Exodus, the Bible

Reciprocity is the responsive state of give and take in a co-dependent relationship between two different conditions. Therefore, *reciprocity* is the state in which part and the whole define each other. It is the coexistent state of interchange in which, like the alternation of thought and move in the process of design, the action of one will bring reaction in the other. Likewise, colours seen in combination have a reciprocating perceptual effect on each other — the impression of one hue, say a strong red, when seen in combination with its complementary, green, will induce the red to appear more saturated, i.e. redder and, conversely, the green more intense. This intensification relies upon interaction — an alternating trade-off that can also be ascribed to the figure–ground relationship in pictorial displays and in the positive–negative dualism of solid and void.

Reciprocity is opposed to the notion of habitable space as a neutral setting. It is a cause and effect operation that envisages architecture as entering into a dialogue, of having its own say, and of existing in its own realm while embodying a special relationship with the life and activities of the user. It sees the context of each architectural setting as impacting on the user and vice-versa. Both are not passive entities but emit and receive energies, forces and pressures that cause upon the other a continual process of evolution and change. This notion is articulated by Peter Zumthor in an article for *Architecture + Urbanism* in 1998 when he describes his approach to architecture not as a message or a symbol but as a 'responsive envelope'. For Zumthor, architecture is the setting for life that is played out within it and around it; it is 'a sensitive container for the rhythm of footsteps on the floor, for the concentration of work, for the silence of sleep'. Such an approach, he proposes, involves a constant questioning of the meaning of particular materials in each architectural context. When we get it right, new light is shed onto both the way a material is generally used and its own inherent sensuous qualities. When we succeed, materials in architecture can be made to reflect the vitality of the user-recipient and to 'shine' and 'vibrate' in reciprocation. Therefore, *reciprocity* occurs when we are in tune with our setting and when the parts and the whole of that setting, including the occupant, define and redefine each other.

See also: **Dialogue • Feedback • Interaction • Interface**

Reconfigure

To *reconfigure* is to recycle the configurative process. The configurative process organizes the parts or elements in a particular form or figure; it is a compositional process that ensures that the identity of the whole is present in the parts, and vice-versa. Therefore, while 'configure' relates to the act of composing and designing, and 'configuration' describes its outcome, *reconfigure* is the process of their rearrangement. Therefore, when heard in design reviews, the term is polite archispeak for 'do it over again, but this time do it differently'.

See also: **Composition • Feedback • Resolved**

Regulating lines   ▮

The choice of the regulating line is one of the decisive moments of inspiration, it is one of the vital moments of architecture.
— Le Corbusier

Regulating lines constitute a design tool that, like the golden section, are used as an invisible geometrical scaffolding on which to order and align the interrelating incidence of architectural mass and its constituent elements. Their use as a means of verifying formal relationships was promoted by Le Corbusier to be one of the crucial architectural design operations. So much so, that in his seminal manifesto *Towards a New Architecture*, first published in 1923, he dedicates an entire chapter to the topic. Citing antecedents in the use of units of measure based upon human dimensions and applied to bring order to the wilderness at the beginnings of building, Le Corbusier argues for a geometry that brings harmony, measure and unity in the face of ´chance, irregularity and capriciousness´.

By retracing the *regulating lines* of the Notre-Dame in Paris and Michelangelo's Capitol in Rome, Le Corbusier demonstrates their application in his own design projects. He describes how a simple geometry can define the mass and its subdivision, and correct the placement and proportion of secondary elements within it — doors, windows, panels, incline of staircases, etc. — down to the smallest detail. He sees the outcome as importing a higher (mathematical) order to his architecture, of bringing monumentality to the scale of a private house and of distancing his architectural design from a surrounding built environment filled with whims and inconsistency.

However, there is a word of caution. The use of such lines of control should be seen as a means to an end and not as a design crutch. Danger lurks in their exhaustive use when order without diversity becomes uniformly dull and monotonous.

See also: **Axis • Composition • Fibonacci series • Golden section • Ley lines • Order • Ordering systems • Proportion**

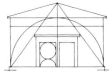

The fundamental geometry of *regulating lines* found on a marble slab in 1882 showing the façade of the Arsenal at Piræus

Resolved   ▮

A design is considered *resolved* when its process of development has been exhausted, that is, when all the key decisions regarding an intention have consolidated and a concept has firmed-up to become fully formed. This is the happy state when the identity of the whole of a design is present in its parts, and the parts exhibit a unifying presence in the whole.

However, some architects will admit that their designs are never fully *resolved*. For example, the Californian design team Morphosis considers each consecutive design project as merely an overture, a prelude in a personal design continuum along which each project is seen as a spring-board from which to provide generative input into the next. This is a process in which the architects will, even beyond the completion of a building, return to a reworking of its drawings and models. Seen as a source of inspiration for the evolution of a new design, these become the subject of a renewed process of analysis. It is from this retrospective means of pushing forward new ideas, from creating and recreating, from mining the new from the old, that the name 'Morphosis' is derived.

For British architect, John Outram, the 'resolution' of a building design triggers a similar retrospective phase which can occur long after his build-ings are constructed. This is a phase when, using hindsight, he embroiders elaborate mythical narratives around them. These become a mechanism for definition — allowing him to develop narratives and myths which inform future work. Outram's illustrated stories gradually coalesce into a longer fictional commentary involving all his completed buildings — a procedure that sees each building as not only making its contribution to the genesis of the next, but also being a part of an as yet un*resolved* bigger picture.

As there are degrees of resolution, most design is considered to be *resolved* when the most important conflicts have been determined. Design can therefore be viewed as a conflict-resolution process. Consequently, it might be argued that an architectural design is never finally *resolved*, but is a continuous process of refinement that can occur long after a deadline has imposed its artificial closure.

See also: **Composition • Reconfigure**

▌Rhyme

Rhyme is repetition with a difference. Linguistically, this means two words have identical sounds, yet are distinct — Venturi famously rhymed, when he turned Mies van der Rohe's 'less is more' into 'less is a bore'.

In architecture, the term can be applied when a motif is repeated, but with subtle alternations. Mannerist architecture, which used orthodox classical motifs in deliberate opposition to their original context, could be said to *rhyme*. A repetition of a light effect or detail within a building, where the impact changes each time, is architectural *rhyme*.

Rhyme schemes are often perceived as architectural because their ordering pattern provides a poem's structure. Elizabethan sonnets were frequently referred to as 'monuments', with Samuel Daniel defining them as 'much excellently ordered in a small roome'. Critics often use *rhyme* in this context of patterning — Rudolph Wittkower has noted that the enclosed rhyme ABBA is echoed in Italian Renaissance architecture, while Adolf Kurt Placzek has drawn attention to the 'ABCCBA rhyme schemes' of brownstone façades.   (CP)

See also: **Articulate • Diachronic • Modulate • Rhythm • Synchronic**

Rhythm ▐

Without rhythm there would be no life, there would be no creation at all. Each creature passes rhythmically through its stages of growth; under the wind's influence, forests, corn fields, and the shifting sands move in rhythm. — Emile Ruder

Rhythm in architecture is a term borrowed from other arts, such as poetry, music and dance. Its use in archispeak transfers meaning from the syncopated flow of words and syllables, musical tones and bodily movement to pattern variations of the repetitious ordering of architectural elements — architectural *rhythm* and harmony giving rise to the allusion of architecture as 'frozen music'.

Alignments of architectural elements, such as columns or windows, repeated at regular intervals forms the basis of the concept of *rhythm*. Each element in the repetition becomes a signal for a measurement that does not necessarily involve equal intervals — their variation evoking an image of musical time. Throughout history the gridplan has provided a framework against which rhythmical variations on a rectangular theme have been played out. A basic one, two, one, two *rhythm* found in the zig-zag decoration of primitive cultures is a universal, pulsating *rhythm* that is found in both ancient and modern buildings. Harnessed to a structure of harmonic and gilded proportions, more complicated *rhythms* involving patterns of subtle variation and relating to the three-part beat of the waltz and the four-part measure of the quickstep have been related to the floor plans and fenestrations of a Renaissance architecture.

Two basic kinds of modern architectural *rhythm* have been observed by Steen Eiler Rasmussen: one metrical and symmetrical like the military two-step, the other 'natural' and asymmetrical like the samba. He cites several architects, including Frank Lloyd Wright and Gunnar Asplund, who composed their buildings using both rhythmical variations. But it was their exploitation of a liberated architectural *rhythm*, expressed in the curves and undulations of their later work, that opened up new paths and made it possible for other architects who, like jazz musicians, extemporize more freely with rhythmical orchestration. When sensed, the rhythmical heartbeat of architecture is often described as its 'pulse'.

See also: **Breathe • Contrast • Diachronic • Modulate • Rhyme • Symmetry • Synchronic**

Robust ▐

Apart from a building's ability to survive the knocks of weather, usage and various forms of vandalism, there is another use of *robust* which has meaning in architectural design. The process from concept to construction of a building is a tortuous and challenging one: not least due to the external factors that can affect its passage. In order to insulate a design concept against such pressures, Louis Kahn talked of the 'seed' of an idea which is so strong that 'nothing can destroy it'.

Like Kahn, we therefore talk of a *robust* diagram, which can withstand the knocks of cost and programme changes — as well as the modern day procurement route. Indeed, the recent shifts in control of ownership of a design from the architect to others have made the idea of a *robust* concept fundamental to the success of an executed design.

An example of such a *robust* 'seed' of an idea can be found in Frank Lloyd Wright's Guggenheim Museum in New York, where the very notion of spiralling down through the building while passing works of art hardly needs a diagram to aid its explanation. The experience was never to be diluted by the detail.

The more recent Peckham Library by Will Alsop was born from a typically *robust* artwork by the architect himself. The idea was immediate: to raise the public library functions high above the ground on raking piloti, creating an equally public space below. Inside, timber reading room pods are suspended above the books. Clear intentions, mould-breaking ambition and impossible for the ravages of the building process to destroy.

(RR-C)

See also: **Design intent • Design genesis**

Peckham Library, London. There is a resilience between Will Alsop's preliminary painting and the finished building.

Sacred space   ∎

A *sacred space* conveys intense meaning communicated through collective memory to an individual or a group in whom it evokes an emotional response. Such a place encompasses an extended cosmological and physical context. These *sacred spaces* are defined by edges and boundaries, which exhibit surface qualities that stimulate our senses, as do the surfaces and forms of the spatial furniture articulating the infrastructure of the spaces. Lighting enhances the meaning of *sacred space* when it illuminates specific areas and plays upon receptive surfaces.

Sacred spaces may take the form of paths, expanding and contracting as they move us from one space to another in a specific direction, or spaces of rest that become focal points within a spatial sequence. Significant transitions, thresholds and entranceways exist along paths and between the spaces connecting them to other spaces or to significant elements existing within the topography or cosmos. Meaningful views, the celebration of cosmic events, the utilization of light, and access with procession through the spatial sequence are dependent upon the orientation of the spaces within the topography.

Ancient builders and contemporary architects agree that orientation is an important design determinant in the placement of *sacred space*. In recognizing the exceptional qualities inherent in *sacred spaces* of both the past and the present, astute designers have the opportunity to use them in the future, not only in the creation of *sacred space* but in the design of all meaningful space.   (MTF)

See also: *Axis mundi* • *Genius loci* • Ley lines

Sunlight floods into the Maes Howe megalithic chamber, Orkney Islands, and the interior of the Mnajdra Temple, Malta (both 3,500 BCE).

Sacrificial   ∎

The act of sacrifice is the giving up of something of value for the sake of the greater good. In archispeak terms it can be explained as follows. Once a building is written and spoken about it thus acquires a cultural dimension; it becomes a matter of architecture. The building disappears into description and discussion; it is 'sacrificed' to language, as it were. It is no longer what it used to be and often seems to have been definitely silenced.

However, there are buildings that do not disappear in what is written and discussed. They remain what they are and where they are; they themselves speak. They make clear what they represent, how their contents are activated and how they remain connected to their cultural origins.

One such building is a hunting lodge on the edge of a vast woodland area near Antonin in Poland, designed by Karl Friedrich Schinkel in 1822–24. Here, one instinctively senses to what the building refers. It proclaims its origin, its intervention in the woods, its culture and the cultivation of the site. It makes one realize that what was taken away did not disappear but, rather, was sacrificed and, admittedly in a princely manner, reactivated. The building glorifies the space cleared in the woods, the landscape, the view of the hunting ground, the hunt, and a time that seems to stand still. It is the glorification of what was and how it was — origin, intervention and sacrifice.   (HM)

See also: **Servant/served**

Karl Friedrich Schinkel's hunting lodge near Antonin, Poland.

Scale

Scale dictates a system of static proportions that strives to control variation. — Mihai Craciun

Scale refers to the proportion used in determining the relationship of a representation to that which it represents. *Scale* has meaning in architecture in two important ways: one involving the making of architecture and the other its perception. The essence of both is relationship. Architecture as built form generally requires the preparation of instructions in the form of models and drawings in a real or virtual space that accurately convey in great detail the size of, and relationship among, all the parts that comprise the work to be built. These drawings and models have precise size relationships to the completed work. They are at specific 'scales' that allow measurement of the drawings and models, which are usually much smaller than the work to be built, to be directly related to that work. Appropriately enough, the measuring device that allows this translation is called a *scale*.

The perceptual aspect of *scale* relies on the eye to do the measuring, to make a relationship. It involves making a connection between the size of what is seen and the size of something known. The known may be actually in the visual field or in one's memory. One of the most common known scalar references is the human body, as a whole or its parts. Similarly, those parts of buildings that are sized to accommodate the human body, such as doors, steps and windows, are good scalar cues. Certain building materials, especially those installed by the human hand, such as bricks and concrete masonry, are good scalar elements. Their size range is small and is controlled by what a person can comfortably handle.

Since humans try to make sense of their surroundings and to orient themselves, architects try to facilitate this, in part by providing good *scale* references and by making spaces that fit people and their activities. In other words, they try to create environments with human *scale*. The terms 'urban *scale*' and 'residential *scale*' describe architectural features that conform to the generally accepted sizes and proportions for those settings. A common criticism of many glass curtain-walled buildings and the spaces surrounding them is their paucity of recognizable *scale*-giving elements.

Sometimes scalar clues are deliberately distorted for effect. A common example is the increase in size of columns, entrances and the like to convey importance, thereby creating monumental *scale*. A false sense of depth can be created by progressively diminishing the size of a stair in all its dimensions as it recedes from the viewer. An unintended distortion that sometimes occurs in speech or writing is where '*scale*' is used when the word 'size' is more appropriate. (PDS)

See also: **Composition • Order • Proportion**

Sciagraphy

Sciagraphy is an outdated term but still holds currency among those generations who pre-date the digital revolution. The term is used to describe the geometry of shadow projection. It stems from the time when, at the end of the nineteenth century, students at the École des Beaux-Arts in Paris mastered this discipline as a central facet of their architectural studies. Making their orthographic drawings more easily understood, the projection and rendition of shade and shadows reinforces the illusion of dimensional depth, emphasizes form, and the surface quality and inclination of planes. Its conventional use in elevations and sections depicts shadows (and shade) responding to a 45 degree angle of bearing from the top left of a drawing.

Like dry-stone walling and thatching, *sciagraphy*, both as a term and a practice, has become something of an anachronism. But there are some modern exponents who are still proud to exercise this skill in hand-made orthographic drawings, especially among Japanese architects, such as Shin Takamatsu and Arato Isozaki.

See: **Convention • Depth cues**

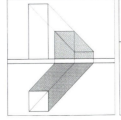 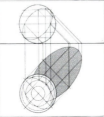

Orthographic construction of the shadow projection of a column and a sphere.

Scrim

Originating in the eighteenth century to describe an open-weave fabric for the lining of upholstery, the term *scrim* was also adopted by stage designers for a screening device that, allowing a variety of lighting effects, provides layers of space to a set design. It has been in use in the theatre for many years and may be where architects discovered it.

In architectural parlance the term is used to describe a 'second skin' membrane or 'lining' that, like a stage curtain, fronts a building façade or a wall. A *scrim* is a superimposed plane, usually delicate or translucent in nature, that provides an intermediate, transitional layer of space to extend the limits of the architectural threshold. When positioned as a secondary elevation on the outside of buildings, the *scrim* creates an ambiguous spatial zone that is neither interior nor exterior in nature.

Notable examples of the *scrim* are the black-veiled façades that peer into the vacant Manhattan site where the Twin Towers used to stand, and the free-standing glass screen fronting the main elevation of Jean Nouvel's Fondation Cartier in Paris. Framing a strip of landscape between street and façade, the screen appears as a kind of secondary and allusory elevational film that has been projected forward of the building itself. The *scrim* is also the stock in trade of the Charleston firm of Ray Huff and Mario Gooden, many of whose buildings, such as their Beach Residence at Sullivan's Island and the Degaussing Facility in Charleston Harbour, South Carolina (shown here), rely upon an additional lattice mantle to define an ambiguous spatial field that blurs the distinction between interior and exterior space.

See also: **Boundary • Edge condition • Framing (enframing) • Parameter • Threshold • Transitional space • Translucency • Zone**

Screening and cooling scrim space around Huff+Gooden Architects' Degaussing Facility in Charleston Harbour and their Beach Residence at Sullivan's Island, South Carolina.

Sculpitecture

Abstraction has abolished the boundary between architecture and sculpture, so that any work of abstract sculpture that encloses a space large enough to enter and move about in is de facto a work of architecture. — Richard Padovan

During the 1990s the work of sculptor Anthony Caro underwent a trans-formation; a shift resulting from his deep interest in the two enterprises of sculpture and architecture. Although separate disciplines, Caro sees them as sharing common aesthetic concerns and, spurred on by the notion that sculpture and architecture can be mutually nourished, he began to erode the view of sculpture as end-product, of self-contained objects that exist both in and of themselves — a condition that positions the spectator on the outside.

While sculpture can defy gravity and fly free, and architecture remains firmly rooted, Caro worked along the boundary between the two disciplines, producing large pieces occupying human scale that allow 'habitation'. These he called *sculpitecture*, i.e. sculpture functioning at the interface between the architectural space it occupies and the inner spaces it provides. The bodily action of moving around and into his work is, he suggests, the physical equivalent of what is happening when we explore visually a piece of sculpture. Caro's 'sculpitectural' pieces extend to occupy the same space as that articulated by architects; they occupy human scale space and interact both with the architecture they house and the people who engage with them. Having collaborated on architectural projects with Frank Gehry and Norman Foster, Caro's *sculpitecture* not only takes us to the frontier of the two disciplines but also hints at the possibilities when architects and sculptors begin to learn from each other.

Other sculptors who seem to strike a chord with architects from the boundary of the two disciplines include Donald Judd, James Turrell, Richard Serra, Dan Flavin and Carl Andre.

See also: **Cutting edge • Multi-sensory space • Place • Scale • Tactile**

Segment   ▮

To anyone brought up in an English public school, where private supplies of tinned fruit were about the only means of warding off scurvy, 'segments' meant mandarins, just as 'slices' meant peaches and 'halves' meant pears — and, until the 1960s, 'stoned' meant apricots. It was difficult, as well, to reconcile those bright orange triangles floating in thin syrup with the actual fruit that appeared every Christmas at home.

In architecture, segmented projects also have a particular flavour. The term traditionally meant part of an arch ('substantially less than a semi-circle', as Pevsner firmly points out) or a sphere, so that Libeskind's Imperial War Museum-North which is based on a divided and reconsti-tuted sphere, could be formally described as a segmented building. But the term can also be used in a metaphorical sense, for projects that assemble units together in giant clusters, such as Soleri's Noahbabel arcology or Buckminster Fuller's Tetrahedronal city. The hives that

Segmented spiral
from a student
design for a walk-up
Museum of the
Twentieth Century.

Archigram planned to plug us into could also be so described. And, like the mandarins, such segmented projects need a supporting medium of ideology to stay afloat and become palatable. (CLM)

See also: **Crystalline** • **Fragment** • **Shard**

Semiology

The science of signs, architectural *semiology* equates the rules and structure of language with architecture. Popular in the 1980s among academics, a few star architects and a host of mediocre imitators, it became the theoretical basis for the post-modern architectural style. Unfortunately, it resulted in a host of cheap 'decorated sheds' appearing, not just on the landscape but also in the architectural press. As part of the larger Structuralist movement in literary criticism, architecture is described in terms of signifiers, signs, semantics, syntax, etc. Design inspiration comes from investigations into the formal structure of language. E. E. Cummings, James Joyce, Lewis Carroll's 'Alice' and others, somehow directed designers to create 'texts' and 'subtexts' within their architecture. Unfortunately, these texts could only be read by a very small group of academics and other insiders. On the whole, buildings remained mute and are now devalued as narrative consumer items. Ironically, it is a continuation of the critique of the poverty of Modernism and Functionalism started by Robert Venturi in the 1960s. For a short time Charles Jencks, Charles Moore, Geoffrey Broadbent, Umbert Eco and others attempted to make the *Semiology* movement legitimate. (EO)

See also: **Narrative** • **Sign** • **Symbolism**

Serendipity

The original meaning of the term *serendipity* has changed over time. The *Oxford English Dictionary* defines *serendipity* as 'the faculty of making happy and unexpected discoveries by accident', whereas Horace Walpole, who first coined the word in 1754, provides a definition using a different etymological root. His definition of *serendipity* as 'a gift for discovery by accident and sagacity while in pursuit of something else' is closer to the aphorism: 'chance favours the prepared observer'.

Horace Walpole (1717–97), the fourth Earl of Orford and son of Prime Minister Robert Walpole, first wrote the word *serendipity* in a letter describing the safe passage of a portrait of Bianco Capello, a sixteenth-century Duchess of Tuscany. Walpole derived the word from an oriental fairy story entitled *The Three Princes of Serendip* who 'were always making discoveries, by accident and sagacity, of things which they were not in quest of'. *The Three Princes of Serendip* ('Serendip' refers to modern day Sri Lanka) was translated from Persian and published in Venice in 1557 by the printer Michele Tramezzino. The story has been the source of many translations and derivatives that have attempted to link the island of Serendip to its meaning. For example, John Barth in his *The Last Voyage of Someone the Sailor* (1991) writes: 'You don't reach Serendip by plotting a course for it. You have to set out in good faith for elsewhere and lose your bearings serendipitously.'

Many important discoveries, such as the accidental discovery of America and penicillin, have been made while in pursuit of other things. Similarly, *serendipity* can also be of value in architectural design. When design is truly innovative, *serendipity* can be nurtured by taking a disinterested point of view during the design process, allowing seemingly peripheral or circuitous events to influence the outcome. Equally, design education should encourage students to practise acts of creative disorientation so that they may be prepared to exploit the virtues of a serendipitous world.   (SB)

See also: Dada • *Dérive* • Surrealism

Serial vision   ■

Our perceived experience of interior and exterior architectural space is primarily a sensual event involving movement — for to pass through an environment is to cause a kaleidoscope of changing sensations — of transitions between one spatial impression and the next. Each experience affects the orchestrated functioning of our senses in a variety of ways — our eyes, ears, nose and skin registering changing stimuli which trigger a flood of brain responses on all levels.

As part of this multi-sensory dynamic, each body, neck and eye movement sets the visual environment in motion. We can look up, down and sideways, and collect information even at the periphery of our field of vision; we can adjust by focusing on points in the far distance and points near at hand. This sequencing of an unfolding spatial experience is known as *serial vision*. Architects, such as Le Corbusier, Frank Lloyd Wright, Steven Holl, Richard Meier and Rem Koolhaas, liken the dynamic of sequential visual perception to a cinematic unfolding of space and, indeed, anticipate this in their design approaches. Gordon Cullen discusses *serial vision* in terms of walking from one end of a street to another at a uniform pace; progress of travel providing a sequence of visual revelations — the impact on the eye of sudden contrasts caused by small deviations and formal misalignments in the nature of a shifting space, causing disproportionate effects in the third dimension. In their *Body, Memory and Architecture* (1977), Kent C. Bloomer and Charles W. Moore refer to the difference between the route one's body takes and the eye's capacity to take in the route in 'larger leaps', explore alternative pathways, or even take it in all at once.

The graphical recording of the unfolding spatial experience in both built and un-built environments is known as 'serial drawing'.

See also: **Animate** • **Multi-sensory perception** • **Picturesque** • *Promenade architecturale* • **Storyboard** • **Visual field**

'Stills' from a series predicting the construction sequence of Daniel Libeskind's proposed Boiler House addition to London's V&A Museum.

▌ Servant/served

**The seminal idea of my work is the constant distinction between the
areas that are served and the areas that serve. And that distinguishes,
in my opinion, modern architecture from old architecture.**
— Louis Kahn

The idea that the functions and spaces of support (the *servant* spaces) that
are necessary but subordinate to the primary spaces of a building (the
served spaces) should have their own distinct expression originated with
Louis Kahn and was first realized in his Yale Art Gallery in 1951. The idea
grew out of Kahn's interest in geometric order and the rational expression
of structure: 'The spaces defined by the members of a structure are as
important as the members. These spaces range in scale from the voids of
an insulation panel, voids of air, lighting and heat to circulate, to spaces
big enough to walk through or live in . . . I believe that in architecture, as in
all art, the artist instinctively keeps the marks which reveal how a thing is
done . . . Structures should be devised which can harbour the mechanical
needs of rooms and spaces . . . It would follow that pasting over the construction, of lighting and acoustical material, the burying of tortured,
unwanted ducts, conduits, and pipe lines would become intolerable'
('Toward a Plan for Midtown Philadelphia', 1953). 'I do not like ducts; I do
not like pipes. I hate them really thoroughly, but because I hate them so
thoroughly, I feel that they have to be given their place. If I just hated them
and took no care, I think they would invade the building and completely
destroy it' ('Order in Architecture', 1957).

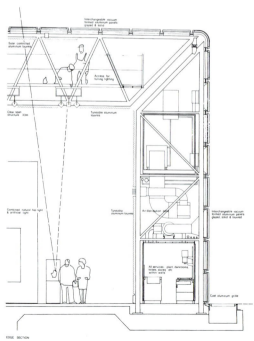

Detail of Foster and
Partners' servant wall
at the Sainsbury
Centre for Visual Arts
in East Anglia, which
serves the needs of
its interior space.

In *Studies in Tectonic Culture* (1995), Kenneth Frampton writes: 'It is hard to overestimate the radical nature of this concern, for prior to Kahn's formulation of the theoretical opposition of "servant and served", contemporary architecture has failed to address the problems posed by the increase in the amount of services being installed in buildings in the second half of the twentieth century.' Writing in his *Deconstructing the Kimball* (1991), Michael Benedikt reinforces the importance of the concept: 'Universal, redirecting, opening up new opportunities . . . It influenced the work of a generation of architects, from Paul Rudolph to Richard Rogers, and continues to do so in smaller ways today in every building that exposes, collects, or gives room and good form to its "services".'

The order created by the *servant/served* concept not only contributes to the poetic appreciation of a building but also adds to the order and understanding of the construction process, thus encouraging the co-operation of the building trades in creating a successful project. The importance of the concept is likely to continue as the complexity and space required for building services expands, and as budgets and environmental constraints become more demanding.   (PDS)

See also: **Kit of parts • Serviced shed**

Serviced shed   ▌

The *serviced shed* is a minimal, industrialized building type with an envelope that provides maximum internal volume, while support systems and functions are localized, usually within the cavities of lightweight lattice steel walls, floors and ceilings. The clear demarcation between functional space and service systems directly responds to Louis Kahn's servant/served principle to provide a subdivisible open interior space ideal for indoor sports, factory production and the display of art.

The *serviced shed* is made feasible by the process of industrial standardization, mass production and a modular design technology that was formerly pioneered by Charles and Ray Eames and was rehearsed in car, aircraft and aerospace production techniques. This represents a vast untapped potential for design exploration. To date, the 'decorated shed' has not yet emerged from the *serviced shed*.

See: **Decorated shed • Kit of parts • Module • Servant/served • Typology**

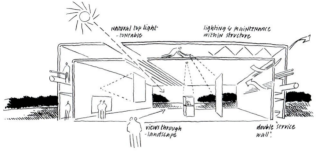

Norman Foster's sketch of the Sainsbury Centre for Visual Arts showing the relationship of service wall to the shed.

Shard

Derived from 'potsherd' — a broken piece of ceramic material — *shard* refers to a broken fragment of pottery or glass. Its architectural usage stems from countless student projects, which, especially in the early 1990s and inspired by Zaha Hadid's more splintered Cubism and in a spirit of organized chaos, assemble design proposals using jagged, dart-shaped forms with fiercely tapered and pointed curved planes. One classic monument to the broken fragment is Renzo Piano's towering *shard* of glass proposal for the 66-storey London Bridge Tower at Southwark. There is also Lebbeus Woods' 'Shard Houses' project, i.e. a proposal for residential towers built on pilings in San Francisco Bay and assembled from locally scavenged *shard*s of industrial off-cuts.

Perhaps the 'daddy' of all *shard* prototypes is Daniel Libeskind's 'plate-smashing' Imperial War Museum-North in Trafford, Manchester. Derived from the notion of the reassembly of three fragments of the earth's crust to metaphor 'a world shattered by conflict', its three main *shard* pieces represent conflict on land, in the air and on the sea. However, relationships between the three interlocking fragments and the site are mathematically and geometrically rooted. For instance, representing a segment of the globe, the domed curves of the *earth shard* find their fictive centres deep in the earth and at the north pole, while the edges of the vertical *air shard* are aligned to a notional line connecting north and south poles.

See also: **Crystalline • Fragment**

Fragmented, *shard*-like planes forming Zaha Hadid's detail of a movement sequence from her Kurfürstendamm 70 project, Berlin, 1986.

Shear

Shear is the action of opposing tangential forces. Tangential forces are ones that act parallel to the surfaces upon which they act, rather than perpendicular. *Shear* occurs in most nailed, bolted and welded connections. It always occurs as two pairs of opposing forces, called couples. If shearing forces act upon vertical planes, the requirements of static equilibrium ensure that equal forces act upon the accompanying horizontal planes. The figure shown below illustrates typical shearing forces in a simple beam. Note that horizontal shear can be a major concern in timber beams because of the presence of grain that causes weakness along the horizontal planes.

Frank Lloyd Wright used the term in a metaphorical sense to explain the difference between an integrated, organic, or interlocking design as opposed to one in which superficial elements, such as decoration, can be 'sheared' away without damage to the basic design. *Shear* can also be a design move that mimics the slippage and distortion that result from an earthquake. In this sense, the term appears in the early writings of Peter Eisenman to describe the structural 'slippage' when two layered volumes appear to slide in opposite directions. The expression of this conflicting force splits a façade into a dual condition: a simultaneous cloaking and exposure of external and internal volume.   (RS)

See also: **Dualism • Tension**

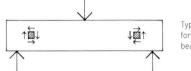

Typical shearing forces in a simple beam.

Sign

Signs represent a non-verbal communication system that operates outside spoken language. A *sign* is arbitrary in nature. A language of signs possibly evolved from the ideograms and pictograms of early writing which, in turn, developed out of the primitive grunts of prehistoric speech, descriptive gestures and associated mark-making. However, although functioning as a language, a *sign*, unlike verbal communication, cannot always be referred back to an interpretative code. Linguist Ferdinand de Saussure and semi-ologists Charles Sanders Pierce and Roland Barthes show that signs can be categorized into three types: 'icon', 'index' and 'symbol'.

An 'icon' is an image or diagram in which meaning is imparted through likeness or resemblance. Therefore, a drawing of a building is recognized by its similarity to our knowledge of the architecture it portrays; a diagram, such as a clock face, a ground plan or a Cartesian grid provide a schema on which events are organized or played out.

An 'index' is a *sign* by virtue of an existential link between itself and its object. For instance, a weather-vane signifies the direction of the wind; the north point infers the compass points, and still photographs appear as paper-thin versions of the objects they represent.

The third category of *sign* is 'symbol'. The symbol is a *sign* that demands neither resemblance nor any existential link with its object of its meaning. Symbols include the Christian cross, the hammer and sickle, the scales of justice and, indeed, verbal language, which, in itself, is a symbolic sound system.

Whether it be icon, index or symbol, the form of a *sign* is termed the 'signifier'; the corresponding concept triggered in its interpretation is called the 'signified'.

See also: **Diagram • Icon(ic) • Semiology • Symbolism**

Sight lines

Sight lines are clear, unimpeded and direct channels of vision between two points connecting an observer with an object or event in view. *Sight lines* are crucial in the design of spaces where public performance or ceremony take place. Anyone who has had the misfortune of sitting behind a column in a cathedral or in the auditorium of one of those old Victorian theatres will have experienced the visual exclusion caused by intrusion in the line of sight.

Visual access often follows lines of axis — *sight lines* from points within a building interior kept open and unobstructed so that a clear line of vision is aimed, framed and maintained from foreground through middleground to a targeted focal point in the distance. Architecture is riddled with intentional and accidental lines of sight, which, like holes in Swiss cheese, cut through individual buildings or bore through urban density. When the axes of these visual pathways are crossed, unexpected vistas explode into view; when followed, they disclose destination.

City *sight lines* function as an aide-mémoire to orientation and endorse the all-important sense of place. For example, from its avenues, the cross streets of Manhattan provide intermittent visual contact with its defining rivers. As in the planning of many major cities, the sites of monuments and important buildings in Paris have the patterns of their *sight lines* carved back into the urban footprint. For instance, the Grande Arche de la Défense in the west Parisian business district is connected to the Louvre in the east by a strict line of sight known as the 'Axe Historique', and the development of the French dormitory new towns, such as Cergy Pontoise and Créteil, are sited on the horizon so that, albeit distant, visual contact with home is maintained by commuters from the heart of the capital.

A powerful example of *sight line* control occurs on the bridged approach to Mario Botta's 'Birdcage House' in Ticino, Italy. The bridge functions like a gun barrel, its sighting device being a framed aperture in the building mass through which a precise view is aimed at an edifice several kilometres away on the opposite bank of Lake Lugano.

See also: **Axis • Framing (enframing) • Ley lines • Linearity • Place • Serial vision • Tension • Visual field**

Simulacrum

If we allow magazine photos or screen images to replace experience, our ability to perceive architecture will diminish so greatly that it will become impossible to comprehend it. — Steven Holl

Simulacrum is an image of something, a shadowy likeness, a deceptive substitute, an effigy. The term describes the extreme post-modernist conclusion advanced by the French sociologist Jean Baudrillard, who, in the early 1970s, proposed that the representational image has historically passed through a series of phases from that of reflecting a basic reality to one of bearing no relationship to any reality whatsoever. Baudrillard further suggests that our reality has corrupted into a virtual adaptation of itself, i.e. a simulated culture of the real in which the image itself generates a new reality. *Simulacrum*, therefore, describes this separate world in which the imaginary duplicates reality. In *The Anaesthetics of Architecture* (1999), Neil Leach describes this world in terms of advertising in which the term 'real' has been commandeered by global companies. This is the make-believe world of the 'real thing', '. . . of industrially manufactured "natural" ingredients', where the concept of "authenticity" '. . . becomes a suspect, counterfeit currency'.

This is the condition for which the term 'hyperreality' came to the fore in the late 1980s, i.e. a sense of living not in a world of work and corporeal objects but in a world of consumption, of hype and a sea of media images, of shifting surfaces and styles, a world where the real has dissolved into a place were all is *simulacrum*. If *simulacrum* is arrived at when the boundary between representation and the reality to which it refers becomes blurred, then it occurs when we immerse ourselves in a movie and, indeed, in digital flythroughs and walkthroughs.

In 1897 in Nashville, Tennessee, a temporary, full-sized plaster replica of the Parthenon was built to bolster the city's nickname of the 'Athens of the South'. Owing to its enduring popularity, the plaster version remained for four years until 1931 when it became replicated by a more durable concrete version. This copy of a copy of the original represents a *simulacrum*.

See also: **Hyperrealism • Pictorial space • Sign • Symbolism • Virtual reality**

Athens of the South. Concrete copy of a plaster replica of the marble Athenian Parthenon in Nashville, Tennessee.

Site appraisal   ∎

Also known as '*site analysis*', the site appraisal is often the first tangible piece of information produced at the onset of the design process. Not only does it represent an analysis of the context for a building proposal, but it also provides a major stimulus for initial thoughts on the development of the architectural form. Therefore, in providing both constraints and opportunities, the nature and characteristics of the site and its existing

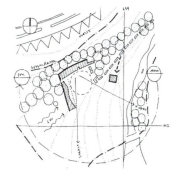

Diagrammatic study of hard and soft site data.

topography (in conjunction with an analysis and interpretation of the brief) can have a profound effect on the shaping of initial ideas.

The facts about a site will include both hard and soft data. Hard data studies local, non-negotiable issues, such as climate, dimensions, boundaries, topology, existing buildings, existing links; soft data studies broader, more subjective, contextual issues, such as sensory, cultural and human aspects, plus site origin, site history and its current significance.

The main function of the *site appraisal* is to filter collected data in order to distil those bits of information that hold direct relevance to the design and positioning of the building form.

See also: **Context** • **Diagramming** • **Filter** • **Mapping** • **Site specific** • **Topology**

Site specific

Architecture is bound to situation. Unlike music, painting, sculpture, film, and literature, a construction (non-mobile) is intertwined with the experience of place. — Steve Holl

Compared with art, music and literature, which can be staged in different locations, architecture is rooted to the place of its setting. Its realization embodies a 'sense of place' that is inextricably tied to the nature of its site. When a building appears to physically engage its setting in such a way that you cannot imagine one without the other, this is termed *site specific*. However, site specificity does not mean that the building 'disappears' but, rather than set itself apart by being raised on Le Corbusier's pilotis or ignoring the setting entirely by 'turning its back', it is an ensemble sensitive to its surroundings in terms of scale, orientation, form and materials — including recognition of a memory of the site itself.

Writing in his *Mind and Image* (1976), Herb Greene describes the human need to relate architecture to its setting as ultimately stemming from a recognition of ecological relationships and the fact that our evolution depends upon co-operation. This co-operation takes two forms: physical co-operation and conservation, both essential for survival; and symbolic co-operation, which reflects valued archetypes in our understanding of links between the man-made and the natural environment. In this latter relationship, symbolic features of a building can invoke historic associations with past occupancy or events.

Prototype buildings, such as American fast food restaurants, are often designed using a process that begins with a stock plan from headquarters that is then adapted by a local architect to be *site specific*.

See also: **Context** • **Engage** (*dégagements*)

Skin

The building skin is the essential expression of most architecture, whether wrapped tightly around the structural form, or inflated to produce a bubble container, or deeply modelled as it contrives to provide an envelope for complex interior organization.
— Michael Wigginton

Like 'skeleton' and 'façade', the term *skin* draws from an architectural vocabulary that draws from the human body-building analogy. Generally speaking, *skin* refers to the outer layer of a building. This is the external cloaking of all the layers of the building envelope that covers roof, walls and underside. Functioning as a separating membrane, external *skin* is the interface between inside and outside. However, another membrane made its appearance when buildings acquired an 'interior *skin*' — a covering of painted linen or wooden panelling applied to prevent visual and physical contact with the crudity of the hitherto internally exposed structure. A *skin* of plasterwork later became traditional in the eighteenth century to provide a washable sealant and to coincide with a developing awareness of health and hygiene.

Writing in *Companion to Contemporary Architectural Thought* (1993), Michael Wigginton has compared inadequacies in the development of the building envelope with the biological interface between the human body and its environment, i.e. the eye and epidermis. He describes the eye as a self-cleaning, lubricated device capable of contracting and dilating in response to changing light levels while fitted with a shutter that can shut down when not in use. He describes epidermis as a self-healing, water-proof and flexible membrane with a porosity that allows cooling and an insulation that keeps its internal working parts to a constant temperature. By contrast, the *skin* of modern buildings is crude and inefficient but, he concludes, the dawn of new technologies begins to pave the way for intel-ligent systems that will allow the *skin* of a building to similarly respond to exterior conditions.

A recent history of external architectural *skin* shows alternating cycles of materialization and evanescence. For instance, a Modernist white paint and reflective glass sought to ephemeralize and dissolve the outer appearance of façades. The more recent return to a positive expression of *skin* reappear in the colour-changing and image-impregnated claddings of Herzog & de Meuron, but only to be dematerialized again in the plasma-screened elevations in the cross streets around Manhattan's Times Square and in the mist of Diller & Scofiddio's 'The Cloud' building in Switzerland (see page 71).

See also: **Envelope** • **Interface**

Smart materials   ▌

Nature is smart — are we smart enough to learn its lessons?
— Julian Vincent

Inseparable from the concept of 'intelligent buildings', the term *smart materials* has been around for some years. Much of the inspiration for this evolving technology draws from nature. For instance, while antler bone is tougher than any man-made ceramic, the humble spider's web — apart from being the beautifully delicate product of incredibly lightweight engi-neering — can withstand the force of a fly travelling at around a metre per second by using small springs oiled by the morning dew. Similarly, in the building industry, materials are designated 'smart' when they interact with their environments and respond to change in controlled ways. For example, the expanding and contracting NASA-developed 'muscle wire' can enable the building envelope to automatically open and close in response to external conditions. Developments in nanotechnology will allow walls to transform from opaque to translucent to transparent or to change colour on command. Using fibre optic technology, windows will transmit light and switch off the lights when there is plenty of light in the sky.

Writing in *Lightness* (1999), Julian Vincent describes the ultimate *smart materials* as those which can design themselves. For example, a smart structure is one that will itself not only detect overload (which is within technological means) but will also automatically compensate through deformation, i.e. by changing shape or by adding material. There is a membrane in development that will soften and change shape as a function of the geometry of its enclosure, and then stiffen again. Based upon studies of strain detectors in insects, an aircraft fuselage is currently being developed that can change its shape and thickness in response to its flying speed in order to reduce vibration and increase passenger comfort. There is also in development a self-repairing concrete in which, should fractures occur, embedded capsules cause a reinforcing material to be released. However, so that the load-bearing properties of a material are not compromised, Vincent suggests that such additives for change should be exclusive of the material. Then, he concludes, 'we have a truly adaptive architecture'.

See also: **Cutting edge**

▌ Space adjacency

Space adjacency is to do with the affinities between areas and rooms in built environments. This refers to the need for spaces in buildings to be proximate to one another because of the ways occupants use the environment.

Space adjacency requirements are defined with the client during the project brief or programming phase, before designing begins. Then these requirements serve as building planning guidelines in physically positioning spaces in the proposed scheme.

Space adjacency analysis addresses three aspects of space-to-space affinities: the relative importance or priority of achieving proximity between particular rooms in the design; physical configurations that will achieve the desired relationships between the spaces; and reasons why rooms need to be near each other. *Space adjacency* analysis also addresses aversion between building areas, that is, situations where spaces should be separated.

Affinities between environmental components of any scale can be studied with *space adjacency* analysis: furniture, areas within a room, spaces, space clusters, departments, functional zones, floor levels, buildings, campuses, and even neighbourhoods, towns and regions.

The matrix is a graphic tool employed to study *space adjacency* requirements during project programming. The matrix grid facilitates systematic decisions about affinities between any single room and all other rooms in the building.   (ETW)

See also: **Diagramming** • **Grid** • **Juxtaposition** • **Matrix** • **Methodology**

Spatiality   ▌

Spatiality refers to our mental perception of space; it is a construct rather than an entity. *Spatiality* refers to the perceived characteristics of space: the void, the nothingness, the 'in between' that when brought into existence and given shape by the solids that define its limits becomes invested with its own apparent qualities. *Spatiality* also characterizes the feeling experienced kinaesthetically in space, the status of existing in the third dimension.

Writing in *Architectural Design and Research* (2000), Rein Saariste identifies spatial form and dynamic as the two key aspects of *spatiality*. Spatial form is primarily sensed through three kinds of axes. Firstly, there is the 'situation axis' that runs through an object in view and on to the horizon. Secondly, the 'system axis' is one around which objects are grouped or one running through closed centres. Thirdly, there is the 'spatial axis' in which *spatiality* is distinguished by a short and long axis in enclosed volume — the long axis making connection with other spaces while also being the carrier of its dynamic.

Saariste subdivides spatial dynamic into tension and transparency. Spatial tension is aroused through contrast: contrast between open and closed, small and large, dark and light, and inside and outside. Meanwhile, spatial transparency can be actual, i.e. in terms of routes or vistas, or assumed, such as when a building gives the impression of being transparent.

When discussing *spatiality* in his *Elements of Architecture* (1990), Pierre von Meiss uses the analogy of radiance. Radiance is a consequence of the presence of matter. Mainly referring to free-standing objects in open space and façade fronts, he describes objects as not only emitting their own spatial requirements but also acting as mediator between the observer and surrounding space. However, although not an exact science, the characteristics of *spatiality* are generated by its defining planes and forms.

See also: **Breathe** • **Multi-sensory space**

Stasis   ▌

The death rate is one per person. — George Valliant

Stasis is the state of coming to rest — at the end of the day, at the conclusion of a journey or a narrative. *Stasis* is the state of equilibrium and repose, the result of a static balance between opposing forces — a type of détente. A single frame in a roll of movie film represents a moment of *stasis*, as an objective sketch freezes a moment in the dynamic of our perception. In medicine, *stasis* refers to the stopping of the normal flow of bodily fluids, typically blood. Structural engineering is about the creation of *stasis*. The dynamic of architecture is driven by the tension between *stasis* and movement. Architectural *stasis* can also refer to the compromise or resolution of conflicting agendas, such as budget and client desires. The ultimate *stasis*, one supposes, is the stillness of death.

See also: **Balance** • **Tension**

Storyboard

When walking around a building, a sequence of aspects can be distinguished, each reflecting a characteristic image. Thus a 'comic strip' emerges, composed of a series of various associations.
— Karel Vollers

The *storyboard* is a visual storytelling format with roots in the comic strip frame and the movie *storyboard*. It is employed 'stop-frame' fashion when the designer wishes to sequentially set out his or her ideas or to take the viewer on a conceptual journey around, towards or through a building design. Usually shown as perspectives, serial drawings can also incorporate a whole variety of drawing types in a frame-by-frame account of time and movement through the space of a design. Other widespread functions of the *storyboard* format include the diagrammatic assembly stages of construction details or structural components, serial photographs taken from a physical model or views generated from a computer model and even the demonstration of predicted phased stages in the on-site construction of a building design (see page 165).

The fragmented nature of the *storyboard* makes it a popular presentation device for communicating movement and change in time and space. When incorporated into presentation layouts it is often superimposed to 'float' above larger drawings, or to appear as a linear component to create a compositional 'plinth' along the bottom of display boards.

The first ever movie *storyboard*, part of which is shown here, was created in 1921–22 by the Hungarian artist Lázló Moholy-Nagy for an unmade film entitled *Dynamic of the Metropolis*. He simply transposed the technique of photomontage to create a design tool for the cinematic medium.

See also: **Composition • Fragment • Narrative • Serial vision • Time line**

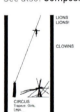 

Frames drawn from the first ever movie *storyboard* designed in 1921–22 by Lázló Moholy-Nagy.

Strip

My kingdom for a Big Mac. — Stephen Friedman.

Along the American commercial *strip* one finds pizza rather than piazza, burgers rather than boulevards, logos rather than landmarks, and neon rather than nodes. Framed by the windshield and animated by the accelerator pedal, the *strip*, while being the brunt of critics, has provided a rich source of inspiration and has spawned countless student projects. While its banal sameness was satirized in Valdimir Nabokov's *Lolita* (1959), one of its champions, Robert Venturi, eulogized the symbolism of the *strip* in his *Learning From Las Vegas* (1972).

He argues for an architecture of the 'decorated shed', and portrays the ugly and ordinary design of the *strip* as a more legitimate vernacular form for our time than the monumental symbols of classic modernism. He also argues that the choice for inspiration for design should be Disneyland, a popular lifestyle and a 'vital mess'. For Venturi, the Las Vegas *strip* serves as a positive example of urban forms that somehow fit the way some people today lead their lives. However, although romanticized in the movie *American Graffiti*, many Americans see the *strip* as visual pollution. Indeed, the alternative view of the *strip* mall is one of an urban and suburban blight on the American city.

However, for those who do not live near one, the American *strip* can, to paraphrase Herb Greene, be seen as a kind of Technicolor dream world of images rendered in plastic and set adrift in a sea of parking lots. Enlisting the sham façade and the sign, its buildings cheap and careless, the allusions are usually superficial and the user feels that he or she is being processed along with the hamburger.

See also: **Context** • **Decorated shed** • **Sign**

Superimpose

Superimpose is another term for 'layering', that is, the overlaying of one object or plane on another. Through the overlapped association of disparate elements (as in the technique of collage), the act of superimposition can cause a new consideration, and open the door to surprise and revelation.

The experience of an architectural superimposition involving opaque, transparent and translucent materials, creates diffusion, overlap, penetration and parallax — bodily movement causing these impressions to animate into a kaleidoscope of experience. A fascination with the visual side-effects of superimposed geometric nets causing degrees of filtered transparency and an optical interference known as '*moiré*', is exemplified in the work of many artists and architects.

Superimposition is a key device in the Deconstructivist blurring of boundaries between film, literature and architecture, and their challenge of a single unified set of images and the idea of an identifiable language. Borrowed from film theory and the concept of montage, the repudiation of hierarchy in the work of, for example, Bernard Tschumi and Peter Eisenman, led to a fascination with a complexity resulting from a fragmentation and distortion.

The successive stages of development in landscape and city are conceived as separate layers that become superimposed over time: the more the layers the greater the complexity of the context. Layering is also a common design tool. For example, Bernard Tschumi's basic design approach for the Parc de la Villette was to design in three distinct and gridded layers to create a superimposed system of lines, surfaces, and points.

See also: **Fragment** • **Juxtapose** • **Layering** • *Moiré* • **Montage** • **Synthesis**

Suprematism

Suprematism is the art movement that has launched a thousand design projects. *Suprematism* was the visionary forerunner to Constructivism, but it was also its counterpart. Proclaimed in Russia in 1915 in his 'Suprematist Manifesto', Kazimir Malevitch announced the arrival of a new and non-objective art and himself as its inventor. Using black and coloured geometric forms apparently hovering and flying in white, limitless space, he claimed to have created an abstract language liberated from nature. This was an abstract language that would become the trademark of the Constructivists who later applied it to industrial and architectural design.

   The *Suprematist* flagship is Malevitch's 'Black Square'. Painted in 1915, this depicts a black square emblazoned on a white background — an image that became his symbol of artistic revolution. For him it illustrated 'the first step of pure creation in art' and represented form as occupying 'universal space'. His concept of painted and gravity-defying abstract forms continued into the mid-1920s when he turned to its three-dimensional expression, making white plaster cubic models called 'arkitektons'. These depicted his utopian vision of a weightless technology — the zero gravity space formerly exhibited in his paintings now being applied to his 'new world' dream of a truly revolutionary architecture.

   Marginalized at the time by Stalin, Malevitch's legacy came to profoundly influence basic design teaching both in Russia and the German Bauhaus. Indeed, the enormous impact of his vision continues to permeate the world of design. For instance, Zaha Hadid's early student projects and later projects often make direct and indirect references to the 'arkitektons'. Her design for 'The Great Utopia' exhibition of Russian *Suprematism* and Constructivism at New York's Guggenheim Museum in 1992, in which she built a habitable version of Malevitch's 'arkitekton', reflects her tribute to a movement that has been so influential.

See also: *Avant-garde* • **Constructivism** • **Futurism** • **Modernism**

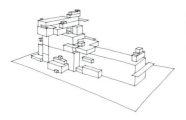

One of Kazimir Malevitch's 'arkitektons' made in 1923.

Surrealism

Founded in 1922 by André Breton with the aim of liberating the unconscious, *Surrealism* was a literary and artistic movement formed from surviving members of the Dadaist movement. Its aim was to emancipate the process of thinking from any preoccupation with reason and taste. In the attempt to create original and provocative confrontations and enlisting the montage tactic of 'shock', they sought the most unusual subject matter in the most unlikely places. One branch of *Surrealism*, epitomized

in the work of Marcel Duchamp, employed *objet trouvé* (found objects)
to establish serendipitous relationships of pure fantasy, while another,
exemplified in the paintings of René Magritee and Salvador Dali, reconstructed dreamscapes and puzzle-pictures in a Superrealist manner.

The architectural branch of *Surrealism* is irrational, metaphorical, yet
figurative. Much of this involved fantastic landscapes, with an ancestry seen
in the engravings of Piranesi and in the paintings of Hieronymous Bosch.
While Max Ernst made drawings and frottages of imaginery cities,
Salvador Dali painted all manner of unexpected buildings, even created his
own and, for a time, was hired as an 'imagineer' by the Disney Corporation.
The architect whom the Surrealists saw as one of their important predecessors was the visionary Claude-Nicholas Ledoux. But there is a proto-
surrealist strand that connects the designs of Art Nouveau architect Hector
Grimaud, through Antonio Gaudí and Marcel Duchamp (who invented
a door that was simultaneously open and closed) to the advocate of a
non-utilitarian 'absolute architecture', Bruce Goff.

See also: **Dada • Serendipity • Sign**

Sustainability   █

Sustainability is one of the most important and valuable concepts to enter
architectural thinking in the 1990s. Unfortunately, this term has been used
to describe such a broad range of ideas and objectives that it seems to
now retain little meaning. Misunderstanding and misuse are rife. This is
unacceptable as the consequences of trivializing *sustainability* are dire.

A succinct and useful definition of *sustainability* is that developed by the
Bruntland Commission, paraphrased as follows: meeting today's needs
without compromising the ability of future generations to meet their
needs. This definition suggests that we are stewards of resources (not
owners) and should be accountable for the long-term and long-distance
effects of our decisions and actions. Further, *sustainability* implies using,
but not depleting or hopelessly degrading, resources that are of limited
availability. Even further, *sustainability* implies a sorting of needs from wants.

Sustainability is a BIG concept; it is a society-wide long-term concern,
not simply an architectural buzzword. It is highly unlikely that a single
building can be designed to be truly 'sustainable'; the accounting of
resources consumed versus those left for future use is unfavourable.
Architecture alone cannot provide *sustainability*. On the other hand, society
cannot achieve *sustainability* without the active participation of architecture and related disciplines — buildings consume too many resources
to be ignored. Thus enter associated concepts such as energy-efficient,
passive, green or even regenerative design. These are steps on the road
to *sustainability*.   (WG)

See also: **Arcology • Ecological footprint • Energy efficiency**

Symbiotic

Symbiotic is the mutually beneficial relationship between different organisms, ideas and communities. The theory of 'symbiogenesis' developed by molecular biologist Lyn Margulis proposes the creation of new forms through permanent *symbiotic* arrangements as the primary means of evolution for all higher organisms. In some cases, two entities will merge and evolve into a more complex design. As described by Margulis: 'Here then is an evolutionary mechanism more sudden than selective mutation: a *symbiotic* alliance that becomes permanent.'

In architecture, symbiosis is a process of combining dissimilar elements that assist one another to create a more meaningful whole. A building and its location may have a *symbiotic* relationship that establishes a particular ordering system. For example, the edge of a building adapts through design. It may be sheltering, porous or diaphanous in relation to its interior requirements and exterior setting. It's like a trellis and grape vine that take part in an architectural symbiosis which evolves into a shaded arbour.

In urban design, differing uses can be combined to create a more evolved urban environment. Hybrid buildings, such as Adler and Sullivan's Auditorium in Chicago, are examples of different building types that are merged into one structure. The 'act of combining' generates new patterns of architectural design and discourse. Symbiosis even occurs in the humble suburban shopping mall where large box anchor stores sustain the existence of smaller boutique style shops. Also, these malls work best if there are several similar shops in a cluster — especially if they sell women's shoes. It's rather like the fast food outlets that spring up next to college campuses.   (CH)

See also: **Composition • Juxtaposition • Transprogramming**

Symbiotic vine-arbour entanglement and *symbiotic* gender fusion in a Branson Coates photomontage for their Body Zone installation in the Millennium Dome.

Symbolism

Flourishing around the turn of the twentieth century, *Symbolism* became an influential movement in the development of later theories of abstraction and surrealism in art, while in literature it became an important precursor of Modernism. It refers to the use of symbols to represent concepts and ideas. To do so, objectivity and direct representation is discarded in favour of the subjective and a synthesis of the many different facets of the reality we understand. Suggesting ideas by means of ambiguous yet powerful symbols, the movement combined a fascination for the mystical, the sensual and the primitive.

By questioning our stereotypes, *Symbolism* mediates between the realm of the consciously understandable and the realm of the unconscious; it is a mediator between the visible and the invisible. But this connection can also work in reverse, i.e. when the viewer projects symbolic meaning back on to what he or she perceives. For instance, when looking at works of art we are constantly faced with the questions: 'What does it all mean? and 'What is the hidden agenda in this work?'. This often indefinable capacity of a picture or a sculpture to make a statement is characterized by the term 'symbolic content'.

The issue of symbolic content in an architectural context is touched on by Richard Weston when, writing in *Building Design*, he describes the tendency of people to invent meanings as a way of coming to terms with, of 'domesticating', unusual built form. This famously happened with Jorn Utzon's Sydney Opera House in Australia. Although the architect had not consciously intended to evoke yacht sails in the massing of his building, the association is so apt that it was bound to stick. Weston also describes the symbolic expression of national feelings of strength and resistance as expressed in the granite bedrock of land masses like Scandinavia and Scotland.

See also: **Analogue • Branding (naming) • Metaphor • Sign**

Symmetry

Symmetry refers to an exact correspondence of form and constituent configuration on opposite sides of a dividing line or plane or about an axis. The most well-known early example of a discussion of *symmetry* in architecture occurs in *The Ten Books of Architecture*, written by Viruivius in about 70 BCE. He used the term *symmetry* to describe the relationship of the whole to its parts to each other and to some module. According to Richard Padovan in his book *Proportion: Science, Philosophy, Architecture* (1999), this idea, while useful in its own right, has more to do with proportion than with a contemporary definition of *symmetry*. In its ancient sense, the term meant harmony, not the mirror-like connotations the word holds today.

Symmetry is generated from three simple manipulations of a basic module in relation to a reference plane, axis or point. The operations of translation, rotation and reflection can, singly and in combination, generate a rich array of forms. By far the most common type of *symmetry* found in architecture is 'bilateral *symmetry*', which consists of a form and its mirror image on the other side of an axis or plane. Bilateral *symmetry* is present in the human body, possibly explaining its dominance in architecture, in much the same way as early systems of measurement and architectural proportion were related to the size and proportion of the human body.

According to gestalt psychology, symmetrical arrangements of objects, particularly bilateral ones, create a strong recognizable grouping that satisfies our need to create order in our perceptual environment. Architects have long recognized the compelling nature of this ordering principle, using it to convey a sense of power, prestige and formality. Thus, bilateral *symmetry* is present in the arrangement of spaces and the composition of the main façades of important private and civic buildings in many cultures. In his book *Elements of Architecture* (1990), Pierre von Meiss says that, for Palladio, *symmetry* was essential for creating aesthetic balance. Most architects today avoid the precarious nature of balancing a scheme about one axis of *symmetry*, choosing instead to use asymmetrical composition strategies to achieve counterbalance.

On another level, *symmetry* in all its forms is a useful tool for creating order in building construction, since it can take advantage of the repetition of like elements inherent in industrialized building processes. One can look for precedence to the natural world, where atoms aggregate to form crystals and molecules through the repetition of *symmetry* — operations that respond to their electrical characteristics, creating richness through variations on a few basic ordering principles. (PDS)

See also: **Balance • Composition • Crystalline • Cubism • Gestalt • Ordering systems • Proportion**

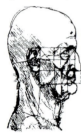

Illustration of a study of *symmetry* on the head of an old man in a drawing by Leonardo da Vinci.

Synaesthesia

Synaesthesia is a phenomenon in which one type of sensory stimulation evokes a response in another sense. For example, the synaesthetic relationship between colour and shape was researched by Wassily Kandinsky in Germany and Faber Birren in the US. Each independently noted that a square was red, a triangle yellow and a circle blue. Colour *synaesthesia* is used as an idealizing agent by admen who understand that red cars drive faster in the mind than similar models in different colours, that instant coffee tastes best when served from red containers, and that our psychological clocks seems to run more slowly in red spaces — thereby assuming we have spent longer in that space than the actual duration.

To vividly experience this sensory cross-linking is to be a 'synaesthete'. Émigré and author of *Lolita*, Akim Nabakov, described his experience in his mind's eye of distinct hues corresponding to each of the alphabetic sounds heard in America in the English of his adopted language. Composers Ludwig van Beethoven, Alexander Scriabin and Sir Arthur Bliss were also synaesthetes, each assigning a personal and precise palette of hues to the sounds of musical notes — Bliss even composing a Colour Symphony with Movements in Red, Blue and Yellow. Synaesthestic crossovers also abound in speech; they can be found in the expression of architecture as 'frozen music' and back again when music is described as 'sound architecture'. Indeed, Erich Mendelssohn described how listening to Bach would trigger his creative design energy, and Frank Lloyd Wright told of the music he heard in his inner ear when in the presence of a moving architecture.

The synaesthetic realm can also be experienced in the virtual world of cyberspace and computer games. Here, each of our senses can be transposed to another: shapes can become colours, colours tactile sensations, tactile sensations can become sound, generating a synaesthestic orgy of sensation.

See also: **Experiential • Interaction • Multi-sensory space**

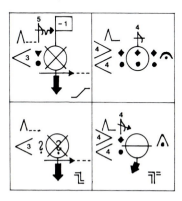

Sound pictures: four frames from a graphic musical score by Stockhausen.

Synchronic

Derived from the Greek *syn* (at the same) *chronic* (time), the word *synchronic* is fundamental to the structurist approach to aesthetics. It can be applied to a variety of situations or events where the observer perceives, appreciates, reacts or judges experiences that are happening at the same time, or are treated together. One such example in the field of colour theory is in the concept of 'simultaneous contrast', where the same grey appears yellowish when surrounded by blue (its complementary colour) or the same grey greenish when surrounded by red. One can call the resultant perceptual change in the hue of the grey as occurring at the *synchronic* level.

When we conceptualize relations in nature which we find aesthetically pleasing, this is called *synchronic* rhyme. This term has been given a vital and new direction in the study of visual aesthetics by the renowned evolutionary biologist Nicholas Humphrey in his articles on natural aesthetics in *Architecture for People* (Byron Mikellides, 1980). When asking us to consider the beauty of a flower, such as the static form of the daisy, Humphrey writes: 'The petals, stamen and leaves are three sets of contrasting elements. Each petal in turn differs in detail from the other member of its class yet shares their distinctive shape and colour and the same is true for the stamen and the leaves. The features that serve to unite each set serve at the same time to separate one set from another. But more than this, while the flowers of one species rhyme with each other, the rhyme is given added sharpness by contrasting rhymes of different species.'

Synchronic rhyme has also been applied in the built environment by Peter F. Smith. In his article on 'Urban Aesthetics' in *Architecture for People* (Byron Mikellides, 1980) he describes how the mind, using the 'chunking routine', seeks out order and pattern in architectural features that are broadly similar. Although of different size and level in façades, the variety of windows and gables, for example, is often 'contained within limits which proclaim order more than anarchy'.

Synchronic rhyme can be found not only in nature and architecture but in all of our sensual experiences: in music, art and poetry.   (BM)

See also: **Contrast • Diachronic • Order • Reciprocal • Rhyme**

Synergy

The word *synergy* was popularized in the architectural world in the 1960s by Richard Buckminster Fuller (1895–1983). Fuller's starting point was the concept of cumulative technical advantage, the engineering principle that says the more efficient a structure is, the smaller will be its demand on resources. Thus a more efficient engine will give the same performance to a lighter car, use less fuel, have more internal space, require smaller brakes and so on, in a virtuous circle. In his own work on geodesic domes, where the use of tensile rather than compressive forces was concerned, Fuller showed that structural systems could be designed down to their lightest, cheapest and simplest forms, so as to enable successive structures to exceed the performance of their predecessors while consuming fewer resources and helping to bring about a 'more-for-less-ing revolution in design'.   (MP)

See also: **Energy efficiency • Ephemeralization • Geodesic • Sustainability • Tensegrity**

Synthesis

Synthesis is the process or consequence of drawing together, building up and the assimilation of separate elements, forces or ideas into a connected whole. It is the process of unification. It is a term that Hegel used to describe the march of progress through the dialectic of thesis and antithesis, resulting in a compromise or *synthesis*.

In music, a synthesizer simultaneously combines signals of different frequencies to create new sound patterns. One note is blended into another. White light is a *synthesis* of millions of hues that constitute the colour spectrum. The layering of trace, the superposition of collage and the succession of montage are all techniques of *synthesis*.

The act of composing architectural form, i.e. the ordering of space and matter in light and material, can be said to result from a *synthesis* of the intellect and the senses. It is bound up in Steven Holl's writings on the intertwining of idea and phenomena, i.e. the fusion of concept and sensation that addresses the primary architectural relationships of history/culture-intervention, place-building, structure-enclosure, etc., in the thinking and making of architecture. These come into interplay after being initiated by the seed of an idea and worked through into sensations of experience, i.e. when an idea has formed and the building is ordered and realized. It is then that the idea ('the outer perception' of the intellect) and experience ('the inner perception' of the senses) entwine to become synthesized in the fusion of the subjective with the objective. *Synthesis* occurs when the essence of a piece of architecture organically melds concept with form — when, as part of the physical, sensory experience of a building, the underlying idea remains as a hidden thread that connects its disparate parts.

Adalberto Libera's Villa Malaparte, located on the island of Capri, is a compelling fusion of architecture and land mass. The building literally becomes a part of the geography, and has been integrated into the landscape to such a degree that there is a seamless transition from natural to built form. The power and eloquence of the idea has generated an architectural *synthesis*.   (CH)

See also: Collage • Composition • Montage • Resolve • Robust • Superimpose

Villa Malaparte, Capri. Adalberto Libera's exquisite conjunction of architecture and landform.

Tabula rasa

I am interested in reading Volume Zero. And maybe, when I get through with that Volume Minus One. — Louis Kahn

Begin as if you have never begun anything before. — Herodotus

In the 'Essay Concerning Human Understanding' (1690), the English philosopher John Locke rejected the traditional belief in innate ideas. Instead, he postulated that the mind is born blank, a clean slate — a *tabula rasa* — upon which the understood world grows through the experience of the five senses. In his schema, knowledge that is gained from the senses is further developed by reflection, thus enabling humans to formulate such artificial constructs as space, time and infinity. These constructs then conspire to prevent the individual from having a totally naive thought. To return to the *tabula rasa* that one perhaps experiences at the moment of birth, one must emulate the enlightened state of the successful Buddhist monk who has emptied his mind of thoughts.

   For the designer, the value of this attempt to reach a state of *tabula rasa* is the promise of something truly original. Unfortunately, the indoctrination efforts of culture, society and the profession conspire to clutter the mind with words, icons, theoretical concepts and precedents. In reaction to this perceived straitjacket, the post-modern project has been about the deconstruction of these 'fictions' and to strive for a state of *tabula rasa*, a phenomenologist's dream. The trick is to be quick, as once achieved, *tabula rasa* will only last for an instant, as the vacuum of thought will be filled immediately by new constructs.   (EO)

See also: **Design genesis • Phenomenology**

Tactility

Since there has been life on earth it is our feet which remind us we are alive. We know we exist when we feel it in the soles of our feet and all of us in infancy begin by learning to walk. — Tadeo Ando

Real primacy belongs to the surface, which in the body is the medium of the senses that have the tightest grasp of spatial reality.
   — Donald Kunze

Tactility joins the term 'materiality' as one of the current archispeak buzzwords (see page 114). *Tactility* refers to the perception of architectural form through touch and, in the face of digital simulation, a restitution of evidence of its tangibility in representation. Although historically playing second fiddle to its sister sense, sight, a serious engagement with *tactility* is making a comeback in the creation of built environment.

   Just as there are three dimensions to colour, there are three dimensions of *tactility*. The first is the actual sensation of physical contact with the surface of an object — a textural sensation only fully realized when moving the hand backwards and forwards at the point of contact. The second dimension is expressed when we pick up an object. In holding the object we gain an impression of its weight — this tactile sensation being recorded by our muscles which make infinitesimal adjustments to the balance of our body. The third dimension of *tactility* is experienced when, using the hands, we explore the entire surface of an object — a haptic perception of its form. This sensation is the most reliable of all our sense organs in acquiring knowledge of the existence of a physical form — feeling is believing!

Tactility also refers to texture which can be enjoyed both optically and by touch. Textured surfaces can span scales of roughness and smoothness and temperature ranges from the warmth of polystyrene to the chill of steel. There are also scales of plasticity ranging from hard and inert to elastic; tactile sensations that can also be accompanied by experiences of pain and pleasure. The thrill of physical touch is exemplified by those who cross the lawn fronting I. M. Pei's National Gallery in Washington DC to stroke the pointed edge of his acutely wedge-shaped building; the result of countless caresses not only disfiguring the immaculate lawn but leaving a permanent grease mark on the wall (incidentally, Pei has come to accept this 'desecration' of his building as a compliment).

See also: **Corporeality • Multi-sensory space**

Tectonics   ▋

The term *tectonics* refers to the art and science of construction. It comes from the Greek word *tekton*, meaning builder or carpenter, from which *architekton*, or master builder evolved. Kenneth Frampton considers *tectonics* one of the three sources of legitimacy for architecture. The other two are *topos* (site) and *typos* (type). *Tectonics* has been associated with the artistic expression of construction since the time of Homer. In keeping with its earliest association with carpentry, Gottfried Semper, in *Die vier Elemente der Baukunst* (*Four Elements of Architecture*, 1851), uses *tectonics* to refer to the lightweight spatial frame of a building reaching into the sky, contrasting it to the stereotomics of the massive form of load-bearing masonry rooted in the earth. Today *tectonics*, and its derivative, technology, apply to all forms of architectural construction, and to human production in general.

Since the end of the nineteenth century the primacy of *tectonics* in establishing the poetic basis or architecture has been challenged by an increased emphasis on architecture as space, and on art and literature as sources of inspiration. Consequently, there is now a diversity of attitudes toward the making and critique of architecture in relation to poetic expression generally, and *tectonic* expression in particular. Approaches range from the suppression of tectonic form and the logic of assembly in favour of scenographic and iconographic imagery (post-modernism, for example) to an overriding emphasis on tectonic expression (Santiago Calatrava, for example). Pierre von Meiss argues convincingly for a balanced approach to the competing demands of technology, the natural environment, and human physical and social needs. He cites Wright, Kahn, Scarpa and Botta as examples of architects who have sought to achieve this balance in their work. In the US the parts of architecture practice most closely related to construction have been co-opted in many cases by developers and construction managers, partly as a result of liability concerns on the part of architects and partly because of their lack of interest in the art of construction. However, there is still a strong tradition for architects to be involved with construction in Britain and Europe. Throughout the world there is increasing concern that the pervasiveness of human technology is overwhelming the natural environment to the ultimate detriment of both human and non-human life.   (PDS)

See also: **Articulation • Composition • Corporeality**

Telos

Telos comes from the Greek word meaning 'end' or 'goal'. From *telos* comes the principle of 'teleology', a theory used particularly in theology to argue that nature is working towards a supreme design. The term derives from Aristotle's passion for classification, which led him to devise a 'Ladder of Nature' categorizing various forms of life according to their relative complexity. Its ascending rungs began with inanimate matter through molluscs, insects, fishes, mammals to reach humankind at the top. Things become what they are, he argued, because of their potentialities. For instance, an acorn is potentially an oak tree, and carries within itself the 'form' of an oak. Therefore, according to Aristotle, we should enquire into processes rather than origins — the goal towards which things tend.

Any object consists of basic shapeless matter, on which a form is superimposed to make it what it is. These 'forms' are related to the Platonic solids, but Aristotle saw them as existing solidly in the objects we perceive, rather than some imaginary 'perfect' world. Therefore, the adaptation of *telos* in architectural currency refers to 'becoming' rather than 'being', and working towards an end rather than the final resolution. The spirit of *telos* is found in the recognition of potential in an embryonic design. It is also found in the common adage which proposes that 'process' is more important than 'product', an observation eloquently echoed by Alfred North Whitehead when he wrote: 'The process itself is the actuality'.

See also: **Design intent • Platonic solids • Thesis**

Temperate

Not often do you find a manifesto from 1624 reused three centuries later, but Sir Henry Wotton's 'Commoditie, Firmness and Delight' as the three qualities of building well were remixed by the MARS Group for their 1938 exhibition in London to promote modern architecture. László Moholy-Nagy, Misha Black, Erno Goldfinger and Ove Arup, and even Bernard Shaw, were involved in the event. Le Corbusier, who visited the show, called it 'a charming display of youth . . . which could not possibly alarm anybody'.

While *temperate* refers to a lightness of touch that avoids excess through sheer restraint (an attribute much applauded in the design fraternity), the quality Corb hit on, knowingly or not, was a certain soft-centredness to English architecture. This is an architecture with an even temper to it that at the worst makes it fudge issues and at best gives it a gentility and even humour. The English have excelled at the folly, from Fonthill to the Festival of Britain, from concrete cows at Milton Keynes to no pub at Poundbury. This *temperate* quality sees architecture as space for living, not for expression, for discussion not didactics. It can encourage a cosiness with the past, and discourage looking too hard at the future. Also, it does not fool everyone: Robert Byron, never one to pull his punches, parodied the MARS slogan as 'commodity, Guinness and tonight'.   (CLM)

See also: **Commodity, Firmness and Delight**

Temporality

Temporality is the ephemeral, the transitory and the evanescent caught up in the moment. *Temporality* is concerned with, or related to, fleeting time but also refers to the secular as opposed to the spiritual. In order to discuss its meaning in architectural terms, we have to examine different conceptions of time. The notion of the 'simultaneity' of present and past was developed by Henri Bergson at the turn of the twentieth century, and was later pictorialized in Cubist and Futurist images whose collages represent in one image successive phases of aspect and movement. Bergson's theory is that the past and the present do not denote two temporal segments but two coexisting conditions. One is the present, which continuously passes; the other is the past which is also continuous and through which all presents pass.

In the past, architecture tended to deal with time and *temporality* as something to be denied, i.e. enlisting monumentality in order to provisionally arrest and freeze its passage. However, the advent of the movies made visible a temporal warping, hitherto only experienced in thought and dreams. Cinematic time is elasticated. It provides the facility to temporally switch back and forth, freeze, slow down and accelerate. Film theorists observe that while the still image, the photograph, implies the past and the concept of 'then', the cinematic moving image implies the present and 'now'. Meanwhile, modern theories see space and time as an inseparable continuum.

Modern times have conspired to increase the *temporality* of architecture. Rising land values, rampant technological innovation and changing consumerism have rendered virtually all building of the twentieth century much more temporary than in the past — it is the era of a disposable 'Kleenex architecture'.

See also: **Continuum • Cubism • Dimension • Moment • Rhythm • Transition**

Tensegrity

Tensegrity structures are mechanically stable, not because of the strength of individual members but because of the way the entire structure distributes and balances mechanical stresses.
— Donald Ingber

Sounding more like a workout regimen to combat road rage, *tensegrity* is a truncated compound of 'tensile' and 'integrity'. It was coined by Richard Buckminster Fuller in the late 1940s when, influenced by the articulated sculptures of Kenneth Snelson, he developed the principle of a structure in which tension is continuous and compression is isolated and discontinuous.

All structures are subject to the forces of stress. The simplest and most basic form of all these stresses is compression, i.e. the direct expression of gravity. Gravity is exploited when we heap brick upon brick to build a wall, the wall rising vertically in compression to hold the roof away from the earth. Tension is in opposition to compression. Although involving compression (because you cannot have one without the other), a preponderance of major elements in a *tensegrity* structure are in tension. Like a spider's web, they are extremely lightweight and efficient.

Fuller's exploitation of tension in his masts, space grids and domes produced lightweight structures of limitless strength. Their lightness results from a minimum of bulky, discontinuous compression members in combination with uninterrupted tension bars or cables in continuous tension. The consequence is that *tensegrity* structures, like Fuller's geodesic domes and spheres, become relatively lighter and more efficient as they increase in size — making it possible for him to conceive of elegant space-enclosing projects of ever-increasing dimension and culminating in his dream of building a protective dome large enough to cover 50 blocks of Manhattan island complete with its skyscrapers.

Not only did Buckminster Fuller invent words, but his name has also been used to describe a new form of carbon discovered in 1985. With a molecule shaped like his geodesic domes, this new carbon is called 'buckminsterfullerene', the term later being abbreviated to 'fullerene' or 'buckyball'.

See also: **Design integrity** • **Geodesic** • **Tension**

Tension

Ut tensio sic vis: one of the principles that hooks all architecture together, despite all attempts to wrench it apart. But tension in this sense is more a term for the engineer, for whom it expresses one of the forces at work in the mechanics of a building. For the architect, the term, by extension, involves the visual or tactile interplay of elements in the design, intended in its turn to heighten the viewer or visitor's response or engagement with the work.

Just as *tension* moves in meaning from a carrier of mechanical work to a conveyance of emotional energy, from technical data to jargon, so as a method of communication it grows in complexity. *Tension* derives initially from contrast, whether in volume, surface, colour or light, but can be generated further by layering, rhythm and progression. Many architects have used such devices to interest and excite their buildings, but among contemporary practitioners the word has a special relevance to the work of Jean Nouvel. An obvious example is his Courthouse in Nantes, France, where a series of grids of decreasing size, like a series of filters, mark the progression from the exterior to the courtrooms themselves, an effect underpinned by the handling of daylighting in the courts as well. The same progression can be found in his simple but powerful Cartier Foundation building in Paris, and, this time in colour, in his housing work in Lille, or in the light vortex in his Berlin shopping centre.

For *tension* in Nouvel's work is not just a feature of the building, it is also a revelation of the intellectual process that underpins their design. The visible results of discourse and analysis, Nouvel's buildings draw their power from the mental effort and engagement that goes into their creation. In other words, *ut tensio sic vis* — the *tension* is proportional to the force.

(CLM)

See also: **Contrast • Dialogue • Tensegrity**

Thereness (thisness)   ▌

'Where's the thereness in this building?', 'What makes this place special?' and 'Where is the there, there?' are common questions often heard in design critiques. *Thereness* refers to the particular character, identity or significance of a building design, or, if lacking, the need for one. *Thereness* fills the void of anticlimax following feelings of anticipation; it is the state that comes with the sense of arrival and emanates from the recognition of heightened presence.

While Christian Norberg-Schultz refers to *thereness* as the *'genius loci'*, the late Charles Moore referred to the feeling as a 'sense of place'. When spatially dramatic moments are encountered — either in buildings or building designs — the architectural *raison d'être* or denouement is realized. When accompanied by a gasp of excitement or surprise, this realization is also described as the 'JC Point', the 'X-spot', or an architectural 'moment' or 'climax'.

In Gordon Cullen's *The Concise Townscape* (1961), *thereness* becomes *thisness* when he refers to uniqueness or the idea of typicality, of a thing being itself. *Thisness* and *thereness* come from attention to detail, small elements in a design being given a life of their own. It also emanates when 'this' is 'that', i.e. when architecture becomes sculpture or when metaphor is realized.

See also: ***Axis mundi • Genius loci •* Locus • Moment • Place**

Theory   ▌

Often burdened with a negative connotation originating in the rhetorical opposition of *theory* and practice (as in 'that may be fine in theory, but in practice it won't work'), the term refers to sets of ideas or thoughts about some aspect of the world, expressed in speech or writing. In its most general sense, it could refer to any collection of ideas, no matter how well or poorly organized or supported.

A good *theory* should consist of connected and mutually supporting statements using terms with clear meaning. If it aims at describing reality, we expect the statements to be true and offer explanations: why do things happen the way they do? At this level, we speak about the 'explanatory power' of a *theory*, closely linked to its 'predictive power', because we test theories for the truth if their explanatory claims make predictions. If the predictions do come true as the *theory* promises, we feel entitled to accept the *theory* as true or valid.

In design, we are especially concerned with theories that go beyond describing and explaining reality into recommending and prescribing what we ought to do, what the world should be like: normative theories. Design relies both on descriptive, explanatory and predictive theories about how the world works (validated by scientific method) and on theories about what the world ought to be like. The latter cannot be tested by the standard means of scientific method; we need other means for reaching a decision on such issues — debate, argument (including appealing presentations as well as weighing pros and cons) — to convince or persuade each other of the merits of design proposals. **(TM)**

See also: **Methodology**

Thesis

Thesis is the short version of 'hypothesis', the key claim to be tested or corroborated in a scientific or academic work. In academia, *thesis* is the term used for the main and final requirement for a degree (usually a master's degree) by means of which the student demonstrates mastery of the subject matter in the respective field, in analogy to the 'masterpiece' of an artisan. Specifically, it aims to prove that the candidate is thoroughly familiar with the vocabulary, recognized 'state-of-the-art' discourse and research in the field, and competent in applying standard tools and methods of investigation. This is usually done by carrying out a complete independent research project, with subject and approach (selection of methods) as well as conclusions and interpretation of findings being the student's responsibility. Its success or lack thereof is established by presentation in a public forum in which it must survive questioning and criticism.

The *thesis* may be considered a rigorous form of testing and, as such, open to criticism. It should be recognized as one of the most effective and comprehensive 'learning by doing' teaching tools that we have. Incidentally, it also introduces the candidate's first contribution to the discipline's overall discourse and establishes him or her as a legitimate participant in the discourse.

Sometimes, *thesis* is used interchangeably with 'dissertation' — the final requirement for a doctorate. Where distinctions are made, the doctoral dissertation is expected to be an 'original' piece of research, making a new contribution to the field, whereas a *thesis* may even consist of re-examining research already done by someone else, correcting weaknesses and flaws, etc. In philosophy, the first step of the dialectical enquiry method proposed by Friedrich Hegel consists of establishing the '*thesis*', confronting the 'antithesis' and arriving at a 'synthesis' representing a higher level of insight. **(TM)**

See also: **Design rationale**

Threeism

I

Ask me my three priorities for government, and I tell you: education, education, education. — Tony Blair

The psychological use of three is constantly employed by media-trained politicians who always make a trio of important points, and by their spin doctors and party machines who issue soundbite press releases in a daily trilogy of digestible doses. This strategy responds to a sense of complete-ness and unity. It also recognizes tolerance levels and the point of infor-mation overload in an audience that finds difficulty in grasping more than three concepts at any one time. *Threeism* also represents the journalistic principle that recognizes that it takes three similar events to cause a trend.

Three is a power number through which, according to Lebbeus Woods, an archaic form of knowledge is classified, defined and communicated. For instance, there are three Aristotelian laws of logic, three figures in the Christian Holy Trinity, three Keplerian laws of planetary movement, three Freudian aspects of the psyche, and three sides to a triangle which describes the shape of the pyramid — the ultimate symbol of hierarchy and power. Classical architecture is also based upon a tripartite scheme: base/shaft/capital.

In Steven Holl's work, *threeism* becomes 'tripleness'. Underpinning Holl's organizational theme of tripleness for his design for the Belleview Art Museum in Washington are three distinct types of lighting condition that correspond to three different gallery spaces on three levels. These are designed in relation to three different concepts of time and three cir-culation options. The form of the museum, of course, is generated from a trident-shaped plan.

See also: **Concept • Issue • Hierarchy**

Steven Holl's Belleview Art Museum in Washington embodies a three-pronged mission: the intersection of art, science and technology.

Threshold

I

A *threshold* is a piece of wood or stone place beneath a door or an entrance. Whether a simple step or a grand and highly articulated space or series of spaces, the *threshold* is an architectural element with deep social and emotional significance. It is a transition zone that marks the passage between outside and inside, the beginning of 'dwelling', in the terms of Martin Heidegger. It is where one crosses the boundary into a 'place cleared for settlement', where settlement 'begins its presencing'. According to Heidegger, the *threshold* is a place in the most basic sense in that it is a highly defined 'location'. There is a directional bias associated with the *threshold*, namely that of moving from a less bounded to a more private, contained space, an idea of entering. Accordingly, from the earliest human settlements to the present, ritual and specific modes of behaviour have come to be associated with crossing the *threshold* — removing one's shoes or hat, paying respect to the protecting deities, exchanging greetings with the host, and, more recently, submitting to security checks.

The physical form of the *threshold* as entry place varies widely depending on the cultural setting. With few exceptions it is clearly defined and its conventions are well understood within a culture. The greater the desire for physical or psychological separation between inside and outside worlds, generally the more elaborate and protracted the *threshold* transition. This is often true of seats of religious, commercial and political power. For example, devices such as doors, gates, monumental scale, elaboration of detail, the use of precious metals, symbols and words conveying prestige and power, ritual spaces, changes in direction, progression from low to high, and contrast between the character of inside and outside space, can be employed to emphasize the separation. A great deal of psychological distance can be achieved even in a small space, as in the case of many urban dwellings in Japan, where house interiors traditionally turn away from the street. On the other hand, the *threshold* can be very subtle, as Pierre von Meiss points out in his *Elements of Architecture* (1990) in relation to a house in Lansing, Michigan, designed by Frank Lloyd Wright. There the transition from the natural landscape to the house interior occurs through a sequence of small, hardly noticeable changes. In the aggressive world of retail selling, *thresholds* are blurred in order to entice a potential buyer to engage the merchandise.   (PDS)

See also: **Dialogue • Boundary • Interface • Interpenetrating space • Intersection • Place • Transition • Transitional space**

Time line

A *time line* is a time-dependent ordering device that represents a linear catalogue of events. Unlike a clock face that records linear time, the plot of a movie or a novel is constructed in its own timeframe — their *time lines* providing a linear parameter in the same way that scale functions on a map. Serial drawings are a good example of *time lines* that selectively record spasmodic events along a conceptual, temporal journey through space. One of the best examples of a graphic *time line* is that by Deborah Sussman for Herman Miller. It comprises a selective calendar of the birth dates of important pieces of modern furniture (including those by Charles Eames), illustrated in conjunction with contemporaneous examples of architecture and industrial design.

Time lines intercept significant points along their chosen trajectory, the sum total of their intersections providing narratives.

See also: **Linearity • Mapping • Narrative • Serial vision • Storyboard**

Topography

The authority of the natural world over the man-made is consummate, though it is part of the human psyche sometimes to disregard this fact.
— Robert Kronenburg

Topography has anatomical connotations as in the mapping of the surface contours of the human body with reference to its underlying anatomy. In archispeak it refers to a detailed mapping or a representation of the natural and artificial features of a town, district or the surface terrain of the site for a building or a settlement. Topographical studies usually function as an integral facet of the prelude to a building design. This is when meditations upon initial thoughts, especially those cultivated from the first perception of the physicality of a site, lead to decisions that can become a frame of reference for invention.

The range of approaches to *topography* are seen most easily in terms of sites with significant slopes. At one end of the range, the site is subordinated to a preconceived idea, such as at San Francisco, when an orthogonal street grid is draped over a hilly terrain. Very often a site is reconfigured to create a level plinth on which to construct a building, whether it be a monumental public building like an ancient Greek temple or a modest private house. At the other end of the spectrum is the strategy of raising a building above the site sufficiently enough to allow the undulation of the land to flow beneath it, touching the site in only a few carefully selected points. This approach is encountered in traditional Japanese houses where foundation posts are sometimes cut to fit the surface contours of a rock that happens to be located where the post comes to rest. Implicit in these approaches is a basic attitude toward the land, its contours and other surface features, and their value compared to the imposition of a building on the site.

See also: **Mapping • Site appraisal • Topology**

Taming *topography*. Draped mesh over the topographical contours of a site.

Topology (topos)

. . . it [topology] is the mathematics of continuity. — Ian Stewart

Together with 'game theory', *topology* is one of the two major conquests in twentieth-century theoretical mathematics. It is a branch of mathematics known as 'rubber-sheet mathematics' concerned with the properties of geometric figures that remain constant, despite the degree of distortion the figure is subjected to — hence, the rubber sheet analogy. Bodies that exhibit a continuous surface, such as a cube or a sphere, are classified as 'group zero'. Bodies with a surface disrupted by a single hole, such as a doughnut or a cup with a handle, are classified as topological 'group one'; bodies with two or more surface disruptions are incrementally classified in groups two, three and so on.

Topology is also concerned with the relationships between sets of spaces as they form connected areas. It includes graph theory and is often confused with set theory, or Boolean logic. In the age of computers, *topology* has come into its own, providing the algorithms that sort out space adjacency to fit through a process of 'topological juggling'. It is growing in importance in this age of complex curvilinear architectural form. For example, the Bilbao Guggenheim Museum was made possible by rubber sheet mathematics.

Topology is also the place where the human body is engaged. In the Aristotelian tradition, topos is the hierarchically structured space in which all bodies find their (common)place.   (EO)

See also: **Interface • Mapping • Skin**

▌Townscape

In Gordon Cullen's seminal *The Concise Townscape*, first published in 1961, he proposed that there is an art of architecture that concerns the creation of dramatic urban environments. Written at the time of pedestrian precincts and of a proliferating new town sprawl, *townscape*, he argues, concerns the art of weaving together urban forms — buildings, trees, water, traffic, advertisements, and so on — in such as way as to create dramatic, imaginative relationships.

An isolated building does not constitute *townscape*; this happens when several buildings are assembled and are collectively experienced. When a cluster of buildings is multiplied into the size of a town, questions as to the relationship of space between buildings assume importance. Consequently, the tools of *townscape* include designing in response to sequential vision, place-making and content — the latter involving the mixture of styles, materials and scales.

Cullen's argument for *townscape* is counter to conformity and the 'diagram city'. He proposed new city patterns created by the warmth and vitality of human ingenuity that offer a sense of place and identity, coupled with an 'awareness of elsewhere'.

See also: **Context • Juxtaposition • Picturesque • Place • Serial vision • Thereness (thisness)**

▌Trace

To live is to leave traces. — Walter Benjamin

Past events can be reconstructed from the traces left by footsteps or vehicles, or from trails. — Wolfgang Meisenheimer

Trace is a filtering process traditionally employed in design that uses transparent film or translucent paper through which parts of an under-drawing are selectively tracked and duplicated in order to advance a design idea. The *trace* procedure is repeated until the process is exhausted and the idea is fully developed — leaving behind an 'archaeological' paper trail of evolving design drawings.

However, there is a much more romantic use of the term which refers to the sign of something having previously existed and, having moved on, leaving its mark. Subtle indications, such as the ripples in sand that register the currents of water or wind, are perceived by architects as deeply poetic. Furthermore, like footprints in the snow, historical *traces* of human activity in the landscape can provide a memory, a potential 'archaeological' anchoring system to inform a future architecture. Fascination with this kind of ghosted inscription also translates into a predilection for certain materials. For instance, the sacrificial nature of certain woods, copper and Cor-ten steel provide perennial attraction — each betraying the action of time with a subtle patina or erosion can be seen as exotic and beautiful. Lead is also a material than can allow human activity to be traced. It was applied to the decks of a Ticino fashion boutique by the architect Martin Wagner so that the impressed pattern of movement of its stiletto heel-wearing clientele would be permanently 'mapped' in its floorscape.

In his essays on the origins of modernity written in the 1930s, Walter Benjamin discusses the interior in terms of an urban detective story: the removed picture that leaves the ghost of its shape framed in grime; the headrest stains on the sofa; the indentations left in a pillow by a now invisible sleeping head or in a carpet by the feet of shifted furniture; all *trace* occupancy. Traces are worn steps; they are clues to what went before; they communicate an interplay between absence and presence.

See also: **Anchoring • Erosion • Ghosting • Memory • Palimpsest • Poetic**

Transition

Usually I make walls thick and let the doorways show the thickness. It is a question of substance. You really feel that you have made a transition from one space to another. — John Pawson

Transition is a shift from one place, state or condition to another. Transitions occur directionally along lines of movement. Movement through architecture is filled with *transition*: transitions in space (from open to enclosed), transitions from city to private dwelling (from public to private), transitions of material, (some seamless, some causing a heightened sense of change), and transitions of activity (work, rest and play).

Exposed to the ravages of time and the elements, architecture itself is in a perpetual state of *transition*. Moreover, like the eddies, currents and waves of high fashion cycles, the expression of architecture finds itself in a constant state of flux, shifting from one ideological standpoint or theoretical approach to another. *Transition* is simply another term for change.

See also: **Boundary • Dynamic • Erosion • Juxtapose • Modulation • Morphing (metamorphosis) • Threshold • Transformation • Transitional space • Zone**

Transitional space

When a space is enclosed, its defining elements, such as walls, doors and windows, belong to both inside and outside. When we elaborate these zones by a change of level, view or material, we create places that, while embodying both conditions, exist as neither 'inside' nor 'outside' and as neither 'here' nor 'there'. These intermediary places both separate and connect, while providing a frame of reference between two realms. To pass through or momentarily occupy these zones is to experience a spatial conduit that, at city scale, is represented by the gateway, the colonnade and the arcade.

Occupancy of *transitional space* at domestic scale can be found under porches, in the recesses of inglenook fireplaces and on window seats that inhabit the thickness of walls. The appropriation of the window as 'place' was famously proposed in Gio Ponti's designs for the 'live in' or 'furnished window' — a habitable viewing frame with a view incorporating seating, *objet d'art* and planting.

Highlighted in *A Pattern Language* (1977) by Christopher Alexander et al, *transitional space* can offer a place for reflection and withdrawal, where inhabitants enjoy a kind of 'private eye' access to surrounding but detached worlds. Occupancy assumes the role of the mythic guardian of the threshold — the two-headed Janus who uses one head to look back and the other to look forward. However, there are less voyeuristic versions. These are the transitional spaces afforded by balconies, verandahs and niches. Being more exhibitionist in nature, they allow occupants to see and, while framing themselves, to be seen as objects of scrutiny.

See also: **Boundary** • **Interpenetrating space** • **Modulation** • **Threshold** • **Transition** • **Transformation** • **Voyeurism** • **Zone**

Transformation

Transformation and again transformation is the eternal entertainment of the eternal spirit. — Goethe

Transformation concerns change in the nature, function or condition of things. In architecture, *transformation* is the name of the game. Designers transform ideas into representations of themselves and thereby give substance to the abstract and indeterminate. As part of this *transformation* process, two-dimensional data are transformed into a three-dimensional physicality, and back again. The *transformation* of concept into a building design converts the intangible into the palpable; *transformation* is 'becoming'.

Similarly, raw materials become transformed into building components for their *transformation* into habitable space. The ultimate building plays its role transforming the site and, hopefully, the users are transformed by its experience.

See also: **Morphing (metamorphosis)**

Translucency

Translucency is the less distinct but discriminating version of 'transparency'. While transparency provides a Modernist and dual revelation of reflection and visual access, *translucency* is more guarded in its disclosure. While transparency removes all doubt and reveals the spectacle of display, *translucency* interposes enigma and ambiguity. Beloved by architects who bask their designs in the glow of luminescence and in the diffused scattering of light, *translucency* provides a screen through which only the ghosting of shadowy movement is filtered. *Translucency* finds expression in the diaphanous qualities of the mesh and the scrim, and in the planes of etched, frosted and prismatic glass. There is also the ubiquitous use of a glass block semi-transparency that offers high light transmission coupled with effective privacy, as famously expressed in the façades of Pierre Chareau's Maison du Verre. Built in 1931, this is Chareau's 'house of light'. The interior glows with light through its translucent walls by day, and at night the whole building is suffused with a warm radiance from within.

While transparency is 'The Full Monty', *translucency* is the Dance of the Seven Veils.

See also: **Crystalline • Diffusion • Filter • Ghosting • Layering • Scrim • Voyeurism**

Transparency

I sometimes wonder if I'm seeing the building or the image of the building . . . — John Nouvel

Transparency refers to the transmission of light so that images can be seen as if there were no intervening material. In their essay on the subject (1964), Colin Rowe and Robert Slutzky identify two aspects of *transparency*: a literal one based on the 'inherent quality of substance, as in a glass curtain wall', and a phenomenal one that is 'an inherent quality of organi-zation', as in the frontal perception of closely related overlapping spaces that appear and disappear in relation to each other. In his *Language of Vision* (1944), Gyorgy Kepes speaks of the phenomenal aspect of *transparency* as 'a simultaneous perception of different spatial locations', creating ambiguity, rather than the clarity suggested by the literal side of *transparency*. Both aspects were first developed by Cubist painters early in the twentieth century. They influenced the subsequent design and interpretation of works of architecture, first by the early Modernists, some of whom, like Le Corbusier, were themselves painters. *Transparency* continues to be an important concept in architecture today.

Rowe and Slutzky characterize the workshop wing of the Bauhaus by Walter Gropius as an example of literal *transparency* because of its emphasis on the reflecting and light-transmitting qualities of its cladding materials. In contrast, they see Le Corbusier's Villa Stein at Garches as exhibiting phenomenal *transparency* because it plays down the intrinsic nature of the materials in favour of the spatial stratification of the building's interior as revealed, and in some cases contradicted, by the treatment of the frontal planes of the façade, especially where they are interrupted to show the planes and spaces deeper within the building. More recently, the early work of Michael Graves and Peter Eisenman, and that of Richard Meier, generally exhibit characteristics of phenomenal *transparency*. Many recent curtain wall buildings display literal *transparency* in their use of carefully detailed glass cladding, whose visual characteristics can be varied by the application of different surface treatments, further expanding the possi-bilities for expression as lighting conditions change. A current variation on the theme of phenomenal *transparency* is the peeling away of the outer layers of cladding to reveal underlying cladding layers, structure, and sometimes layers of space and enclosure beyond the frontal cladding plane.   (PDS)

See also: **Ambiguity • Crystalline • Cubism • Frontality • Layering • Modernism**

Transprogramming (crossprogramming, disprogramming)

Transprogramming is one of three terms coined by Bernard Tschumi used for describing the intentional combination of building programmes or archetypes, especially those that seem inextricably incompatible. The term can be specifically applied to the relationship between the function and the actual use of a given set of specific spatial relationships and/or building typologies. This will often take the form of an overlay of a secondary use on the primary spatial function of the building type. In his book *Architecture and Disjunction* (1996), Tschumi cites the reference of a planetarium and roller-coaster. By combining apparently dissimilar programmes, a new archetype is extracted, or produced. The new archetype becomes the model for further iterations, or 'trans-programmes' of the archetype. A more current and relatively common example of *transprogramming* is an airport and shopping mall.

Crossprogramming* is a programming exercise that applies a given set of spatial configurations to a programme specifically not intended for it. Similar to a typology displacement, this design methodology is specifically used in architectural preservation for the adaptive reuse of historic structures. Tschumi cites the application of a church building used as a bowling alley. More commonly, *crossprogramming* is at the core of many urban revitalization efforts, such as a warehouse space usurped into condominium housing or a factory building reused as restaurants or retail outlets.

Disprogramming is the most complex of the *transprogramming* genre. It provides for the blending or combining of two or more programmes or archetypes, whereby the spatial configuration of one programme is combined or melded into a second programme's potential spatial configurations. Tschumi describes *disprogramming* as programmatic 'contamination', but it may be more aptly considered as a 'grafting' of two programmes, where the revised second programme can be extracted from the inherent contradictions contained in the first programme. Conversely, the second programme's spatial configuration may be applied to the first programme in order to yield the desired architectural programme. *Disprogramming* is a complex exercise, often done strictly as an academic exercise. However, it is from this type of examination of the design process that Le Corbusier's 'Machine for Living' is thought to have evolved. (MAT)

See also: **Brief • Disjunction • Dualism • Juxtapose • Symbiotic • Typology**

Typology

The adage that suggests 'there is nothing new under the sun' underscores the notion that no new architecture is created without reference to a pre-existing source. Derived from the Greek word *typos*, type refers to 'model', 'matrix' or 'mould'. The body of antecedents provides types against which new design concepts can be modified or evolved. Therefore, like the word 'genre', used to describe established categories of content in literature, film and fine art, *typology* refers to the distillation and classification of existing building types and urban forms as prototypes in terms of function and efficacy.

Later fuelled by the Jungian notion of archetypes, *typology* initially developed around the turn of the nineteenth century as a process of classifying groups with common characteristics as applied to subjects such as entomology and ornithology. It also became an important design strategy with Jean Nicholas Louis Durand (1760–1834) and his contemporaries who attempted to rationalize historic styles according to type. In his *Encyclopédie Méthodique* (1825), Quatremère de Quincy, describes 'type' as presenting 'less the image of the thing to copy or imitate than the idea of an element which ought itself to serve as a rule for the model'. Quatremère goes on to distinguish 'type' and 'model'. While, on the one hand, 'model' is an object to be copied in its own likeness, 'type', on the other hand, is capable of change used in developing a design and can be fundamentally modified and evolved. By creating links with the past, the typological approach reinforces tradition and lies counter to a Functionalist approach in which 'type' was treated as a new phenomenon.

Analytical *typology* describes the various elements of a building or a city and how these elements compositionally fit together. The study of *typology* can provide a platform on which to base possible design decisions and, depending on the situation, generate new design types.

See also: **Archetypal image** • **Context** • **Icon(ic)** • **Mapping** • **Matrix** • **Morphology** • **Precedent**

▌ Utopia

Utopia is a meaningful program for action that comes out of thought that 'transcends the immediate situation' — something that can 'break the bonds' of established society. — Karl Mannheim

Utopias are 'invisible cities', imagined perfect places, idealized states of possibility, envisioned in the minds of designers and writers like Italo Calvino. The term was first used as the name of an imaginary island by Sir Thomas More in his book published in 1516. In More's dream, Utopian islanders were governed by a perfect political and social system — a system later given a new and anatomical twist in George Orwell's satirical *Animal Farm* (1949).

Utopian ideas make visible the invisible world of the ideal. They emerge from thoughts of consequential change; idealistic dreams that summon up images that may radically alter the world. Various *utopias* have been imagined in the form of ideal cities. For example, those emanating from the dreams of Ebenezer Howard, Le Corbusier, Frank Lloyd Wright, and the group known as Archigram, although unbuilt, were influential and have been clearly documented to represent change. However, all realized that, if there was to be radical change, their plans had to be attended by political and economic agendas.

Based upon decentralization, with communally owned land, suburban in nature, and with all needs accessible, Howard's radially planned 'garden city of tomorrow' (1896) later inspired Le Corbusier's La Ville Radieuse (1935). Unlike Howard, Le Corbusier proposed a 'vertical garden city' peppered with high-rise blocks. In the same year that Le Corbusier published his Radiant City, Wright's vision of *utopia* was set out against a grid and called Broadacre City. Like Howard's Garden City, Broadacre City was anti-technology and promoted an agrarian way of life; it was concerned with universal ownership and presented a decentralized sprawl. On the other hand, drawing from 1960s pop culture with themes such as mass communication and mobility, Archigram renounced a static architecture in favour of a dramatized and choreographic technology expressed in their Walking City. Influenced by science fiction and NASA imagery, Archigram's vision came, in turn, to inspire the 'high-tech' imagery of Piano and Roger's Pompidou Centre in Paris. Meanwhile, Paolo Soleri's Arcosanti in 'Aridzona' is another attempt at realizing a form of *utopia*.

See also: **Archigram • Arcology**

Value

Together with 'hue' (the redness, blueness or greenness of a colour) and 'chromacity', or 'saturation' (the strength of a colour), *value* represents one of the three dimensions of colour. *Value* refers to the 'weight' of a colour and, as such, represents the lightness and darkness of its tone in the visual field. Colour psychology research conducted by the Swedish Colour Centre Foundation in Stockholm points to *value* as the key dimension in our understanding of colour meaning. For example, compared with their darker counterparts, lighter colour *values* seem less heavy, appear more distant, and give an impression of being less expensive.

Value in pictorial representation denotes the relationship of one part of a picture to others in respect of light and shade, the part being characterized by a particular tone (or appearance of weight). In other words, *value* is the register that communicates the degree of absence and presence of light. Pictorial treatments of extreme expressions of light and dark *value* are called 'chiaroscuro'.

An understanding of the deployment of *value* systems in graphics and, indeed, in the three-dimensional experience, brings greater control of compositional structure. For instance, in our everyday perception, heavier *value*s appear naturally to occur in the lower region of the visual field as a stabilizing factor. Meanwhile, regions of equal *value* can appear bland while high concentrations of contrasting *value* hold the power to grab attention by generating visual excitement.

'Value added' is a common phrase used today as an explanation of the utility of architectural design. *Value* is also used as 'worth'; *values* are ideals or morals.

See also: **Composition • Contrast • Depth cues**

Vernacular

... the most important movement in architecture today is the revival of the vernacular and classical traditions and their reintegration into the mainstream of modern architecture in its fundamental aspect: the structure of communities, the building of towns. — Vincent Scully

In speech, *vernacular* refers to the language or dialect of one's native country, while its use in architecture is concerned with everyday, ordinary buildings rather than their monumental counterparts. *Vernacular* describes a traditional language of building, usually of unknown authorship, constructed from local materials to suit their native setting, indigenous climate, and specific local needs. Being built from locally available materials, such as stone, clay, timber and thatch, *vernacular* buildings in the UK — like those the world over — make little reference to mainstream style or to any prevalent theories of architecture.

'Neo-*vernacular*' emerged in the UK and Scandinavia in the 1950s — especially in the 'contextualism' of Alvar Aalto and his respect of site context, memory, route, etc. It describes an architecture resulting from the subjection of the language of *vernacular* form to an architectural style or design theory. Meanwhile, 'psuedo-vernacular' is a pastiche architecture without integrity, and simply mimics and inflates the appearance of handmade traditional buildings.

See also: **Context** • **Typology**

Vignette

When heard in architectural discussion, the word *vignette* invariably refers to the smallness of impression or view, such as a short descriptive essay or character sketch. Although originating from the floral embellishment of illuminated manuscripts, the term nowadays stems from reference to the early days of photography and the popularity of small oval-shaped head and shoulder portraits, usually contained within a shaded or faded border.

Today, in archispeak, a *vignette* loosely refers to a small freehand sketch, a thumbnail drawing, or a photograph — with or without a definitive frame of reference or edge. *Vignette* has also been heard as a reference to small-scale models, and also describing a sudden glimmer of insight. However, the spontaneity of such drawings and quick sketches in presentations is often applauded by reviewers who find them a pleasing antidote to the more professional-looking computer graphic and the highly-polished perspective drawing. Indeed, their presence in a presentation is worthy of consideration because they can bring a sense of the human touch to a design proposal and they also help to introduce variegation to a range of presentation techniques.

See also: **Contrast**

Virtual reality

Perhaps the most striking transformation effected by these (digital) technologies is the change in our perceptions of materiality, space, and information, which is bound directly or indirectly to affect how we understand architecture, habitation, and the built environment.
— Elizabeth Grosz

'Virtual' is one of the most common adjectives heard in current architectural debate. The popularity of the phrase *virtual reality* (often abbreviated to VR) stems from the early 1980s and its association with computer-generated 'virtual environments' in which a person can navigate, explore and interact. The settings simulated in the computer are also referred to as 'virtual spaces' or 'virtual worlds' — their experience ranging from a screen-based, non-immersive and out-of-body experience to a total-immersive experience. The latter experience often involves computer-linked 'Darth Vader', helmets which find their genesis in the pioneer work into flight simulation in the early 1970s by Ivan Sutherland at the University of Utah. The helmet can feedback user movement, location and angle of view to a visual system, while the later advent of sensory body suits and Datagloves transmit tactile feedback.

Other *virtual reality* domains include the 'virtual classroom', the virtual community' and the 'virtual company' that can videoconference a 'virtual meeting' in the 'virtual office'. 'Virtual shopping' is already with us; this allows shoppers to perambulate a simulated mall, making purchases en route, the actual goods later being delivered to their homes.

In architecture, the digitally generated walkthrough and fly-by of a virtual building design have become so established that they are now commonplace. Indeed, there is even evidence of a hardening resistance to their apparent ease and slickness. Furthermore, the ability to recreate a realistic simulation using the computer has caused a reaction in some quarters accompanied by the call for a return to freehand drawing.

See also: **Cybernetics • Cyberspace • Hyperrealism • Simulacrum**

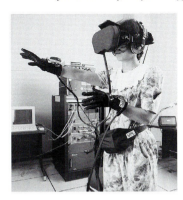

Dress code for full immersion in the virtual world.

Visual field

An infinite number of perspectives projected from an infinite number of viewpoints could be said to make up the spatial field of the phenomena of a work of architecture. — Steven Holl

Humans move in the horizontal plane. For this reason their optical capacity is mainly laterally directed to take in the principal danger zones. As a consequence of this age-old inherited exertion, our field of vision is more extensive in the horizontal dimension than in the vertical dimension. Indeed, compared with that of fish and birds that take in information equally from all directions, our field of vision is elliptically-shaped with a strong bias towards the horizontal. However, compared with the dynamic of our visual field, which alters with every movement of the eyes, head and body, the framed pictorial *visual field* in drawings and paintings is fixed.

The limits of our binocular (two-eyed) *visual field* is horizontally more than 180 degrees and vertically more than 130 degrees. Within this central cone of vision, the range for accurate shape and symbol discrimination is 30 degrees and, depending upon the quality of the viewing condition, colours can be discriminated accurately in a field extending out to 60 degrees. When we look at a scene, the eye cannot focus on more than one very small point at any one time. Visual data received outside the focused centre of vision become progressively less determinate as they range out to the blurred outer reaches of our peripheral vision where we also find the almost unnoticed intrusion of our eyebrows and nose. Therefore, a scene is never viewed 'at a glance'; rather, it is reconstructed via a scanning sequence involving head and neck movements during which the eye flits continuously from point to point to 'paint-in' and complete an almost instantaneous visual reconnaissance of the situation.

The *visual field* becomes important when attempting to determine the degree of intrusion caused by development along fringes of pristine land-scape like North Florida beaches, or the insertion of highways through designated areas of natural beauty.

See also: **Constancy scaling • Depth cues • Focal point**

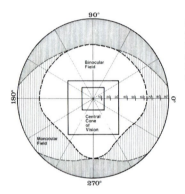

One reason for the lateral tendency of our *visual field* is the almost unnoticed intrusion of our eyebrows and nose (shown by the darker hatching) on the field of view.

Vital signs

Vital signs are measures that describe the factors contributing to the per-formance of a building in maintaining safe and healthy human occupancy.

The term *vital signs* refers to a way of thinking about buildings (specifi-cally building design and resulting performance), developed and espoused by the Vital Signs Curriculum Project of the University of California, Berkeley. The concept is simple — to use occupied buildings as laborato-ries from which real-life lessons about how buildings, building compo-nents, and systems actually work may be extracted. The vital signs approach has been used in both educational and practice settings, with students and with design professionals. Several libraries of *vital signs* case studies have been developed and are publicly accessible (see links below).

The *vital signs* approach to learning from buildings consists of several sequenced steps: a walk-through of a building to identify areas of interest or concern; development of hypotheses regarding selected issues; design of investigative methodologies to test the hypotheses (often using low-cost portable instrumentation); analysis of collected data; development of conclusions; and, ideally, publication of a lessons-learned case study.

The *vital signs* approach may also be used to study virtually any aspect of building performance that can be isolated for analysis — from curb appeal to daylight factors, to equipment operating schedules, to shading performance, to energy efficiency. The instrumentation lists assembled for such studies have opened new avenues for assessing buildings and system performance. A *vital signs* investigation is an interesting way to kick off the design process for a new building, system or component, essentially leading to learning from unpublished procedures.   (WG)

http://arch.ced.berkeley.edu/vitalsigns/
http://www.uoregon.edu/-aoc/
http://www.aa.uidaho.edu/bldvital/NBMToolDay/

See also: **Energy efficiency** • **Post-occupancy evaluation (POE)**

Voyeurism   ▮

I know you're out there, I can hear you breathing. — Max Miller

Voyeurism is the act of obtaining sexual gratification from observing the sexual activities or sexual organs of others. It also refers to the powerless or passive observer, such as the immobilized spectator portrayed in Alfred Hitchcock's movie *Rear Window*, who, with the look of a detective, uses his eyes (and binoculars) to travel about the incidents being played out behind the windows of facing apartments. Like James Stewart's character, we avidly watch popular voyeuristic reality television shows like 'Big Brother' (that ironically refers to the unseen eye of Orwell's *1984*), while daytime television soap operas provide their own form of *voyeurism*, the internet has also generated a whole new breed of *voyeurism* — the mini-DormCam.

Detached from our other senses, the voyeuristic gaze is often discussed in terms of cinema and photography, such as Cindy Sherman's intrusive photographs of herself masquerading as different female stereotypes in a parody of different and uncomfortable *voyeurisms*. This sense of looking on, unobserved, is also discussed in architectural terms by Beatriz Colomina in her book *Privacy and Publicity* (1996). In the context of buildings and projects by Adolf Loos, particularly his house design for the entertainer Josephine Baker, she describes architecture as not only providing a platform that accommodates the secret view but as a 'viewing mechanism' that frames its inhabitant.

Architecturally speaking, keyholes, wall apertures, translucent screens, up-views into glass swimming pools, mirrors (one-way and two-way) and skylights provide opportunistic conduits for the intimacy of the voyeuristic gaze. In a voyeuristic sense, Colomina suggests, architecture becomes a kind of 'body apparel' through which provocative glimpses of its occupant may be captured.

See also: **Filter** • **Sight lines** • **Threshold** • **Transitional space** • **Translucency** • **Transparency**

▌ Walkability

Only thoughts which come from walking have any real value.
— Nietzsche

Walkability concerns the provision of healthy, safe, secure and pleasant pedestrian walkways between destinations required for human lifestyle maintenance. *Walkability* refers not just to outdoor recreational needs but also to those to and from the shops and school, known as 'pure walks', and to pedestrian journeys to and from the subway, bus stop and the parking garage.

Good *walkability* is seen as a criterion of 'liveability'. It exists in those towns and cities where a network of sidewalks and pathways provide continuity, variety and choice of perambulation. While not meaning pedestrianization, *walkability* does refer to the ability to stroll along routes that, while being relatively free from the barriers imposed by heavily trafficked roads, offer degrees of individual activity and social interaction.

Walking is arguably the most empowering form of travel since it presents a strong temptation to deviate from the path, to pause and examine, to reconsider and to look again. The ability to stroll around the city is the preoccupation of the '*flâneur*'.

See also: *Dérive* • *Flâneur* • **Porosity**

▌ Working wall

Borrowed from its use to describe the servant element of the serviced shed (see pages 167 and 168, respectively), the term has been reapplied to describe an archetypal design strategy. It refers to the attraction of the potential of access, circulation and habitability of the void contained by a wall, and a resulting linear architecture that hangs, projects from, or is clustered about the primacy of a spinal support. Historical prototypes of the *working wall* include The Great Wall of China and the occupied wall protecting the medieval city. They emerge from a tradition of load-bearing masonry constructed to a thickness that allows habitability.

To design within the confines of the cavity, or the '*poché*', provides a discipline that is both attractive and challenging to the designer eager to

Garden wall. Hodder Associates' National Wildflower Centre at Knowsley, near Liverpool.

demonstrate his or her skills in a tight spatial situation. It accounts for the ubiquitous 'habitable wall' project and its cousin, the 'habitable billboard'. Essentially linear in footprint, the *working wall* is an archetype that, like the circular plan and the 'crossbow' plan, is a design generator that many students seem to need to exorcize at one time or another before moving on. It is a fascination that reflects a kind of 'Die Hard' approach in which the secret cavities, ducts and voids of a building are seen as habitable.

Built precedents of the working wall include Nigel Coates' Taxim Restaurant in Istanbul, Stephen Hodder's National Wildflower Centre in Knowsley Park (shown here) and Charles Moore's temporary and the-atrical 'Wonderwall' for the 1984 World's Fair in New Orleans, which, being only 10 feet wide, contained ticket kiosks, fast food outlets, video arcades, stages and rest rooms.

See also: **Erode** • **Edge condition** • **Linearity** • *Poché* • **Serviced shed**

█ xyz space

While the Euclidean system is useful, predominantly for manipulating space as well as the people and objects in it, its building-block approach to spatiality is nonetheless inadequate to our quotidian experience. — Donald Kunze

Its space (planimetric space) is made up of physical, two-dimensional, flat surfaces. Its rhythm, the elementary harmony of the natural numerical series 1, 2, 3, 4 . . . — El Lissitzky

xyz space is orthographic space defined by first- and third-angle projection, which imagines a design idea in plan, section and elevation form as suspended within an imaginary glass box. To do so, it uses coordinates derived from the Euclidean progression of dimensionality, i.e. point, line, plane and solid.

Writing in *Chora 1* (1994), Donald Kunze describes our acceptance of 'xyz thinking' as being so ingrained that we have begun to distance ourselves from the primacy of any direct sensory experience. For example, in *xyz space* we determine events in a language of pictorial abstraction that uses orthographic coordinates as spatial codes that are 'non-perceivable in nature's patches and horizons'. Kunze suggests that our physical body and its primacy of vision and touch (our retina and skin having the tightest hold on spatial reality) rarely experiences three dimensions or three-dimensional objects in *xyz space*. Furthermore, our eyes have to be taught culturally how to recognize the third dimension in nature and, he suggests, such learning blindfolds us to other ways of seeing and portraying space.

Our conditioning to *xyz space* is well documented. For instance, one of the more obvious side-effects is our ability to see optical illusions — a state of affairs that is not evident in societies perceptually unskilled in this form of spatial representation.

See also: **Cartesian grid • Euclidean space • Grid**

Yin-Yang   ▮

In ancient Chinese philosophy, *Yin* is the passive principle of the universe, characterized as female and sustaining and associated with earth, dark and cold. Its complementary, *Yang*, is the active principle, characterized as male and creative, and associated with heaven, heat and light. Although challenging political correctness, the duality of *Yin-Yang* belongs to an ancient Taoist philosophy proposing that the achievement of balance and harmony in the human body and its environment will dictate relationships between odd and even, warm and cool, and the five elements: earth, water, fire, wood and gold.

As in the practice of acupuncture, in which the body is pricked at a point complementary to that of an ailing organ, and in the preparation of Chinese food, which involves counterbalanced amounts of cool (*Yin*) and warm (*Yang*) ingredients, so too are traditional Chinese architecture, interior design and garden design subject to a symmetry and formality to achieve equilibrium. This is a design language informed by *Yin-Yang*, and one based upon a symbolic system that respects the significance of the compass points, of contrasting the human-made with the natural, of rough with smooth, round with square, and meandering with straight. Its aim is to generate 'qi', i.e. the force of nature that, when expressed in our setting, produces energy and balance in the mind and body. Sounding more like a Chinese takeaway, feng shui is the art of detecting qi in a room, a building or a site.

Easily dismissed today as a New Age fad, aspects of a feng shui geomancy, such as prospect, appropriateness of materials and colour, and the placement of furniture, were famously encountered by Norman Foster and Partners in their design for the Hong Kong and Shanghia Bank in Hong Kong, when a feng shui master was brought in as part of the design team.

See also: **Balance • Dualism • Positive–negative space • Symmetry**

Zeitgeist

Architecture is the will of the age conceived in spatial terms.
— Mies van der Rohe

Literally translated, *zeitgeist* means 'time spirit' or 'spirit of the age'. Georg Wilhelm Friedrich Hegel (1842–1928) first articulated a theory of the *zeitgeist* in his *Philosophy of History* (1956). He described the *zeitgeist* as an instrument of the Absolute, a force beyond the control of humankind. It was seen as the mechanism behind the dialectic of history. Hegel associated the *zeitgeist* with the development of the universal mind. He postulated that great persons are the means whereby the universal spirit — the Absolute — realizes its ends, especially in art, religion and philosophy (one wonders if he includes architecture in the above).

In early twentieth-century architectural discourse, the new *zeitgeist* became a rallying cry for the rise of Modernism and the rejection of history. The leading spokesperson for this attitude was Nikolaus Pevsner in his influential *Pioneers of the Modern Movement* written in 1936. Ironically, the concept of the *zeitgeist* eventually became synonymous with historicism — which Charles Jencks has described as having 'the awful habit of surviving lethal attack'. Fortunately, the notion of a *zeitgeist* has now been declared illusionary in this age of post-modern thought. Thus, the current *zeitgeist* is that there is no *zeitgeist*. **(EO)**

See also: **Modernism**

Zen

Zen refers to the direct experience of beauty in simple, ordinary life as a fully aware and conscious human being. It is the attitude that life is an aesthetic experience that is not to be judged and the direct experience of beauty in simple, ordinary life as a fully aware and conscious human-being. In *Zen*, 'mindfulness practice' means bringing one's complete and full attention to whatever one is doing, and maintaining that complete and full attention, moment by moment by moment, regardless of what one is doing. Being able to bring one's full attention and consciousness to a task requires personal commitment and training. It does not come from somewhere else and it cannot be bestowed by someone else.

There are many *Zen* stories that illustrate this essential principle ingredient of enlightenment, and at the same time demystify the notion of enlightenment as some other special place to be, where one is eternally calm and peaceful. True enlightenment is achieved in this life, right where you are, all the time. There is no other place you need to be. By being able to bring out your full attention, complete consciousness and awareness to whatever the task is at hand, you are able to do any task. As the *Zen* saying goes: 'If you can cut the carrots (mindfully), you can rule the kingdom'. **(LP)**

See also: **Existential • Experiential • Phenomenology**

Zoning   ∎

Zoning is one of a series of spatial organizational tools, such as axial lines, grids, and systems of measure and proportion that can be traced back to the set of design instruments derived from Euclidean geometry. *Zoning* concerns the imposition of territorial limits, but not of spatial content. It is a means of compartmentalizing the indeterminate and is a strategy that enjoyed a resurgence in the 1960s and 1970s when, associated with a Functionalist design approach, it became applied to schemes requiring flexibility in the design of urban plans and large buildings. In such designs, *zoning* provides an initial design tool for shaping an indistinct programme. It can be applied as a provisional strategy without making committed declarations as to how the scheme is to be fleshed out.

The zoned composition of, particularly, American cities into demarcated areas of use, such as residential, industrial and commercial, was heavily criticized in the 1950s by Lewis Mumford and also by Jane Jacobs in her book *The Death and Life of Great American Cities* (1961). Despite their lack of order, both argue for mixed zones that provide vitality and architectural interest. Meanwhile, at the scale of the public park and private housing, the montaged arrangement of clearly demarcated zones of activity is the stock-in-trade of architects such as Bernard Tschumi and Rem Koolhaas.

See also: **Collage • Composition • Edge condition • Functionalism • Juxtaposition • Montage • Order • Ordering systems • Parameters • Space adjacency**

Zoomorphic   ∎

Zoomorphic deals with the animalization of inanimate objects. For example, Jaguars, Mustangs, Cougars and Panthers prowl our highways, and occasionally spotted is the legendary Robin. Apart from branding automobiles with the animalistic attributes of swiftness or brute force, animal bone-structures lurk in the bridges of Santiago Calatrava and Ian Ritchie, and also in the metaphorical and concept-generating wings, fins, scales and crustacia of countless student design projects.

The notion of animal forms as a source from which to inform human-made structures was popularized in D'Arcy Thompson's book *On Growth and Form* (1961). Meanwhile, plenty of literal and abstract representations of mammal, bird and fish forms abound in the built environment — from Frank Gehry's fish in Japan and Cesar Pelli's 'whale' in Los Angeles to Herb Greene's 'Prairie Chicken' in Oklahoma.

See also: **Analogue • Animate • Morphing (metamorphosis) • Metaphor**

Chicken shack. Herb Greene's Prairie House (1962), Norman, Oklahoma.

Archispeak: Further Reading

Abbot E.A. (1952). *Flatland: A Romance of Many Dimensions*. Dover Publications, New York.

Alexander C., Ishikawa S., Silverstein M. (1977). *A Pattern Language*. Oxford University Press, New York.

Antoniades A.C. (1992). *Poetics of Architecture: Theory of Design*. Van Nostrand Reinhold, New York.

Aston M., Rowley T. (1974) *Landscape Archaeology*. David & Charles, Newton Abbot.

Banchoff T.F. (1990). *Beyond the Third Dimension: Geometry, Computer Graphics, and Higher Dimensions*. Scientific American Library, New York.

Barth J. (1991). *The Last Voyage of Someone the Sailor*. Hodder & Stoughton, London.

Barthes R. (1993). *Camera Lucida*. Vintage Classics, London.

Beer S. (1972). *Brain of the Firm: The Managerial Cybernetics of Organisation*. Allen Lane, London.

Benedikt M. (1991). *Deconstructing the Kimball: An Essay on Meaning and Architecture*. SITES/Lumen Books, New York.

Benedikt M. (1987). *For an Architecture of Reality*. Lumen Books, New York.

Beukers A., van Hinte E. (1999). *Lightness*. 010 Publishers, Rotterdam.

Bloomer K. C. & Moore C.W. (1977). *Body, Memory, and Architecture*. Yale University Press, New Haven.

Brookes A. (1998). *Cladding in Buildings*. E & FN Spon, London.

Brookes A. (2003). *Innovation in Architecture*. E & FN Spon, London.

Ching. F.D.K. (1979). *Architecture: Form, Space & Order*. Van Nostrand Reinhold, New York.

Collins J. & Mayblin B. (2000). *Introducing Derrida*. Totem Books, New York.

Colomina B. (1996) *Privacy and Publicity*. The MIT Press, Cambridge MA.

CEC (Commission of the European Communities) (1990). *Green Paper on the Urban Environment*. European Commission, Brussels.

Cullen G. (1961). *The Concise Townscape*. Architectural Press, London.

de Bono E. (1970). *Lateral Thinking: A Textbook of Creativity*. Penguin Books Ltd, Harmondsworth.

Descartes R. (1637). La Geometrie in Sorrell T. (2000). *Descartes: A Very Short Introduction*, Oxford University Press, Oxford.

Dodds G., Tavernor R. (eds) (2002). *Body and Building: Essays on the Changing Relation of Body and Architecture*. The MIT Press, Cambridge MA.

Dondis A.D. (1973). *A Primer of Visual Literacy*. The MIT Press, Cambridge MA.

Doxiades C.A. (1966). *Between Dystopia and Utopia*. Trinity College Press, Hartford CT.

Debord G. (1983). *Society and Spectacle*. Black and Red, Detroit.

Durant S. (1986). *Ornament*. The Overlook Press, New York.

Eco U. (1986). *Travels in Hyperreality: Essays*. Pan in association with Secker & Warburg, London.

Euclid. *The Thirteen Books of the Elements (1956)* . Dover Publications, New York; abridged edn, Everyman's Library, London, 1933.

Farmer B., Louw H. (eds) (1993). *Companion to Contemporary Architectual Thought*. Routledge, London.

Fisher T. (Aug.1993). 'The Avant-Garde, Past and Future'. *Progressive Architecture*.

Forty A. (2000). *Words and Buildings: A Vocabulary of Modern Architecture*. Thames & Hudson, London.

Frampton K. (2002). *Body and Building: Essays on the Changing Relation of Body and Architecture*. MIT Press, Cambridge MA.

Frampton K. (1995). *Studies in Tectonic Culture: The Poetics of Construction in Nineteeth and Twentieth Century Architecture*. The MIT Press, Cambridge MA.

Friedman S. (1989). *City Moves*. McGraw-Hill Publishing Company, New York.

Frutiger A. (1989). *Signs and Symbols: Their Design and Meaning*. Studio Editions, London.

Gelernter M. (1993). The Concept of Design and its Application to Architecture in Farmer B., Louw H. (eds) (1993). *Companion to Contemporary Architectual Thought*. Routledge, London.

Gibson W. (1993). *Neuromancer*. Harper Collins, London.

Gilloch G. (1996). *Myth and Metropolis: Walter Benjamin and the City*. Polity Press in association with Blackwell Publishers, Oxford.

Greene H. (1976). *Mind & Image*. The University Press of Kentucky, Lexington.

Grosz E. (2001). *Architecture from the Outside: Essays on Virtual and Real Space*. The MIT Press, Cambridge MA.

Hall E.T. (1966). *The Hidden Dimension*. Doubleday, New York.

Haraguchi H. (1989). *Comparative Analysis of 20th-Century Houses*. Rizzoli, New York.

Hayward R. & Mcglynn S. (1992). *Making Better Places: Urban Design Now*. Butterworth Architecture, Oxford.

Hayward R. & Oliver P. (1990). Architecture: An Invitation. Blackwell, Oxford.

Hegel G.W.F. (1956). *The Philosophy of History*. Dover Publications, New York.

Hitchcock H-R. & Johnson P. (1932). *The International Style: Architecture Since 1922*. W.W. Norton, New York.

Hume D. (1739-40). *A Treatise on Human Nature*. Everyman´s Library, London, 1911.

Jacobs J. (1961). *The Death and Life of Great American Cities*. Vintage Books, New York.

Jencks C. (Feb. 2003). 'The New Paradigm in Architecture'. *Architectural Review*, London.

Jencks C. (1977). *The Language of Post Modern Architecture*. Academy Editions, London.

Jenks M., & Burgess R. (eds) (2000). *Compact Cities: Sustainable Urban Forms for Developing Countries*. Spon Press, London.

Jenks M., Williams K., Burton E. (eds) (1996) *The Compact City: A Sustainable Urban Form?*. E & FN Spon, London.

Kahn L. (1957). 'Order in Architecture'. *Perspecta 4*, Yale.

Kahn L. (1953). 'Toward a Plan for Midtown Philadelphia'. *Perspecta 2*, Yale.

Kepes G. (1944). *Language of Vision*. Theobald, Chicago.

Leach N. (1999). *The Anaesthetics of Architecture*. The MIT Press, Cambridge MA.

Le Corbusier. (1946). *Towards a New Architecture*. Architectural Press, London.

Leupen B., Grafe C., Kornig N., Lampe M., de Zeeuw P. (eds) (1997). *Design and Analysis*. 010 Publishers, Rotterdam.

Lloyd Morgan C. (1998). *Jean Nouvel: The Elements of Architecture*. Universe Publishing, New York.

Lloyd Morgan C. & Zampi G. (1995). *Virtual Architecture*. B. T. Batsford Ltd, London.

Lynch K. (1960). *Image of the City*. The MIT Press, Cambridge MA.

Mann T. (1992). *Building Economics for Architects*. Van Nostrand Reinhold, New York.

Mann T. (2003). *Time Management for Designers*. W. W. Norton & Company, New York.

McKean J. (1994). *Crystal Palace*. Phaidon Press Ltd, London.

McLuhan M. (1964). *Understanding Media*. Routledge & Kegan Paul, London.

Mikellides B. (1980). *Architecture for People*. Studio Vista, London.

Mitchell W.J. (1995). *City of Bits: Space, Place and the Infobahn*. The MIT Press, Cambridge MA.

Mitchell W.J. (1992). *The Reconfigured Eye*. The MIT Press, Cambridge MA.

Nabokov V. (1997). *Lolita*. Penguin Books, London.

Newman O. (1972). *Defensible Space: Crime Prevention Through Urban Design*. Macmillan, New York.

Nicoliades K. (1941). *The Natural Way to Draw.* Houghton-Mifflin, New York.

Norberg-Schultz C. (1963). *Intentions in Architecture.* The MIT Press, Cambridge MA.

Norberg-Schultz C. (1979). *Genius Loci: Towards a Phenomenology of Architecture.* Rizzoli, New York.

Orwell G. (1951). *Animal Farm.* Penguin Books Ltd, Harmondsworth.

Padovan R. (1999). *Proportion: Science, Philosophy, Architecture.* E & FN Spon, London.

Paulof J. A. (1999). *Once Upon a Number.* Allen Lane Publishers Penguin Press, London.

Pawley M. (1974). *The Private Future.* Random House, New York.

Pawley M. (1990). *Theory and Design in the Second Machine Age.* Basil Blackwell, Oxford.

Pawley M. (1990). *Buckminster Fuller.* Trefoil Publications Ltd, London.

Pawley M. (1998). *Terminal Architecture.* Reaktion Books Ltd, London.

Pawson J. (1996). *Minimum.* Phaidon Press Ltd, London.

Perez-Gomez A. & Parcell S. (eds) (1994). *Chora 1.* History and Theory of Architecture Graduate Programme, McGill University, Montreal and London.

Pevsner N. (1986). *Pioneers of History.* Viking Press, New York.

Poggioli R. (1983). *The Theory of the Avant-Garde.* Bellnap Press of Harvard University Press, Cambridge MA.

Pollard C. (2002). *Bedtime.* Bloodaxe Books Ltd, Northumberland.

Preiser W.F.E., Rabinowitz H Z., White E.T. (1988). *Post-Occupancy Evaluation.* Van Nostrand Reinhold, New York.

Rowe C., Slutzky R. (1964). 'Transparency, Literal and Phenomenal', *Perspecta 8*, Yale.

Rowe C., (1976) *The Mathematics of the Ideal Villa and Other Essays.* The MIT Press, Cambridge MA

Saariste R. (2000). 'Agram: architectural grammar' in *Architectural Design and Research: Composition, Education, Analysis.* Thoth Publishers, Bussum.

Scott G. (1974). *The Architecture of Humanism.* W. W. Norton, New York.

Scruton R. (1979). *The Aesthetics of Architecture.* Methuen & Co. Ltd., London.

Sommer R. (1969). *Personal Space: The Behavioural Basis of Design.* Prentice Hall, Englewood Cliffs, NJ.

Spiller N. (1998). *Digital Dreams: Architecture and the New Alchemic Technologies.* Ellipsis, London.

Steenbergen C., Mihl H., Reh W., Aerts F., (eds) (2002). *Architectural Design and Composition.* Thoth, Bussum.

Sullivan L. (1900). *Kindergarten Chats.* Shultz, New York.

Thompson D'A. W. (1917). *On Growth and Form.* Cambridge University Press, Cambridge; abridged edn 1961.

Tschumi B. (1996). *Architecture and Disjunction.* MIT Press, Cambridge MA.

Venturi R. (1966). *Complexity and Contradiction in Architecture.* Museum of Modern Art, New York.

Venturi R., Brown D.S., Izenour S. (1972). *Learning From Las Vegas.* The MIT Press, Cambridge MA.

Vitruvius. *The Ten Books on Architecture.* (translated by Rowland I.) (1999). Cambridge University Press, Cambridge and London.

Vitruvius (1960). *The Ten Books on Architecture.* Dover Publications, New York.

Vollers K. (2001). *Twist & Build.* 010 Publishers, Rotterdam.

von Meiss P. (1990). *Elements of Architecture: From Form to Place.* E & FN Spon, London.

Watkin A. (1925). *The Old Straight Track.* Methuen & Co. Ltd, London.

Weston R. (1996). *Modernism.* Phaidon Press Ltd, London.

White E.T. (1983). *Site Analysis: Diagramming Information for Architectural Design.* Architectural Media Inc., Tallahassee.

White E.T. (1997). *Images of Italy.* Architectural Media Inc., Tallahassee.

White E.T. (1999). *Path, Portal, Place: Appreciating Public Space in Urban Environments.* Architectural Media Inc., Tallahassee.

Wiener N. (1961). *Cybernetics: or Control and Communications in the Animal and the Machine.* The MIT Press, Cambridge MA.

Williams C. (1981). *Origins of Form.* Architectural Book Publishing Company, New York.

Williams K., Burton E., Jenks M. (eds) (2000). *Achieving Sustainable Urban Form.* E & FN Spon, London.

Woods L. (1997). *Radical Reconstruction.* Princeton Architectural Press, New York.

Wotton, H. (1624). *Elements of Architecture.* (facsimile edn. 1968). University of Virginia Press, Charlottesville.